FASCIST
AND ANTI-FASCIST
PROPAGANDA
IN AMERICA

FASCIST AND ANTI-FASCIST PROPAGANDA IN AMERICA

The Dispatches of Italian Ambassador Gelasio Caetani

Pellegrino Nazzaro

CAMBRIA PRESS

YOUNGSTOWN, NEW YORK

Library of Congress Cataloging-in-Publication Data

Nazzaro, Pellegrino.
    Fascist and anti-fascist propaganda in America : the dispatches of Italian
Ambassador Gelasio Caetani / Pellegrino Nazzaro.
        p. cm.
    Includes bibliographical references and index.
    ISBN 978-1-934043-66-0 (alk. paper)
    1. Fascism—United States—History—20th century. 2. Anti-fascist
movements—United States—History—20th century. 3. Propaganda—
United States—History—20th century. 4. Caetani, Gelasio, 1877–
1934—Political and social views. 5. Italian Americans—Politics and
government—20th century. 6. Fascism—Italy—History—20th century.
7. United States—Relations—Italy. 8. Italy—Relations—United States. 9.
United States—Politics and government—1919–1933. 10. Italy—Politics
and government—1922–1945. I. Title.

    E743.5.N35 2008
    320.53'307309045—dc22

2007051889

*To the loving memory
of my father and mother
for their anti-Fascist tenacity*

TABLE OF CONTENTS

PREFACE

The gestation process of this work goes back to years past. It went through three stages.

A bit of historical background will set the first stage—the stage linked to the political history and career of my father. Under Mussolini, paramilitary organizations and a Fascist nomenclature emerged in Italy. These included *arditi* (crack troops), *squadristi* (Fascists engaged in punitive action against the enemies of Fascism), *mazzieri* (Fascists armed with stilettos and guns), *manganelli* (truncheons or nightsticks), *fasci di combattimento* (fighting groups), *Fasci del Littorio* (Lictor's *Fascis*), *Milizia Volontaria per la Sicurezza Nazionale* (Voluntary Militia for National Security), *ras* (local boss), *gerarca* (hierarch), *sovversivi* (subversives), *fuorusciti* (political exiles), and the *Brigate Nere* (Black Brigade).[1]

This takes us to the brutal attack on my father, Vincenzo Nazzaro. While he was still a bachelor, a gang of nationalists, *arditi* and *mazzieri*, armed with guns and stilettos, beat him viciously. It was Holy Trinity Sunday, 1920. Vincenzo Nazzaro, one of the local founders and activists of the *Partito Popolare Italiano* (PPI), founded by Sicilian priest Luigi Sturzo in 1919, was actively engaged in presenting to the local public the ideas and the program of Sturzo's manifesto *Al Liberi e Forti*. The *mazzieri* brutally assaulted Vincenzo Nazzaro. Those who witnessed the assault remembered that his face had been transformed from that of a handsome man to the face of the biblical *Ecce Homo*. Vincenzo Nazzaro survived the brutal attack, and religious people who knew him attributed his survival to divine intervention by the statue of the Holy Trinity, venerated in the town's monumental church.

The Nazzaro family pursued the indictment and prosecution of the *mazzieri*, who were found guilty of criminal association with intent to commit murder (*associazione a delinquere a scopo di delitto*) and sentenced to several years in jail. However, in the aftermath of the Fascist March on Rome (October 1922) and the appointment of Benito Mussolini as prime minister of the Italian government, *Il Duce* granted an amnesty and set the jailed criminals free.

Vincenzo Nazzaro married Giovanna Crispo in 1926. (The Crispo family had emigrated to the United States in 1901.) In the aftermath of the assault, the Nazzaro family lived under constant threat. Fascists considered them *sovversivi* (subversives) and kept them under constant control. Often threatened, my father was forced to appear at the *Dopolavoro*, the center where Fascists convened after work. From 1940 to 1956, my father taught at the local *Scuola Statale di Avviamento Professionale Industriale "Carlo Poerio."*

During WWII, he was subjected to more severe control and threatened with dismissal from his teaching position. It was a difficult period for the entire family. After receiving tenured professorship at the school, he retired from active teaching in 1956 and emigrated to the United States in 1957.

My own educational experience at the local high school influenced the second stage of the present work. Students received a good dose of weekly Fascist indoctrination there. We learned *"Mussolini ha sempre ragione"* ("Mussolini is always right"); *"Credere, Obbedire e Combattere"* ("Believe, Obey and Fight"); and *"Il Mito e' Fede, e' Passione. Non e' necessario che sia una Realta'"* ("The Myth is

Faith, is Passion. It is not necessarily a Reality"). But most disturbing were Mussolini's bravadoes: *"Non piangete prima del tempo! Non fasciatevi la testa prima di averla scassata."* ("Don't cry beforehand, do not bind up with bandages your head before it is broken," May 26, 1927) and *"L'opposizione e' necessaria: non solo ma vado piu' in la' e dico: puo' essere educativa e formativa."* ("Opposition is necessary. But I go beyond it and say: it can be educational and formative," June 7, 1924). I remember that we, the children of anti-Fascist or presumed anti-Fascist parents, were forced to sit in the back of the classroom. From there, we became more vocal in our opposition against Fascism, asking constantly, "What is Fascism and why is Italy Fascist?"

A preliminary answer to these questions came during my very challenging years at the gymnasium and lyceum, where history and philosophy were interwoven. From Greek and Roman history, philosophy, and literature, to the Enlightenment, to the American and French Revolutions, we were introduced, in a systematic and chronological way, to the ideas of democracy, liberty, equality, constitutionalism, popular sovereignty, Marxism, Socialism, and Fascism among others.

The professors covered a historical and philosophical arch that included Herodotus, Thucydides, Polybius, Plato, Aristotle, Plutarch, Cato, Sallust, Livy, Tacitus, Cicero, St. Augustine, St. Thomas Aquinas, Machiavelli, Hobbes, Locke, Montesquieu, Voltaire, Rousseau, Burke, Smith, Ricardo, Mill, Marx, Hegel, Kant, and Tocqueville down to the history and philosophy of the first half of the 20th century. It was, indeed, the most illuminating and challenging intellectual experience of my academic and educational life.

On registration day at the University Federico II of Naples, I still remained uncertain as to which doctoral degree to pursue: medicine— my mother's preference—or jurisprudence—my father's preference. I opted for jurisprudence, a four-year *curriculum studiorum*. The written dissertation and specialized topics for oral presentation and analysis (*tesine*) required a fifth year. The multidisciplinary curriculum determined my decision. Under Italian National Law, a Doctorate in Jurisprudence (Ph.D.) gives title to three equally significant careers: legal, diplomatic, and teaching in history and philosophy.

During my five years at Federico II, I had the privilege to study under distinguished scholars. Among them, Giovanni Leone became prime minister of Italy and then the elected president of the Italian republic. Francesco De Martino, who later held ministerial positions in the Italian government during the period of the Center-Left Coalition (*Il Centro Sinistra*), had written *Storia della Costituzione Romana* to international acclaim. Biagio Petrocelli was later appointed justice of the Italian Constitutional Court. Alessandro Graziani, a victim of Fascist persecution, was a distinguished scholar of political economy. Rolando Quadri was a scholar in international law and organizations.

Another significant experience for me was to study under Ugo Rocco, a distinguished professor and brother of Alfredo Rocco (*Dizionario Enciclopedico Italiano*, Vol. X, "Rome," 1970, p. 484; and *Enciclopedia Italiana*, Vol. XXIX, "Rome," p. 529). Originally a Nationalist, Alfredo Rocco had shaped the juridical system of Fascism and its constitutionalism.

The study and analysis of *Il Progetto Rocco Nel Pensiero Giuridico Contemporaneo* (Cedam, Padova, 1930) introduced me to the analysis of Fascism and totalitarianism by Italian and international scholars such as H. A. Smith, University of London; W. T. S. Stallybrass, Oxford University; E. Bise and Alfred von Overbeck, Frieburg University; F. Collin, University of Louvain; H. Donnedieu De Vabres, University of Paris; A. Khoehler, University of Erlangen; J. A. Roux, University of Strasbourg; Andor Kovats, University of Debrecen; Pierre Garraud, University of Lyons; and Giulio Battaglini, University of Pavia, among others. In these and other works, Alfredo Rocco's doctrine and theories underwent severe scrutiny. It became evident to me that the Italian Nationalists and their political ideas had become the legal cornerstone of the Fascist totalitarian state. Alfredo Rocco's new jurisprudence, implemented with the consent and approval of Benito Mussolini, was one of the most significant elements of the post-1925 establishment of the totalitarian regime.

Any historical analysis of Fascism must concentrate on Alfredo Rocco's hermeneutics of National-Fascism, let alone his responsibility for the implementation of the *Stato Totalitario* (Totalitarian State) in Italy.

The title of my dissertation was *Il Principio di Disponibilita' del Processo Penale* (Legal and Constitutional Rights of Plaintiff and Defendant). The tesine dealt with "*Il Mezzogiorno e Sturzo*" (Southern Italy and Sturzo) and "*Mercato Comune ed OECE*" (Common Market and the Organization for European Economic Cooperation). Synopses of both tesine were published, respectively, in *Politica Popolare*, Naples, Anno IV, January 1958, p. 2, and in *La Vita del Mezzogiorno*, Roma-Benevento, Anno 52nd, nn. 4–5, February 25, 1960, p. 3.

The third and final stage initiated when I registered at the *Facolta' di Lettere e Filosofia* of the University to research history and philosophy. During the two years at the Facoltá, I joined the Centro di Studi Sturziani, directed by Ferdinando D'Ambrosio, a member of the Italian Parliament. At the Centro, I researched the *Mezzogiorno* (Southern Italy) and the problem of Italian emigration abroad, especially to the United States. The research gave me an in-depth understanding of the problem of the *Mezzogiorno* through the works of F. S. Nitti, L. Sturzo, A. Gramsci, G. Salvemini, G. Fortunato, P. Villari, E. Corradini, and N. Colajanni, among others. (For a complete bibliography on Italian emigration, see Grazia Dore, *La Democrazia Italiana e L'Emigrazione in America*, Brescia, 1964). In the first round of research on the *Mezzogiorno*—the most intense period of my professional career—I became immersed in local and provincial archives to investigate the social, economic, and political impact of Italian emigration.

The Provveditorato agli Studi di Benevento hired me to teach in the state school system, *Scuole Medie* and *Istituto Magistrale*. In 1960, I received an offer to teach in the United States and left Italy in 1961. In 1963, I was hired in the College of General Studies, now

College of Liberal Arts, at the Rochester Institute of Technology where I continue as professor in the History Department.

In 1968, I began extensively researching Fascism, anti-Fascism, and Italian emigration abroad at the *Archivio Centrale dello Stato* in Rome, and continued doing so thereafter for several years. The present work is the result of this research.

Pellegrino Nazzaro
Rochester Institute of Technology

ACKNOWLEDGMENTS

I would like to express my sincerest thanks to Peggy Noll, Staff
Assistant for the Departments of Fine Arts, History and Philosophy
in the College of Liberal Arts at RIT for her effective communica-
tions with the editorial board of Cambria Press and to Dorothy E.
Conway for reading the preliminary galley proof of the manuscript.
To both my thanks and appreciation.

FASCIST
AND ANTI-FASCIST
PROPAGANDA
IN AMERICA

INTRODUCTION

Three names stand out significantly in the historiography of Fascism and anti-Fascism in America: Gaetano Salvemini, John Patrick Diggins, and Alexander DeConde.

Gaetano Salvemini published *Fascist Dictatorship in Italy* (1927) and *Mussolini Diplomate* (1932). (Italian editions of the latter appeared in 1945 and 1952 under the title *Mussolini Diplomatico*). *Under the Axe of Fascism* followed in 1936. *Fascist Activities in the United States*, a 1940 pamphlet, became *What to Do with Italy*, written with Giorgio La Piana and published in 1943. The Center for Immigration Studies published *Italian Fascist Activities in the United States* (1977), edited and with an introduction, by Philip V. Cannistraro. According to Cannistraro, Salvemini displayed a balance between objectivity and political realism. The credibility of Salvemini's arguments against Fascism springs from solid probatory evidence.

Salvemini believed that we should judge political leaders by the political environment in which they operate as well as by their achievement—or lack of achievement—while in office (see *Gaetano Salvemini*, 1959, p. 29). Ennio Di Nolfo (*Mussolini e la Politica Estera Italiana*, 1960), considered Salvemini the first historian to detail convincingly Mussolini's idiosyncrasies in foreign policy. Present and future generations of scholars must consider Salvemini one of the major historians of Fascism and anti-Fascism.

The second important author, John P. Diggins, published *Mussolini and Fascism, The View from America* (1972). This comprehensive analysis of American views of Italy covers America's fascination with Mussolini's ideas, Fascist propaganda in America, and American and Italian-American resistance to Mussolini and Fascism. Present and future scholars of Fascism and anti-Fascism in America will continue to rely on this fundamental and important work.

Third, Alexander DeConde published *Half Bitter, Half Sweet, An Excursion Into Italian American History* (1971). Based on extensive research of primary sources, the work is considered a comprehensive and scholarly study of the diplomatic and political history of Italian-American relations from 1700 to 1970. This comprehensive analysis provides students and scholars with a fine selective bibliography on the subject.

Since 1970 a constellation of new publications on Fascism and anti-Fascism has appeared in the United States and in Italy, spurred by interest in ethnicity and ethnic studies, and literature on the subject continues to flourish. In general, historians and researchers agree that the definitive history of Fascism and anti-Fascism in the United States has yet to come. In *Blackshirts in Little Italy, Italian Americans and Fascism, 1921–1929*, published in 1999, Philip V. Cannistraro recognizes exactly that: the history of Fascism and anti-Fascism in the United States, "despite some recent advances is still to be written." Perhaps the present or next generation of scholars will address this challenge.

Neither Salvemini nor Diggins wrote, and perhaps never intended to write, a definitive history of Fascism and anti-Fascism in the United States. Their works fall within the category of documentary and critical historical analysis and represent the *vademecum* for those who plan to write such a definitive history of Fascism and anti-Fascism in the United States.

The task requires a collective and collaborative effort built on the knowledge of the historiography of both countries—Italy and the U.S. Moreover, it must be integrated with and corroborated by a patient and systematic consultation of documents and sources still buried in the archives of Italy, the United States, and other countries such as England and France, through which Italian émigrés and *fuorusciti* (political exiles) journeyed on their way to the United States.

Linguistic skills will give researchers not only first-hand access to sources still hidden in public and private archives but also an understanding of linguistic *sfumature* (nuances). The historian's mission remains to discover the truth, free from manipulation, interposition, ideological or national bias, and sanitation.

Fascism scholars must consider all contributions toward research, however small, seemingly irrelevant, dated, or updated. Interpretations and conclusions deserve respect notwithstanding historical and critical analysis.

The present generation of scholars tends to emphasize an interdisciplinary approach and analysis of historical events. The new trend of scholarship appears to move in the direction of multidimensionalism. In the age of globalization historians tend to adopt the method of total integration whereby neither limits nor frontiers exist. Surely, this approach will provide extra dimensions to the historical process and help those who will write the definitive history of Fascism and anti-Fascism in the United States. They must, however, apply what the late Renzo De Felice used to call *la misura della storia* (historical balance).

In the summer of 1968, I began research in the Archivio Centrale dello Stato di Roma, Italy, with the assistance of Dr. Guido Guerra. That documentary evidence led to the essay, "L'Immigration Quota Act del 1921, La Crisi del Sistema Liberale e l'Avvento del Fascismo in Italia," delivered at the III Symposium Di Studi Americani (May 27–29, 1968), sponsored by the Istituto di Studi Americani of the Universita' di Studi di Firenze. The proceedings of the symposium appeared, under the auspices of the Consiglio Nazionale delle Ricerche, in the book *Gli Italiani Negli Stati Uniti* (1970). The English version of my paper was published in the *Journal of European Economic History* (Banco di Roma, Vol. 3, Number 3, Winter 1974, pp. 705–23) under the title "Italy from the American Immigration Quota Act of 1921 to Mussolini's Policy of Grossraum: 1921–24."

Several American colleagues participated in the symposium, and their papers were also original and covered a variety of topics: Italian emigration, political participation and leadership, community integration, ethnic interests and conflicts, criminality, assimilation, and civic participation. To put it into context, with this symposium, Italian–American historiography in the United States had abandoned the confines of localism and provincialism and had entered the realm of national and international discourse.

My research continued and more essays followed based on archival documents. One of the publications contained the *Manifesto of the North American Anti-Fascist Alliance*, edited and translated in English and Italian and published in *Labor History* (Summer 1972) and in *Affari Sociali Internazionali,* n. 1–2, 1974.

The late professor Renzo De Felice published "L'Atteggiamento della stampa cattolico-moderata Americana verso il Fascismo prima e dopo la Conciliazione" in *Storia Contemporanea* (Anno II, n. 4, 1971, pp. 717–37), later reprinted in the book *Modernismo, Fascismo, Comunismo, Aspetti e Figure della Cultura e della Politica dei Cattolici nel '900,* a cura di Giuseppe Rossini (1972, pp. 47–67).

"Fascist and Anti-Fascist Reaction in the United States to the Matteotti Murder," was published in *Studies in Italian American Social History, Essays in Honor of Leonardo Covelli* (1975, pp. 50–65).

The essay "Modigliani's Visit to the United States and the American Labor Party" (13 Articles for the *New Leader*, June 18, 1927–October 15, 1938) appeared in *Rivista di Studi Politici Internazionali* (Anno LII, n. 206, 1985, pp. 241–78).

My archival sources convinced me to organize my research more systematically, and I began working on the present book. In the meantime, the present generation of scholars began emerging: Ronald

H. Bayor, Stefano Luconi, Philip V. Cannistraro, Claudia Damiani, Gian Giacomo Migoni, Anna Maria Martellone, Grazia Dore, Gianpiero Carocci, Gianfausto Rosoli, Donna R. Gabaccia, Alexander J. De Grand, and Emilio Franzina, among others. They have given a further impetus and added new dimensions to the study of Italian American Fascism and anti-Fascism in the United States. Their research and work indicate the life and vibrancy of the historiography of Fascism and anti-Fascism in America.

I based this book on first-hand, original, and archival documents uncovered in Italian and American national archives. It presents to the national and international audience of scholars and readers a clear view of the causes of the dissemination of Fascism in the United States from 1922 to 1940.

While some sectors of America's public saw in Fascism an ideological movement requiring alignment and conformity to Mussolini's doctrine and discipline, most Italian-Americans welcomed Fascism as a movement that emphasized Italian patriotism and a newly found national identity—an antidote to and defense against American nativism, xenophobia, and the paranoid stigma that victimized the entire Italian-American community.

The book underscores the notion that none of the activities of the Italian-American Fascist associations organized in the United States had political designs. Contrary to some interpretations, still in vogue, Fascism in America never assumed conspiratorial tones. Fascist organizations in the United States were plagued by factionalism, internal struggles, and heterogeneity. Moreover, the presence in the United States of a vocal anti-Fascist movement, the International Anti-Fascist League of North America, prevented Fascism from developing an efficient propaganda network throughout the United States. Beset by internal factionalism, personal feuds, ambassadorial and consular conflicts, and frequent clashes with anti-Fascist groups, Fascism in the United States never emerged as a political ideology capable of creating an alternative to American democracy.

This study details how in December 1929 Mussolini disbanded the Fascist League of North America. Thereafter, the period 1930–1940 saw a constant deterioration of the myth of Mussolini in the United States. G. E. Modigliani's visit to the United States, the anti-Fascist opposition of L. Antonini and S. Romualdi, and the Ethiopian War, among other issues, dealt a decisive blow to the faltering fortunes of Fascist propaganda in the United States. Italy's aggression against Ethiopia spurred a strong anti-Fascist reaction in the United States, especially among the African American community.

CHAPTER 1

ITALY FROM THE AMERICAN IMMIGRATION QUOTA ACT OF 1921 TO MUSSOLINI'S POLICY OF *GROSSRAUM*, 1921–1924

With few exceptions, American scholars view the phenomenon of immigration through the lens of U.S. socioeconomic development. "As Americans," E. Schuyler points out, "we have only a platonic interest in the amount of emigration from Italy, the causes which produce it and the real or probable effects on the prosperity of that country."[1] It seems, however, that historians have neither analyzed sufficiently the motivation behind this attitude nor considered the international repercussions of 1920s U.S. anti-immigration legislation, particularly on the domestic consequences suffered by Italy.

American historians justify the passage of the Quota Act of 1921—also known as the Johnson Bill—on the basis of economic crisis. In fact, between 1918 and 1921, the United States went through an economic crisis, followed by recovery, succeeded by a second crisis during which prices soared, and the cost of living went up 77 points to a high of 105, based on the index of 1914. Exports dropped from $8.2 billion in 1920 to $4.3 billion in 1921. The price of farm products declined, and production dropped seriously. In the industrial field, a decline in production followed low consumer demand and resulted in the unemployment of 6,500,000 people. However, the same phenomenon affected all nations bearing the consequences of World War I. Postwar fallout caused the American economic crises of the time—not immigration.[2]

RACIAL PREJUDICE OR ECONOMIC NECESSITY?

Between 1919 and 1921, historians contend, the war-boom economy followed by two economic crises ultimately justified the restriction of immigration, and so goes the argument for the Johnson Bill. Such a conclusion seems unwarranted. From the last quarter of the 19th century to the first decades of the 20th century, no alarming symptoms of impoverishment rankled society after cyclical periods of economic depression. From a report presented by Louis Dublin to the Commission of Immigration and Naturalization, Oscar Handlin concludes: In periods of economic instability, immigration reached very low quotas and therefore did not play a major role in unemployment. Practical common sense on the part of potential immigrants halted their immigration to the United States during economic crises; those already here returned home in times of low wages and depression.[3] Immigration did not play a hand in causing or heightening the economic crises confronting American industry in the early 1920s.

The fact that the Johnson Bill favored immigration from northern populations and limited immigration from southern Europe, the Middle East, and Asia, certainly hints at racial and national motives for its passage. Many Americans judged all Mediterranean races inferior and morally far below those of northern Europe. They believed so-called inferior southern European races would adulterate the Nordic blood of America.[4] This intolerance grew along with a rapid influx of foreigners and led to unjustified and exaggerated fears among the American public—as well as federal authorities. The Immigration Restriction League, the American Legion, the Daughters of the American Revolution, and several labor organizations professed, organized, and directed such prejudiced thinking for several years. Ultimately the nativistic Ku Klux Klan also picked up and adopted this attitude.

American hostility had already reared against Italian immigration before passage of the Johnson Bill in May 1921. In March, federal authorities at the Port of Philadelphia had imposed a quarantine of twelve days on the ships *Regina d'Italia* and *San Rossore*, each carrying 1,600 passengers. In New York they had imposed a longer quarantine on the *Duca degli Abruzzi*, which carried 1,500 passengers. These moves followed reports by two American physicians, Fama and King, which told of epidemics of bubonic plague and exanthematic typhus in Italy. According to unpublished documents in Rome's Central State Archives, the two American doctors' reports on health and hygiene in Italy in 1921 were inaccurate and of no serious account.[5] The American consular authorities at the port of embarkation of the three ships had issued sanitary certificates, which proved and guaranteed rigorous sanitation practices aboard the ships and guaranteed that passengers migrating to the United States had been deloused and washed before embarking.[6] Nevertheless, in the above-mentioned cases, although American authorities had issued clean certificates, tendentious denunciations of others carried the day. Alarming and unfounded telegrams were sent to the United States, and consequently the Italian vessels were treated with hostility in American ports by citizens and federal authorities. This situation prompted an immediate and strong response on the part of Italian consular authorities in Washington.

In an urgent report, the Italian chargé d'affaires in Washington, D.C., Dr. Saluzzo, cabled the Italian government (telegram no. 17515, dated March 14, 1921) warning Prime Minister Giovanni

Giolitti that the American doctors' reports of exanthematic typhus plaguing Italy threatened a decrease in visits by well-to-do tourists to Italy; discouraged Italian emigrants from coming to America for fear of a long quarantine in American ports and possible difficulties in disembarking; prompted more American demonstrations for limiting Italian immigration; harmed passengers aboard the vessels; and damaged Italian maritime companies because Americans planning trips to Europe would avoid taking passage on Italian ships.[7] On May 19, 1921, the American Congress, with a Republican majority, passed the Immigration Quota Act, which President Wilson had previously vetoed; on May 11, 1922, Congress extended it for two additional years.

CONSEQUENCES ON ITALIAN DEMOGRAPHY AND MARITIME BUSINESS

Beyond any doubt the Immigration Quota Act damaged the Italian nation and wreaked havoc on maritime business and ultimately the country's political structure. The Italian government had always relied upon emigration as a safety valve to alleviate overpopulation and unemployment, especially in the regions of central and southern Italy. It now had to face emergent and serious consequences. On May 1, 1921, Giuseppe De Michelis, head of the Emigration Bureau, a division of the Italian ministry of foreign affairs, delivered a memorandum to Prime Minister Giolitti informing him of the imminent application of the law restricting immigration to the United States. The memorandum pointed out the considerable reduction in the annual quota of Italian immigrants, which in the past had reached very high levels.[8] In the first quarter of 1921, 100,000 Italians emigrated to the United States; after the passage of the new law, only 42,000 Italians would be admitted to the United States between May 21, 1921, and July 1, 1922. This drastic decrease would stagnate Italian emigration, rock Italy's internal economic situation, and shake the stability of the Italian government.

In a United Press International news conference on May 12, 1921, Prime Minister Giovanni Giolitti called attention to Italy's plight: its dense population—almost 400 inhabitants to the square mile—and insufficient resources to sustain itself, and said the American Restriction Immigration policy had dealt a severe blow to his country. In fact, only one-fifth of Italy's land could be properly cultivated, only two-fifths could be partially tilled, and the remaining two-fifths consisted of barren rock and mountains. Before the war, 600,000 people left Italy each year for other countries. Italy's international trade deficit amounted to more than $200 million. However, the deficit had been more than overcome by wealth returned to the country by emigrants, whose remittances amounted to over $200 million, and the money brought into the country by foreign tourists, which amounted to $120 million each year. Emigration and tourism, Italy's two cash cows, historically rewarded the country with hefty returns.[9]

Italy's overall socioeconomic situation, with its perennial, near-stagnant sluggishness, worsened after the American Restrictive Immigration policy. Unskilled labor in Italy made up the core of unemployment. Agriculture absorbed 50 percent of the labor population, industry 30 percent, and trade and commerce less than 10 percent. Expansion of the agricultural economy had suffered serious setbacks. For instance, the output of wheat and corn dropped from 52 and 25 million quintals respectively in 1911, to 38 and 22 million quintals in 1920 (one quintal equals 100 kilograms or about 220 pounds). The overall economic crisis and its resultant inflation, labor unrest, and growing unemployment, intensified after a series of domestic incidents. General strikes between 1919 and 1921 led to widespread looting of stores and to workers' occupation of major factories (September 1920).[10]

This unstable socioeconomic situation forced Italian governmental authorities to take drastic measures to reduce fallout from the Johnson Bill. De Michelis points out, "the American Restrictive Law was going to bear serious repercussions in Italy. The Italian government ought to take immediate measures to reduce the consequences to a minimum economic loss." To this end, the head of the Emigration Bureau suggested a series of devices. First, passports should be issued with absolute preference for employable men. Second, only those men who could send money back home immediately would be sent overseas. To prevent a decrease in the money sent home from emigrants in America, elderly persons, women, and children should postpone their emigration—and their reunions abroad with relatives—in favor of able-bodied males. These tactics were intended to alleviate the burden of unemployment at home and to accelerate the flow of money from abroad into the Italian treasury—money important for the government as well as for private enterprise.

The effect of the restrictive law on the nation seemed very bound up with the effect on Italian maritime interests: "The most important problem," reported De Michelis, "is to find out how the Italian shipping companies can bear the consequences of the law." Fourteen national ships were under contract for transportation of passengers to North America. The new law compelled these ships to limit the number of emigrants to 600 per trip, a mere half the number they had carried previously. The financial loss would be too great for them to remain in operation. These companies, in a meeting held at the Emigration Bureau, suggested mothballing half their ships, rather than operate them at a loss.[11]

The suggestion, if accepted, would have deprived half the currently employed shipping personnel of their jobs and would have made Italian unemployment even more acute. Bureau and government representatives deemed this move politically unwise. The government supported De Michelis' suggestion of raising passenger and freight rates to compensate for the loss of revenues. This solution would have simplified the task of the government, which was more concerned with the problem of unemployment. Of course the emigrants, who were already in financial difficulties, would carry most of the economic burden. The normal rate of freight had been 1,600 lire (over $500). The suggested increase to 2,600 lire would compensate for company losses. Since the increase was considerable, the head of the Bureau urged the government to persuade maritime unions to share the financial burden. The Bureau feared that if the emigrants carried the increased cost entirely, many would have to give up the idea of emigrating.

A third series of problems complicating the situation concerned foreign ships—from five French and three English companies—involved in the transportation of Italian emigrants. Their presence, the eventual competition, and the refusal to withdraw willingly from Italian ports made imperative an intervention by the Italian government. Since those ships operated under foreign flags, the Italian Societies of Navigation, Transatlantica Italiana, Navigazione Generale Italiana, Transoceanica, Lloyd Sabaudo, Cosulich, and La Veloce, on May 4, 1921, presented a request to the Ministry of Industry and Commerce asking for immediate governmental intervention.

They pointed out the considerable decline of emigration, the consequent economic losses suffered by the companies, and the competition created by the presence of foreign companies in Italian ports. To reduce the losses of Italian maritime companies and the national economy, they recommended that the Italian companies receive exclusive rights to transport Italian emigrants and the foreign companies be temporarily excluded so long as the Johnson Bill remained in effect. In evaluating the plight of the companies, the government gave serious consideration to the expenditures they had made in improving and expanding their fleet and port facilities, especially at Genoa and Naples.

At first the government suggested the companies compete in northern European shipping markets, but the companies rejected the proposal. European shipping tonnage already exceeded the demand, and little room was left for competition. Besides, the Italian ships would have been at a distinct disadvantage. Northern European companies had the advantages of shorter trips, better supplies, and national protection.

On May 19, the Honorable Tommaso Tittoni, undersecretary of industry and commerce, sent an urgent request to Prime Minister Giolitti to take action concerning the practical consequences of the

Johnson Bill for shipping companies. The undersecretary urged the adoption of the following measures:

1. Grant the Italian Maritime Companies the exclusive right to transport emigrants from the Italian ports until the end of July 1922.
2. Increase the price of freight for the next 12 months to compensate for the decrease of emigrants.
3. Increase the price for passengers traveling in first and second class.
4. Reduce maritime personnel.
5. Reduce the wages of the crews.
6. Abolish the 2 percent reduction in salary (established by the recruiting contract), in favor of the seamen.[12]

On May 21, the chief secretary of the Council, Dr. Berio, presented to Prime Minister Giolitti these proposals with a personal note stating: "In my opinion, in the present situation we have no other choice but to accept the proposals of the Maritime Companies."[13] Prime Minister Giolitti agreed, adding: "I give my approval to these proposals, above all to the one which grants the Italian Maritime Companies the exclusive right of transporting emigrants. Nevertheless, we must find a way to prevent the emigrants embarking from foreign ports." Giolitti gave the impression that barring Italian emigrants from non-Italian ports would solve major consequences for Italy posed by the Johnson Bill. However, the serious consequences which the American decision would have on the political, social, and economic life of Italy could not have escaped a man of his political and parliamentary experience. Without the safety valve of emigration, surplus manpower had to be absorbed within the Italian semi-industrial system.[14]

GOVERNMENTAL CRISES AND ECONOMIC UNREST

No solution would have been effective without a drastic governmental change. The Italian Liberal Party drew its support from industrialists, the intellectual middle class, and landholders interested in keeping the status quo without radical socioeconomic change. Moreover, such a program would have required the support of the new political forces that emerged with the election of May 15, 1921, which had heavily shifted the political axis. In that election the Liberals, fearing the election of the Socialists and Populars who advocated radical changes, sought support from Fascists and Nationalists on the right, through the so-called National Blocs. In spite of armed opposition, punitive expeditions, destruction, plunder, and murder on the part of the Fascist Squads, the Socialists and Populars together maintained their positions.

At the same time, having gained some respectability from the election, Benito Mussolini, founder and leader of the Fascist Party, and 35 Fascists elected to the Chamber of Deputies set to work achieving parliamentary independence from this temporary alliance with the Liberals. The Fascists adopted a position of intransigence and obstructionism in the Chamber and flaunted an unwillingness to support a government headed by Prime Minister Giovanni Giolitti. The prime minister's unrealistic calculations to seek Fascist and Nationalist support through the National Blocs proved a failure. Fascists and Nationalists continued to assert that the liberal- democratic parliamentary system was incapable of solving Italy's problems. Mussolini's demagoguery boasted that the nation's political vacuum and the parliamentary impasse, which failed to provide a viable and stable government, required a Fascist solution: seizure of power through revolutionary or violent means if necessary. Mussolini never hesitated to assert his unique leadership ability; he presented himself as a leader who could not consider anyone higher than himself.

Therefore, after a serious evaluation of the political significance of the May election, Giolitti realized that no government could be formed without Fascist and Nationalist support. Moreover, the Fascist and Nationalist propaganda of national regeneration and of law and order had touched a deep nerve in the Italian populace. Therefore, on June 27, 1921, Giolitti submitted his resignation.

His successor, Ivanoe Bonomi, had to navigate the stormy waters of a political and constitutional crisis and face, in some sectors of the peninsula, open civil war. The Bonomi government did its best to heal internal wounds, at least at the surface. It tried to smooth over political differences and to eliminate competing political factions. However, the Bonomi government fell at the end of February 1922, and was succeeded by two Facta governments (February 26–August 1 and August 1–October 30), which, as it turned out, were the last two democratic governments of the constitutional regime in Italy.

Plagued with economic difficulties, the Facta governments faced high prices and continued demands to solve the problem of unemployment. The internal crisis undermined the foundations of liberalism and democratic institutions and prevented the Facta governments from remedying any social or economic ills. Moreover, Facta's analysis of Italian political and economic problems and complexities paled in insignificance to Mussolini's belligerent actions and violent shouts. In his own bombastic words:

> We want Italy to become a Fascist country...Those who accuse us of aiming at an agrarian slavery should see now with their eyes the crowds of authentic laborers and genuine people with shoulders, legs and arms strong enough to carry on the future successes, the fortunes, and the sacred destinies of Italy. Only cowards and criminals could accuse us of being the enemy of the people, when we have been born of this very class and experienced with our own arms hard work. We want the redemption of Italian workers, at home and abroad... There is already a living and dramatic contrast between the Italy of weak liberal politicians and the healthy, strong, vigorous, uncompromising Italy which is preparing herself to give the coup de grace to all the weaklings, the potboilers, the old scum of the Italian society.[15]

Led by Mussolini, the Fascists ordered farmers, cafe owners, and shopkeepers to lower prices. In Naples, they imposed a reduction of 50 percent on food prices. In Florence, Black Squads threatened retaliation against shop owners who did not lower their prices. In the meantime, they forbade organized labor to strike. Union headquarters, cooperatives, and Popular and Socialist clubs were destroyed or burned. When strikes occurred, the Fascists became strikebreakers. They even ordered the government led by Facta to enact ordinances forbidding and preventing strikes.[16]

In September 1922, State Treasurer Giuseppe Paratore asked Facta to meet with the new Emigration and Unemployment Commission. In the meantime, winter threatened with its inevitable seasonal increase of unemployment. The long and detailed report sent by Paratore to Facta by the end of September casts light on the unemployment situation in Italy.[17] According to the National Employment Bureau, by June 30, 1920, unemployment had reached 105,831. By July 1, 1921, the number had risen to 388,744, and by September 30, 1921, to 470,542. These figures increased steadily until February 1922, when unemployment reached 606,819. But Paratore's report rejected these figures as elusive. In fact, the Employment Bureau limited registration to unemployed men, considered the only source of family wealth and support. Therefore, his report pointed out, for every unemployed man in a family, at least three persons endured the consequences. The total number of people directly affected by unemployment, then, could reach in excess of 2,000,000. The industrial situation loomed as even less promising. Official reports of the ministries of Finance and Industry assessed the general condition as precarious. International indexes showed that among the nations on the winning side of the war, Italy alone had suffered an increase in the cost of living (*Revue d'Economie Politique*, July–August 1922). Yet, these indexes pointed out that Italy occupied the tenth position on the international scale of price-index, followed by Germany, Bulgaria, and Poland, all of whom were desperately fighting inflation. More importantly, between 1920 and 1922, the overall wholesale price index rose by 20 percentage points. The industrial commodities index and that for farm products rose strongly, signaling a key indicator of inflation. The following figures were reported in major Italian cities in mid-September 1922:

Rome	130.17
Milan	114.69
Turin	113.80
Lucca	119.03
Como	118.23
Vicenza	119.30

In the meantime, labor forces—organized as the General Confederation of Workers (2,150,000 members), the Italian Syndicalist Union (300,000 members), the Italian Confederation of Labor (1,823,491 members), the Italian Union of Labor (200,000 members), the Syndicate of Railroad Workers (200,000 members), and numerous small organizations—represented a continuous threat. By the end of 1921, of any European country Italy suffered the most serious consequences from strikes, resulting in the loss of over 16,398,227 working days that year.

In addition, the cooperatives, which had been of great help to the low-income classes and had indirectly contributed to the regulation of prices in the domestic market, had almost disappeared—destroyed or paralyzed by Fascist terrorism. "The practical solution," Paratore insisted, "of the unemployment problem, in the present situation, has to be found in emigration." Emigration symbolized the necessary key to a better economic and political future for Italy. Emigration had saved southern Italy to a great extent before the war, and now emigration was urgently needed to cope with the disastrous phenomenon of unemployment. Germany and Austria had already eliminated all foreign workers from their labor markets, and other European countries, such as Switzerland, refused to accept any more foreign laborers due to their own situations. The Johnson Bill indeed created enormous difficulties and once enacted, made the unemployment problem in Europe in general, and in Italy in particular, not only serious, but catastrophic.

The Italian government, through the Emigration Bureau, had to look everywhere to place as many workers as possible, even attempting to send emigrants to Peru, Brazil, Paraguay, Argentina, and the rest of South America. Brazil, which already had a generous immigration policy, agreed to accept many more Italian workers. Regulations issued by Paratore prevented emigrants from making their own choice about their destination. He also instructed the Bureau to overlook a country's sanitary, social, and juridical conditions.

By September 1922, Italy badly needed the safety valve of emigration, which would have relieved the tense economic situation, solved the problems of unemployment, and alleviated class hatred. At that time Italy's internal deficit totaled 112,025,700,000 lire, while the debt to foreign countries had soared to 21,245,000,000 lire in gold, ten times higher than Italy's prewar debt. As he had outlined in his previous report to Luigi Facta, and a month later, in the early days of October, Paratore warned the prime minister by telegram: "Dear Facta, I urge you to convoke the Commission of Emigration and Unemployment: winter is at hand. Yours, Paratore."[18]

In response, on October 9, 1922, Facta sent a telegram to the ministers of finance, labor, industry, agriculture, and liberated lands that read as follows: "Please come tomorrow, Tuesday, at 4:00 p.m. to the first meeting of the Committee for the Study of the Problems of Emigration, which will be held at the Palace of the Prime Minister. Facta."[19]

There is no record that the meetings took place on that date. A letter from De Michelis to Facta referred to an Emigration Committee Meeting scheduled for October 28, but due to the sudden development of political events, that meeting was indefinitely postponed. "I was notified by His Excellency Carlo Schanzer," De Michelis wrote, "that tomorrow I should have participated in the first meeting of the Interministerial Committee for Emigration, which was formed in one of the last sessions of the Council of the Ministers. But I was just informed that the meeting would not take place at the present."[20]

On October 30, 1922, Victor Emmanuel III, king of Italy, appointed Benito Mussolini prime minister and minister of internal affairs. Up to this point, Mussolini had held no governmental positions. He was simply the leader of the 35 Fascist deputies elected in 1921 and of the newly formed National Fascist Party. Nationwide, Mussolini was known more for his promise of national regeneration and restoration of law and order in Italy than for his political achievements. The same day Mussolini appointed all other ministers but reserved for himself the ministry for foreign affairs. Fascism held power, with thanks to the nation's economic situation for its final rise. Mussolini had the support of the agrarian middle class and the industrialists. He also organized young men between the ages of 17 and 25 into paramilitary Black Shirt units. United they formed a disciplined and enthusiastic force opposing the traditional politics of Liberalism, Socialism, and Popularism. Mussolini's success depended on his promises of social order, economic improvement, and, above all, solving the problem of unemployment.[21]

The Downfall of Liberalism and the Fascist Strategy

Restrictive immigration measures approved by the American Congress intensified Italy's socioeconomic crisis and led to the downfall of Liberalism. The whole Italian political system—based upon uncertain postulates—collapsed. The Liberal program of slow reforms proved inadequate to cope with the postwar economy. Previously, the Liberal government had pleaded for and solicited emigration quotas to meet the consequences of Italy's fast-growing population, especially in the southern regions. Sound reforms had not been attempted to solve structural imbalance and eliminate the permanent disequilibrium between upper and lower classes. Not even when the restrictive American immigration policy became effective did the Italian government introduce effective measures to minimize the consequences of its severe blow. Liberal leaders continued to think of themselves as the champions of democracy in Italy. Taking advantage of dissension and division plaguing other Italian political parties, Liberals adopted a pretence of stability, invulnerability, and capacity to effect law and order. But beginning in 1921, the governments, controlled by a Liberal majority and seriously challenged by economic and social unrest, collapsed one after another. On the other hand, Mussolini started deeply penetrating middle and lower classes.

Fascism, which between 1919 and 1921 had been "an aggregation of negative forces, men and ideals," began taking advantage of the situation and managing its strategy. "Fascism," wrote Salvatorelli in 1923, "represents the struggle of the middle class bourgeoisie, wedged between capitalism and the proletariat, as the third man between the two contestants. This strategy explains the apparent contradictory duplicity of Fascism."[22]

In reality, there was only one Fascism. But, since it maintained a fight against two opposing groups of social forces (plutocracy, bourgeoisie, old ruling class, and profiteers on the one hand, and Socialists, anticlericals, Populars, and strikers, on the other), people believed Mussolini when he claimed Fascism would never allow the exploitation and oppression of the working classes, rather, it would fight for their welfare and prosperity. Thus, it happened that the class struggle he had prophesied became instrumental in rallying most of the oblivious working forces around his program. The rallying together of such forces could take place only in the midst of such an unstable economic situation.

According to G. DeMaria, Fascist events became historically relevant relative to the very serious economic crisis striking Italy and Europe.[23] As has been well summarized by F. S. Nitti, from 1921 on, Italy needed capital, schools, serious industrialization plans, and, through emigration, an outlet for its unemployment and demographic virility. Any decision aimed at restricting Italian emigration abroad would produce damaging effects in Italy.[24] This explains, to a certain extent, why the American Quota Act spurred the advance of Fascism. Fascism acted as a centripetal force, which successfully rallied industrial workers, teachers, students, farmers, landowners, state and private employees, and war veterans. By the end of October 1922, at a Fascist rally in Naples (Oct. 25–26, 1922), party Secretary-General Pasella, reported that Fascism could count on more than 650,000 followers. According to Bolzan's speech in Naples, Fascism was

"Unitarian in its theoretical postulates and rural in its human expression."[25] Anna Kuliscioff, wife of Italian Socialist F. Turati, told her husband of her impression of disciplined militarism and daring courage manifested by the Fascists, ranging from 17 to 25, she observed at the Milan and Ferrara rallies. She reported to her husband in Rome that "the Fascist forces were regimented not for the destruction of Socialist cooperatives, rather their objectives seemed aiming at higher goals... They appeared to represent the mobilization of the unemployed to protest against unemployment and the central government."[26] Marxist historian Angelo Tasca has carried his analysis in this direction. Examining Italy's overall domestic situation, the author concludes that "the economic breakdown and a con-catenation of negative circumstances altered the course of events...Moreover, industrial depression caused a vast amount of unemployment, aggravated by the slowing down of emigration."[27] Another Italian historian, G. Salvemini, rightly argued that unless the problem of Italian immigration into the sparsely populated areas of the world were solved in a spirit of good faith and solidarity, all talks of peace and international cooperation (while Italian immigrants were excluded from the United States, Canada, and Australia) would cause the world to "to play into the hands of Fascist propaganda."[28]

It seems clear enough that new demands for modified social order increased with the deterioration of the economic conditions. Italy's economic and social structure, including its agricultural and industrial unrest, must be held at fault. The influence of economic maladjustment played an important role in the Fascist coup d'état. Though dissatisfaction and unrest had been features of Italian life throughout the entire nineteenth century, criticism of its socioeconomic structure turned particularly bitter in the 1920s. The discontent felt prior to this period is difficult to explain because it had been inarticulate and voiceless. Indications can be inferred from the facts of population movement, emigration particularly, and continual antigovernmental manifestations of workers, peasants, and commoners, described as "anarchic tendencies aiming at controlling private holdings." On the contrary, public dissent and protest displayed open dissatisfaction against intolerable conditions of oppression and exploitation. This explains why emigration assumed such mass proportions between the last quarter of the nineteenth century and 1921. Because of the socioeconomic situation and the perennial conditions of prostration, demoralization, and exploitation, peasants and commoners resorted to protest against usurers, deceitful lawyers, excise men (*gabellotti*), and avaricious barons (who represented the political class). They hoped to revenge themselves by some day returning home wealthy. This explains too why Italian emigration abroad assumed, to a certain extent, a temporary nature. Evidence of the practical aspects of these contingencies of Italian emigration can be seen in the fact that emigrants' remittances helped their families, improved their economic conditions, and contributed in balancing Italy's deficit of exports and the unfavorable balance of payments. But the Quota Act struck a staggering blow to the hopes of those Italians who sought economic improvement through emigration. The restrictive law eventually determined and was in turn reflected in the political organization of the nation. As the situation of economic maladjustment persisted, the Italian people became increasingly more critical. In 1921 and 1922, groups of literary men, on the one hand, and political parties, on the other, expressed their concern. They offered different panaceas, but none brought a practical solution to the problem.[29]

Fascism operated in the midst of this pandemonium. The peculiar character of Italian people, as far as crowd behavior is concerned, exploded in indignation and open rebellion against Liberalism, its philosophy, and its governmental system. Slogans, myths, programs of immediate reforms, and catchwords started circulating wildly and purposely. Italians looked for Utopias around every corner. Violence, economic unrest, indignation, and dissatisfaction were the order of the day. It seems very dubious to infer, as American scholars have done, that Fascism as "another revolution" or "a revolt of the declasses" triumphed in this period.[30] Fascism, instead, never triumphed as a revolution. It never abandoned the laissez-faire doctrine, which always held an important role in the agrarian and industrial arrangements of the Corporate State.[31] Hence, it seems more appropriate to think of Fascism, especially between 1922 and 1924, as a *rivolta ideale* (ideal protest)—one that succeeded as a direct consequence of post-World War I crises in Italy. Thereafter, indeed, Mussolini's Fascism never actually went through the historical experience of a revolution. This inability of Fascism to become a revolutionary ideology explains, to a certain extent, the rise of dissent (*dissidentismo*) among the Fascist *gerarchi*, primarily groups led by C. Forni, A. Padovani, G. Calza-Bini, and A. Misuri.[32] The party struggle and anti-Fascist opposition eventually led to Rocco's Fascist Laws (*Leggi Speciali*) and to a police state after 1924. As Chabod said, the origins of Fascism cannot be reduced to rigid historical formulas. Rather, they should be projected against the background of economic unrest, unemployment, and apparent class disequilibrium. The origins of Fascism cannot be *monocausalized*. The restrictive American law of 1921 went far to add to Italy's critical socioeconomic situation and did nothing to relieve its population pressure.[33]

Mussolini and the American Immigration Restrictive Policy

For several years after coming into power, Mussolini made every effort to cope with the restrictive American law on immigration. Once every week from 1922 to 1924, he met with his advisers to study and discuss the interrelated problems of unemployment and emigration. In a speech delivered in Milan, on April 2, 1923, he defined emigration as a "physiological" need for the Italian people,[34] and at a dinner for the American ambassador in Rome, Richard Washburn Child, he affirmed: "It will not surprise you if I insist on a problem which concerns us directly: I mean the problem of emigration. I limit myself to saying that Italy would be happy to see a relaxation of the Immigration Bill, which would allow an increased flow of emigrants to North America, and the use of American capital to finance Italian industries."[35]

The American Congress reacted to Mussolini's request through Samuel Davis McReynolds, a member of the House of Representatives. On April 8, 1924, he declared that "no foreigner has any vested right in the United States of America. We have the right to pass such laws as we may see fit for the protection of our country." Moreover, reviewing the content of a press conference held by an Italian deputy, Ludovica, who had criticized immigration restrictions, McReynolds exploded:

> It is sufficient to say that Ludovica's interview would have been in better taste and more thoroughly appreciated by the American people had he made some statement as to when the Italian government intends to pay the United States the $2,000,000,000 which she owes for borrowed money. This is the gratitude which they seem to express...This question (of immigration restrictions) should be decided from an American standpoint. (Applause) It is not what is best for foreign countries, but it is what is best for America, her civilization, her refinement, her social conditions, and her government.[36]

On May 15, 1924, at the International Conference on Emigration organized by Italy with the participation of fifty nations, Mussolini described emigration as a necessary instrument for the solution of the Italian economic problems. Mussolini hoped to convince the American government, with the support of other countries, to remove the restrictions. He had failed to convince the president of the United States, Warren G. Harding, by way of Italian ambassador in Washington Gelasio Caetani, that the immigration restrictions discriminated against the Italians, who had greatly contributed to the development of the United States.[37] He later complained in a speech to the Italian Senate, on November 15, 1924: "We have been rudely struck by the Immigration Act. It is enough to say that we cannot remain idle, because we do not know where to send our surplus of humanity. The year 1924 has caused us serious concern on account of this restrictive and almost prohibitive law which America has issued against Italy."[38]

The astute Mussolini knew well how the restrictive American law snarled Italy's economic future. Therefore, when the American Quota Act became fully effective, Mussolini's Italy started striving to find work for its surplus population, no longer absorbed by foreign countries. Mussolini thought he could solve this problem and its practical consequences by acquiring new colonies. In embarking Italy upon the adventure of the *Grossraum*, Mussolini knew that Italy needed "sun and earth" for its surplus of humanity. Mussolini felt deeply concerned for Italy's necessity "for desiring new colonies and the strength to conquer them." As he stressed in an interview with the *Daily Express* on January 12, 1927, Italy, after the American restrictions became effective, had been left with the alternatives: "Either expand or explode."[39]

CHAPTER 2

EARLY FASCISM IN AMERICA AS QUEST FOR *ITALIANITÀ*

Between 1922 and 1924, the meaning of the word *Fascism* underwent a deep change in the United States, due primarily to different kinds of pressure. Whereas American radical Socialist and Communist groups interpreted Fascism as a serious threat to popular democracy and freedom, other sectors saw in Fascism an ideological movement, which required patriotic alignment and conformity to Mussolini's discipline. Therefore, as a foreign-inspired movement it was considered ominous and alien to American tradition. However, among Italian-Americans in a broader sense it designated patriotism and represented a newly found national identity. In organizing themselves into Fascist associations, Italian-Americans awakened a moral concern for patriotic and national pride. Furthermore, in this period, Italian-Americans used Fascism in America to rebut anti-Italian nativistic propaganda and to relax the paranoid stigma on the Italian community in America. Whatever interpretation Fascism received in American circles, among the Italian-Americans its reaction was

never motivated solely by political and philosophical appeal. Moreover, it never assumed conspiratorial tones intended to undermine
and eventually destroy American democratic institutions. It became,
rather, an ideology around which Italian-Americans could rally,
unite, and assert ethnic identity. Thus, many embraced Fascism as
the appropriate antidote to American nativism. In fact, from 1920
on, when anti-immigration organizations intensified their propaganda against southern European immigration, attitudes about
Italian inferiority and criminal behavior intensified. Aware of the
calamitous consequences of such propaganda, Italian-Americans
started looking for concerted action to create a pressure movement
for significant and international recognition. Between 1922 and
1924, Italian-Americans considered Fascism the ideal philosophy
to pursue national identity and patriotic regeneration. As soon as Fascism became known for programs of Italian domestic regeneration
and reconstruction of national pride abroad, Italian-Americans recognized in it a platform for Italian primacy in negating stereotyped
nativistic propaganda.

On January 1, 1923, *La Stampa Unita*, an Italian-American newspaper edited by Clement G. Lanni and published in Rochester,
New York, cheered Mussolini's decision to incorporate the commissariat for the emigration into the ministry of foreign affairs. The
decision did not appear as a normal bureaucratic reshuffle; rather, it
was interpreted as a wise political move. In fact, Mussolini's decision aimed at condemning as intolerable the stereotyped mentality
that considered the Italian worker abroad a mere production tool.
On the contrary, with national and international protection of Italians abroad under the direct responsibility of the ministry of foreign affairs, emigrants would be considered an Italian force, bearing,
among many characteristics, the ideal of *Italianità*: "The emigrant
considered merely as a worker and not as an Italian citizen is a product of a Socialist mentality that we can no longer tolerate. Fascism
will get rid of it, and soon."[1]

On January 14, 1923, Luigi Barzini, Sr., who had been for 25
years a member of the staff of the *Corriere della Sera* newspaper

of Milan, arrived in New York to become editor-in-chief of a new Italo-American newspaper, *Il Corriere d'America*. The first number of the newspaper had been published in New York City on December 27, 1922. The idea of introducing in America a newspaper with a national and international breadth was envisaged as making Americans of Italian extraction "better Americans" while preserving their Italian heritage. The newspaper was intended neither as an organ of Fascist propaganda nor as a soapbox for any political party or movement. According to Barzini, a primary objective of the newspaper was to correct the misunderstandings that existed "among Italians about Americans and among Americans about Italians." Barzini advocated a new spirit; both Italy and the United States needed love and will to do good. In line with these peculiar objectives, the newspaper would prove sufficiently that Italy and America had more in common than historical diversities and radical differences: "American civilization has just as much to gain from what Italian civilization can bring it in the future as it has gained from the contribution of Anglo-Saxon civilization in the past."

As far as the ethnic boundaries were concerned, Barzini stressed *Il Corriere d'America*'s peculiar objectives "to bring the lessons of American civilization home to the people of Italian blood living here, to urge them not to set themselves apart and cultivate the feeling of foreignness, but to identify themselves with life around them."[2]

A few days later, speaking at a dinner sponsored by the Italy-America Society of New York, Prince Gelasio Caetani, the new Italian ambassador to the United States, stressed with vigor that Mussolini considered no country closer to the United States than Italy. In Caetani's words, Mussolini's intentions toward America were neither imperialistic nor bellicose. Instead, he aimed at restoring peace and prosperity "in this much-tormented world" in collaboration with the American nation. These were, in the opinion of Caetani, the immediate objectives of Mussolini's diplomatic strategy. How, asked the ambassador, could Mussolini be embroiled in international controversy with the United States if his primary concern for the economic and financial reconstruction of Italy could hardly divert his attention and preoccupation from domestic issues? Italy's political situation remained somehow fluid. Work ought to be made for those who had no jobs. Increased emigration had become an indispensable requisite for the readjustment of Italian affairs. How could the precariousness of the domestic situation drive Mussolini, at least at this time, into a provocative Fascist propaganda campaign in the United States?[3]

None of the activities of early Fascism in the United States seem politically oriented. On March 21, 1923, Professor Dino Bigongiari, head of the Italian section of the Department of Roman Languages at Columbia University and director of the Fascist Branch of New York, asserted that the objective of Fascism in America was to combat radicalism and criminality. Fascism's aims were channeled to promote good citizenship and the welfare of Italian war veterans and to redeem "the Italian population of the United States from its evil elements, criminals and bootleggers, who have brought discredit upon their fellow Italians." Only incidentally, affirmed Bigongiari, were Fascist organizations of North America helping the cause of Mussolini and Fascism in this country.[4]

In March 1923, in Cleveland, Ohio, Italian-born residents formed a branch of Fascists of North America. Two thousand members described as seeking "more social than militaristic propaganda" joined the association.[5] Meanwhile, in Youngstown, Ohio, a group of prominent Italian-Americans organized, on March 21, a branch of the Fascists of North America with the "avowed purpose of stamping out an alleged Black Hand organization."[6]

> Hence, early American Fascism was not conceived around vested political and imperialistic interests. Rather, it was purported as the sole instrument of a true Italian risorgimento abroad. According to Mario Missiroli, it was due "to Mussolini and to the Black Shirt revolution if Italians scattered all over the world were enabled to find again their national pride." Quoting Mussolini's speech in Milan, in April 1923, Missiroli claimed that since his advent to power Mussolini had substituted *Italian abroad* for the word *emigrant*. And Missiroli continued: "Fascist Italy became the true Fatherland for the Italians who reside abroad, the country of their dreams and desires, the

Fatherland which does not forget and is ever present in the hour of need. Italian colonies gathered in their numbers around Fascist groups formed abroad and it became clear that Fascism and Fatherland were henceforth synonymous."[7]

Indeed, the Italian community of America saw in Fascism the opportunity to open horizons for ethnic aspirations. These aspirations, undoubtedly, would modify the structure and traditional American makeup of the Italian community. Therefore, they cherished Mussolini as the chief architect of Italian grandeur abroad. Mussolini's ambitions in America never transcended a patriotic activism among the Italian-Americans. He never stressed political ambitions or programs aimed at a pro-Italy militant Nationalism. Rather, he wanted a Fascism for Italian-Americans that would introduce a significant, but uncommitted, non-political, international organization that might help Italian-Americans find national identity.

On November 4, 1922, a few days after he was summoned by King Victor Emmanuel to form a new government, Mussolini addressed a message to all Italians living in the United States. Recalling the historic event of the celebration of the fourth anniversary of Italian victory in World War I, he invited Italian-Americans to unite and organize themselves into *Fasci* to disseminate the virtues of Italy beyond the boundaries of the Fatherland. Through these organized and cohesive groups, the Italian-Americans would gain further recognition for their role in American civic and economic life. Moreover, Americans would increase their sympathy for, and trust of, Italian-Americans because "your presence and role in America will be undeniably regarded as a contributing factor in the prosperity and the progress of the adopted country."[8]

As early as 1923, Giuseppe Bastianini, secretary general of Italian Fasci in foreign countries, disclosed that well over 150 Fascist organizations had been created abroad. Over 85 had been founded in the United States. In giving his full report and overall assessment on the Fasci abroad before the Grand Council of Fascism on February 16, 1923, Bastianini painted a good overall picture and indicated future prospects looked bright and promising. Moreover, Fascist organizations abroad had fulfilled the task assigned them by Fascism and the Italian nation. Conferences, centers of studies, educational meetings, and events of all kinds continued to take place to illustrate the role of Fascism in the process of national awakening and regeneration beyond the boundaries of Italy. In that same meeting the group unanimously approved a document dealing with the objectives and role of Fascism abroad. As it will be pointed out time and again, this document will represent the *vademecum* of Fascism's role in the world. A preamble preceded the five articles forming the document. Mirroring Fascist concern for Italians abroad, it insisted on the sacredness of national identity and pride among Italian colonies throughout the world. The Grand Council of Fascism attributed a great deal of importance to the formation of Fascist organizations abroad; it formulated the theory that the existence of Fascist organizations would lead to a stronger cohesion among Italians, and their activities would bring a revival of patriotism and nationhood among the sons of Italy. Moreover, it committed Fascists abroad to the creed of noninterference in and respect for the political structure and constitutional principles affirmed by host countries. The five articles are worth citing:

1. Fascists who reside abroad should be obedient to the laws of the country whose guests they are; they should set a daily example of their obedience to their fellow countrymen and to the citizens of the nation in which they live.
2. They shall not take part in the home politics of the country which gives them hospitality.
3. They shall not create discord within Italian colonies.
4. They shall set an example of public and private probity.
5. They shall uphold and defend their original country, defending its heritage and civilization.[9]

In January 1923, Italian Ambassador Caetani dubbed Fascism in the United States "a delicate affair if not a risky adventure." Uncompromising and prickly, Caetani quarreled with everyone in Rome, asserting that Fascism in America would never develop into a fully pro-Italy oriented organization. While in Italy Fascist organizations could be controlled through a strong political apparatus and eventually rectified with coercive and even violent means, these same measures could never have been applied in the United States. Americans would bristle at the dissolution of a Fascist group by force and coercion and would see such behavior as a reflection of Fascist behavior used in Italy to subdue the opposition. The ambassador considered people of low moral standards the most unfortunate weakness of the *Fasci* in America. For example, Agostino De Biasi, editor of the newspaper *Il Carroccio*, heartily endorsed Fascism, nonetheless, he was considered a scoundrel and held in contempt by the U.S. Italian community. On the other hand, eagerly indoctrinated himself with Fascist ideas and enthusiasm, Ambassador Caetani did not advocate repression of Fascist activities in the United States. In many respects, Caetani visualized Fascism in America as a philosophy in motion and in contradiction giving birth to political opposition—a situation not unlikely to produce an alternative to the American democratic system. Therefore, he set forth rules and strategies on managing a campaign "to infuse Fascist ideology among the Americans and the Italian-Americans." His campaign meant waiting for the right moment "to channel the American public opinion in the mainstream of Fascism."[10]

With an unusually intellectual American background acquired as a Columbia University student, Ambassador Caetani had been exposed to the best of American political and public thought. Moreover, he had kept abreast of current opinion in the U.S. and proved himself an able ambassador in handling Fascism there. On January 28, a few days after the first assessment of the situation of *Fasci* in America, Caetani sent Mussolini a lengthy telegram of recommendations for the future of Fascism in the United States. According to the document, Fascist organizations were increasing, especially in those areas where many Italians lived. Some local organizations seemed to grow from spontaneous and local initiatives. The overall striking reality, however, was that Fascism was expanding daily. Since the movement was having wide-reaching effects, the ambassador looked for Mussolini's opinion on the matter. Also, he wanted to know whether the Italian government planned to direct Fascist activities in the United States. At the same time, Caetani wanted to inform Mussolini of much more than the track record of Fascism in the U.S. Though he could scarcely predict the results of Fascist activities in the U.S., he had a strong feeling that active participation by Italian leaders in the internal affairs of American Fascism would spur adverse American public and governmental reaction.

Accordingly, Caetani cautioned Mussolini against miscalculating American reaction to Fascism in its midst. Also, the ambassador wanted to convey the message that unweighed or premature reactions by the Italian authorities would lead to serious diplomatic consequences. Although Americans grew increasingly sympathetic to Fascism daily, in Caetani's opinion the issue required subtle handling. First, Americans still viewed Fascism as a patriotic awakening of Italian-Americans. Second, Fascism in America was used as a parameter to assess Italian Fascism and to express normative values on Mussolini's political and governmental activities in Italy. To perpetuate this American tribute to Fascism, Caetani invited Mussolini to broadcast word that Fascist activities in America would be rigidly restricted to the diffusion of Italian culture, sport, philanthropy, and national identity. Fascist organizations would refrain from becoming centers of political propaganda: "Fascism in America must be viewed as a genuine and spontaneous phenomenon of Italian revival. In this context, it should avoid forging organizational links with Italian governmental and political groups. Moreover, it should not be encouraged or supported by the Italian Embassy." Finally, Caetani suggested that Fascism in America, on account of its large-scale unpreparedness, should not be viewed by the Americans as an international gendarmerie with conspiratorial muscle.[11]

Chapter 3

Fascism in America: Conspiracy or Quest for Italian-U.S. Solidarity?

By March 22, 1923, the mood had changed. Ambassador Caetani sent Mussolini an informative memorandum on this date about American reaction to Fascist organizations in the United States. According to Caetani, the growth of Fascist organizations had by then created an atmosphere of pessimism in the U.S. and had generated serious backlash among some segments of Americans. Fascism, regarded earlier as a spontaneous resurgence of patriotism among Italian-Americans, found itself suddenly under fire. In an abrupt change, the American press had begun to present Fascism as an international conspiracy and a serious menace to American democracy. The Italian ambassador saw in the yellow journalism of William Randolph Hearst the beginnings of a denigratory campaign against Fascism. Though the motives remained unclear, the events enabled Caetani to tie them all together in a seamless package. He detected a campaign artfully

manipulated to spur criticism of and adverse reactions toward
Fascism.[1] No one now doubts the enormous influence the New York
press had on twentieth-century political ideologies, in particular
Socialism and Fascism.

For a decade and more (1919–1930), individual citizens, news
media, and state and federal authorities had generally formulated
their own ideas on the basis of their beliefs. Without any doubt,
this tendency had received enormous impetus from the close relationship of the news media in New York and popular sentiment.
Many felt that Americanism and American institutions were under
massive political pressure, and some people probably associated
Socialism with the hated Russian police state. Fanning the flame
of fears, the press cultivated among its readers the myth of the Red
Terror.

The news media began to question Fascism's insurgence as a form
of extreme Nationalism among Italian-Americans. Significantly,
the press in New York attempted to present Socialism and Fascism
as members of the same conspiratorial club. The passing of anti-
Socialist bills in April 1920 aimed at outlawing the Socialist Party
and disenfranchising Socialists in the U.S., curbing activities of the
National Security League in defending the Constitution and principles of Americanism against the "Red Menace that threw its bloody
shadow over all Europe" were clear symptoms of the tense atmosphere
in New York at that time. There were those who felt, a little dizzily,
that a Red revolution threatened New York in 1922 "to impose upon
this State a minority dictatorship." However, could a handful of "Red
rascals" stage a revolution and proclaim Red rule in the U.S.? "Well,"
maintained the united patriots, "let us review history: the beloved
regime of Diaz in Mexico was overthrown by 20,000 men; the Czar's
regime was overthrown by 50,000 and Kerensky's by 100,000."

The conspiratorial tone of Fascism in the U.S., inflated by
the mainstream press and by the Italian-American anti-Fascist
press, was blown out of proportion in November 1929. At that time,
Marcus Duffield's article, "Mussolini's American Empire" appeared in *Harper's Magazine*, followed immediately by a resolution

presented to the U.S. Senate by Alabama Sen. J. Thomas Heflin denouncing "certain foreign countries especially interested in striking down vital American institutions and changing our form of government."[2]

This marriage of the news media and popular sentiment produced anti-Socialist and anti-Fascist ideological trappings but escaped Caetani's attention and analysis. It might appear incongruous, but Fascism produced some frantic consequences that eventually undermined its credibility in the United States as a patriotic, uncommitted, nonpartisan movement. Some facts are at hand. Hearst's anti-Fascist campaign—with the full cooperation of other New York newspapers—began the day after the inauguration of the Fascist Association of New York (March 17, 1923). The New York Association, founded by Umberto Menicucci in 1922, with its 10,000 members symbolized the pulsing heart of Fascism in America.

The press shared to the fullest extent a fearsome bias against Fascism and broadcast reports of its treacherous and conspiratorial nature. Media takes on Fascism included tales that (1) Mussolini directed the work of Fascist agents in New York; (2) the Italian government had provided Fascist agents to spread throughout the United States; (3) the Italian ambassador in Washington had granted permission to Fascist associations; and (4) American *Fasci* aimed at creating in the U.S. a vast network of pro-Fascist activities.[3] The press implied these activities were encouraged by immigrants who maintained Italian citizenship and, moreover, the latter tried to convert naturalized Italian-Americans to Fascism.

Leading Italian-American figures and nationwide organizations joined the choir of protest and condemned Fascist militancy in the United States. New York State Senator Salvatore A. Cotillo considered Fascism as a movement "out of place in the United States." In a speech delivered in Albany, New York, on March 25, 1923, he remarked that Fascism in America was the receptacle of Italian war veterans who had left Italy in the aftermath of World War I. If American citizens of Italian extraction were earnestly engaged in Americanization, Cotillo said, they should reject Fascism as incongruous, ominous, and un-American. Moreover, any propaganda weapon introduced in this country to awaken in Italians national pride and cultural heritage would represent an act of duplicity to the nationwide acclaimed Order of the Sons of Italy. Strong in its 300,000 members, with 40,000 in New York City, he contended, that organization could better serve the interests of Italian-Americans than could Fascist activities and propaganda. The time had come, Cotillo asserted, when "the Fascists of the United States understand that America has no use for them. And even if they are not a political society, their very name, their affiliation to the Italian organization are here absolutely out of place."[4]

Fascism as a strictly political entity produced a sense of frustration in the United States. As a matter of fact, the sixteen lodges of the Order of the Sons of Italy in Cleveland joined in rejecting Fascism as a patriotic ideology. They viewed Fascism as an alien phenomenon imported from Italy into the United States.[5] However, this exemplifies the difficulty Americans had in separating political ideology and national identity; what Mussolini had postulated in America could not happen. He erred in trying to introduce in America an uncommitted, non-political international organization to support and enhance national identity among Italian-Americans. He erred in trying to separate Fascism and politics and in presenting to Americans only one face of this two-pronged philosophy.

He undoubtedly knew too little of the history of American thought and action, which would not support or have any confidence in his generalizations. Most people listened unsympathetically to Mussolini's claims that Fascism in America aimed at national revival and identity among Italian-Americans. Mussolini's vague duplicity created difficult problems for Fascism and Italian-Americans alike. In fact, naturalized Italian-Americans were said to have been compelled by Mussolini's agents to promise obedience to local Fascist organizations even though they had declared allegiance to the U.S. Constitution. The *New York Herald*, however, went further in an article titled, "Fascists Invade United States in World Expansion." The newspaper warned Americans and the federal government to look carefully into the record of Fascist activities in the U.S. Headlines treated American Fascism as a revolutionary ideology with the aim to rule America, undoubtedly the newspaper's generalizations tended to conceal by vague language some problems posed by Fascism. The section of the article dealing with Menicucci's interview reflects traditional clichés about Fascism, such as:

1. Fascism encourages vitalization of Italy in America by artists, scientists, workers, persons in commercial and industrial pursuits and everybody who works for civilization.
2. Fascism honors the victory of Vittorio Veneto.
3. Fascism supports cordial relations between Italy and America for peace and prosperity.
4. Fascism promotes mental and physical development in accordance with programs supported by Mussolini.
5. Fascism insists that Italians in countries other than Italy understand the duties of Italian citizenship and obey the laws of the countries in which they live.
6. Fascism honors the unity of Italian veterans of American and Italian armies.
7. Fascism supports aid for immigrants, helps prevent unemployment, and encourages the Americanization of Italian immigrants.[6]

Anti-Fascists considered Menicucci a political charlatan who sought enthusiastic disciples among Americans and Italian-Americans. This only added confusion to the puzzle of Fascism in America.

The traditional American theory of Fascist conspiracy handed down to media, investigators, and historians, began in 1923 and reached explosive moments in 1929 with Duffield's article and again in 1939 with the Dies Committee's report. Duffield's and Dies' allegations, fundamentally the same, railed against Fascism in 1923 and later advanced the idea of a Fascist menace that planted agents provocateurs in the United States. The reports directly linked the government of Italy with Fascist agitation in America.[7]

The conspiracy thesis survived into the 1930s. Even though little evidence exists to bolster the theory, Alan Cassels later (1964) mimicked Duffield's and Dies' stance. Cassels' analysis neglected to separate fact from opinion and reality from propaganda. These inconsistencies have led the American scholar to perpetuate the myth of Fascism in America as "an exportable commodity...among the Italian-Americans in the months following Mussolini's accession to power."[8] Such inconsistencies suggest a reassessment of the nature and goals of Fascism in the United States between 1922 and 1940. The issue of monocausation, i.e., Fascism as a conspiratorial phenomenon, has been too stringent and appears deeply rooted in the minds of twentieth-century American scholars of Fascism. This quasiaxiomatic proposition has prevented an unbiased historical investigation of the nature and role of Fascism in America in the early period (1922–1924). Moreover, little has been said of the role of Italian-Americans and their reaction to Fascism in the United States.

Indeed, Fascism needs to be examined in its diversified components, since no common matrix motivated the phenomenon. In its early period, Fascism in America did not have a subversive or imperialistic connotation. The U.S. secretary of state on December 27, 1929, seemed to have discarded completely the conspiratorial thesis: "The investigation of the incidents referred to in the article in *Harper's Magazine* has been completed by this Department and it has not revealed any activities on the part of any residents in this country of Italian extraction or on the part of any Italian officials which were directed against this government or against its institutions."[9]

As Mussolini saw it, rather than serving as an instrument of subversive propaganda, early Fascism would serve a twofold strategy: first, it ought to reevaluate the Italian community in the U.S. and stir Italian national identity; and second, it ought to lay down the foundations for a geopolitical entente. On November 11, 1922, the weekly magazine, *Literary Digest*, recognized the issue: "Of particular interest to American readers is Mussolini's expectation of forming an economic entente between Italy and the United States."[10]

Some facts about Mussolini's strategy in the early 1920s need to be added to this case study. Rejecting Woodrow Wilson's internationalism as political metaphysics, Mussolini's theory of imperialism became unique. On New Year's day of 1920, he purposely wrote: "By no means are there such things as an Italian, a French or English imperialism. By the term imperialism I mean the eternal and immanent rule of life. Imperialism is nothing more than the desire to earn a livelihood. This is an aspiration that each individual wants to accomplish in the world today. Whatever its basic cause, imperialism today must be democratic, peaceful, economic, and spiritual."[11]

Between 1922 and 1924, Italian Fascism, in the national and international context, was still very much a myth—a myth of security and national order—and it had not achieved international prominence. In many respects, even in Italy, it was a neologism. As an intensely national creed, it stressed the grandeur of the nation. "From now on," asserted Mussolini, "the countries of the world will understand that the myth of Fascism is in building Italy as an important nation to Europe and to the world alike."[12] Even Enrico Corradini, chief exponent of an aggressively imperialistic policy in the 1910s, after the Nationalist-Fascist merger in February, 1923, abandoned his intransigent line of expansionist and imperialist policy. In editorials in *Popolo d'Italia* in 1923, Corradini repudiated his traditional old-fashioned imperialist outlook. According to Corradini, Italian imperialism abroad was nothing more than a vital component of a Nationalist philosophy of life that had regenerated in the Italian nation the faith and the strength to earn moral and national respect in the world. Corradini affirmed, in 1924, that the Fascist state was going to raise Italy above the other countries of the world. "We must seek," asserted Corradini, "Italy's moral and political regeneration. We must look at the problems of the world with an eye closer to the necessities of Italy."[13] What these examples really indicate, however, is the impossibility for Mussolini and Italy, in the early period of Fascist control, to seek imperialistic expansion and subversive interference in the Western Hemisphere.

Within this national and international context, on March 21, 1923, the Italian ambassador presented to American Secretary of State Charles E. Hughes, a verified and assuring version of the role, the nature, and the goals of Fascism in America. According to Ambassador Caetani, the secretary of state had appeared deeply concerned about the content of the communiqué issued in Rome by the Grand Council of Fascism in its February 14 meeting. The secretary of state seemed dismayed at the issue of requiring loyalty to Fascism on the part of American citizens of Italian extraction. According to the secretary of state, allegiance to the Constitution of the United States ought to be total and uncompromised. The American government, moreover, would not tolerate a double standard for Italian-Americans, i.e., allegiance to the Constitution *and* loyalty to Fascism. The Italian ambassador remarked that the Italian communiqué had severely forbidden the Fascist organization's intervening in the political affairs of the American government at all levels. The unfair allegations made against Fascism had complicated the situation much more than imagined. Exaggerated and outrageous charges had been made against many Italian-Americans who had never hesitated in their allegiance and patriotism toward America. Furthermore, if the situation of the *Fasci* in America had briskly deteriorated and their future made unpredictable, premeditated actions were responsible. Perhaps the leading source of resentment and confusion in evaluating the activities of the *Fasci* in America had been spurred by the enthusiastic response of its members. In Caetani's judgment, "mercenary exploiters and hostile provocateurs" had staged unjustified campaigns of opposition and encouraged resentments aimed at making Fascism less palatable to the American public. A flaw in U.S. Fascism was its quivering emotionality that turned into condemnation when any action by a Fascist was criticized as a potential threat to Americanism.

Judged in this light, 1920s Fascism in America seems to have received credit for something it could never fulfill, and the entire issue of conspiracy became disproportionately inflated. In fact, Fascism in America could not go beyond a form of Nationalistic revival: first, because of its peculiar weakness, i.e., the absence of cohesion and leadership; and second, because Fascism, especially among Italian-Americans, served as a dividing force that produced jealousy and outbursts rather than unity and collaboration. Voicing his personal disappointment about the situation of Fascism in America, Ambassador Caetani indignantly concluded: "Fascism in America, as it stands now, does not do any good to Italy, to the Italians in America, and to Fascist doctrine at large."[14]

This general climate of aversion toward Fascism appears to have heavily influenced the American government and the Congress. Strong feelings of Fascist invasion of America prompted governmental investigations, and the Senate showed evidence of a deeply rooted aversion toward Fascism. A few days following the inauguration of the Fascist association of New York City, Utah's Democratic senator, William H. King, called for mass deportation of those naturalized Italian-Americans who had expressed sympathy toward Fascism:

> The Italian-American naturalized citizens betray their oath of allegiance to the American Constitution the very moment they become members of a Fascist organization. Fascism as American, indigenous phenomenon must be retained as a foreign born ideology. Moreover, Fascism is contrary to our fundamental principles of liberty and government by vote. If by December (1923) the organization appears to have assumed nationwide proportions, I shall seek congressional legislative action against those naturalized Italian-Americans who are still affiliated with the organization. Hence, I shall ask for their deportation to Italy. An organization that is under foreign control cannot exist here, since its scope is clearly un-American and antinational.[15]

The press played a large role in setting the stage for this situation. The precipitous rise of rumors of an incumbent Fascist conspiracy in America trumpeted by the media made a nonpartisan and objective evaluation of Fascist goals in America impossible. G. Ward Price, English writer and ambassador at large, laid out the whole issue in a retrospective analysis in 1938. According to Price, large sectors of the press in democratic England and the United States moved in the wrong direction when evaluating Fascism. Instead of putting national interests first, its outlook was motivated by vague and visionary principles: "Because Germany and Italy have evolved a new national system which rejects many of the theories and practices traditional in Britain and the United States, many British and American newspapers assume that these regimes are tyrannies imposed by force...It must be admitted that American newspapers have taken greater pains than those of European countries to investigate the authoritarian regimes in Germany and Italy."[16]

To make things worse, at the beginning of April, Captain Giovanni Gangemi, of the Bureau of *Fasci* Abroad in Rome, sent dispatches inviting consular agents throughout the United States "to designate trust-worthy persons to head local Fascist associations." The reaction on the part of the Italian ambassador in Washington, Caetani, was immediate and harsh. He sent an urgent dispatch to Mussolini denouncing "the serious consequences that such an imprudent act would bear upon Italo-American relations."[17] Continuing on his mission to inform, on April 6, the ambassador held a press conference in Washington in which he again assured American authorities that Fascism in America merely represented a natural quest for Italian revival and identity for millions of Italians living in the country. Since Fascism had never had political goals in sight, he pleaded with Americans to visualize Fascism as a great appeal to the Italian-Americans for spiritual, national, and moral pride. Caetani warned that further attempts to misrepresent Fascism in America as a conspiratorial, un-American, and antidemocratic ideology would be shortsighted, outrageous, and hypocritical. He was quite certain that anti-Fascist propaganda had been staged by Socialists and Communists who saw in the triumph of Fascism the most powerful obstacle for expansion of Bolshevism in the world. Concluding his remarks, Caetani pointed out that aversion to Fascism represented Americans' inability to understand the values of such an ideology; the majority of Americans had not yet mastered the renaissance of manhood that Fascism sought. According to Caetani, American antipathy to

Fascism was so deeply rooted that many still confused Fascism with Bolshevism. Others even associated Fascism with capitalistic reaction. Briefing Mussolini about the press conference, the ambassador suggested that Italian authorities refrain immediately from interfering in the internal affairs of the *Fasci* in America.[18] Mussolini's reaction was immediate. Perhaps he did not want to jeopardize the position of the Italian-Americans. Moreover, mindful of the suspicions that Fascist activities had raised in the United States, he sent a telegram to Caetani containing the following significant statement: "Let the American government know that Italian Fascism has no intention whatsoever to interfere in the internal affairs of the American government at any levels. The Fascist party is ready to order the dissolution of the North American Fascist Association if, by any means, its existence should undermine the relations between Italy and the United States of America, that I want to be of a highest cordiality."[19]

On April 24, the U.S. State Department, with instruction number 344, ordered the American ambassador in Rome, R. W. Child, to gather information on Fascist activities abroad. On May 15, Ambassador Child sent a lengthy memorandum in which he stressed that Fascist organizations ought to be regarded as spontaneous manifestations growing outside Italy. Though a program for their "stimulation and partial control" was managed in Italy, nevertheless, the idea of "keeping Italian Nationalistic spirit alive in foreign countries, especially in the United States" continued. As far as the nature and goals of Fascism in America were concerned, the ambassador saw in them a platform for political recognition of Italian-Americans. In fact, the Italian community had started moving in the direction of operational political unity. The movement, initiated by the previous Italian ambassador in Washington, Vittorio Rolandi-Riccio—who certainly could not be accused of connivance with Fascism—had recognized in Fascism the epitome of newly found national identity. The whole process aimed at channeling Italian-Americans toward a nationalistic affiliation that would make them politically committed, but in unity and not as single individuals. This important aspect stood out clearly from Child's memorandum: "I desire to add that ever since the United States elections of 1920, there has been a deepseated belief in Italian political circles that the Italian population in the United States may be made a unified political factor."[20]

The American Embassy in Rome, headed now by Henry P. Fletcher, sent another lengthy report to the secretary of state in Washington on May 9, 1924. Ambassador Fletcher had met Guido Solazzo, vicesecretary general of Italian *Fasci* in foreign countries, who briefed him on the aims of Fascist organizations abroad, especially in the United States. Solazzo's assessment did not contradict previous statements by Mussolini, Bastianini, and Caetani. According to Solazzo, the growth of Fascism abroad represented a spontaneous manifestation of patriotic revival emanating "from the desire of Italians, living abroad and who sympathize with the Fascist movement and believe in the principles of Fascism, to form organizations which would enable them more effectively to express this sympathy and adherence." However, Fascist organizations abroad had been sufficiently instructed to refrain from interfering in political activities of countries where they were located. Also, they had been instructed to cooperate in every way "to foster good relations between their mother country and the country of their residence." On the particular issue of Fascist activities in the United States, Solazzo gave assurances that the Italian government wanted to see good relations firmly maintained between Italy and the U.S. Moreover, he assured, the Grand Council of Fascism would neither suggest nor support any political involvement of Fascist organizations aimed at undermining the democratic status of the United States. In reality, such involvement would be considered an attempt to set up an *imperium in imperio* (a state within the state) and would violate the principle of American sovereignty.[21]

Between the second half of 1923 and the end of 1924, Mussolini left no stone unturned to generate sympathy for Fascism and for Italy in the United States. On June 28, 1923, he gladly participated in a testimonial dinner offered by the American Embassy in Rome for the inauguration of the Italian-American Association. After a vibrant introduction, he remarked on the difficulty on the part of foreigners to fully grasp the nature and the goals of Fascism as a new ideology. Mussolini flattered Ambassador Child profusely, saying he alone represented an exception to the rule. In Mussolini's words, Child had mastered the philosophy of Fascism in its totality as "exaltation of strength, wisdom, discipline, responsibility and hierarchical authority."[22]

Relentlessly strategizing, by the end of June Mussolini had arranged through diplomatic channels a royal visit to the United States by the king and queen of Italy. The visit was planned to take place in early 1924. The trip was canceled due to the sudden death of President Harding, but Mussolini had already spelled out the objectives of the monarchs' visit in a letter sent to the King on June 29, 1923. According to the document, the visit was intended to bring economic benefits to Italy. In a moment when the overall European economic situation was precarious, Italy had to seek economic and financial help from the United States. Moreover, the presence of the royal family in America in the midst of the Italian-American community would most likely awaken national pride. Also, closer and renewed amicable relations with Americans and their government might contribute to loosening the rigidity of the newly adopted immigration restriction.[23] Mussolini knew full well the necessity to maintain amicable relations with the United States and avoid altering the diplomatic course. He seemed never to underestimate the consequences that negative impressions or reactions on the part of the Americans would have on Italy.

After the issue of Fascist conspiracy had been disseminated by the press, Mussolini's immediate task was to prevent confrontations with American authorities, which would inevitably aggravate the situation and further alienate what sympathy Fascism still enjoyed among segments of the American public. This, in the long run, would have undermined completely the pursuit of attainable goals that Mussolini still considered feasible. He wanted to embark both countries on a new international course. However, to pursue this new course, Mussolini knew that he needed to dispel from the mind of the Americans the deeply rooted conviction that he was trying to pursue a policy of imperialism in America through his Black Shirts. As he stressed on January 19, 1924, to Maria Fermolini, a correspondent for an Italian-American newspaper, Americans had been negatively impressed by "the picturesque and romantic appearance of the Black Shirts, neglecting the idealities, the courage, and the enthusiasm they represented."[24] Alleged Fascist conspiratorial imperialism in America became again an object of analysis on March 6, 1924. In an interview with Oscar de Carvalho Azevedo of the Latin American Telegraphic Agency, Mussolini reiterated his ideas on the issue: "The alleged Italian imperialism has never existed. Italy is willing to pursue a policy of committed friendship with all the nations of the world. Italy's policy will be peaceful without being necessarily pacifist."[25]

On February 24, Mussolini instructed the Italian ambassador in Washington to seek the support of the president of the United States for a new national and international course the Italian government intended to inaugurate on behalf of the economic necessities of Europe. To implement the new course, the United States ought to make available its capital and natural resources, while Italy would provide man power. This collaboration, if carried out with wisdom and self-respect on both sides, would produce far reaching effects in the world and in Europe in particular: "Associated in a myriad of industrial and commercial activities, Italy and America will have a solid lead on European countries and will control the economic outlet in the near Middle East."[26] This historical reassessment of the nature and role of Fascism in America between 1922 and 1924, makes evident that Mussolini's aims in America were not conspiratorial, and historical and diplomatic developments prove that Fascism never assumed conspiratorial tones. The conspiracy thesis appears to be extravagant and destitute of historical foundations. Mussolini's aims seemed to transcend both Italian and American boundaries. He wanted to secure for Italy a position of political and economic control in Europe. Such a position could develop only with the assurance on the part of the United States that Italy would be provided with capital and economic assistance. A policy of Italian-American solidarity would mark the beginning of Italian preeminence in Europe. However, in Mussolini's opinion, a durable and concrete Italian-American collaboration needed to be sustained through the revival of national heritage and pride of the Italian-American community.

Mussolini plainly meant an Italian expansion toward the East, as was unequivocally spelled out on February 21, 1921, in a speech delivered to the Council of Ministers dealing with the forthcoming annexation of Fiume to Italy: "Italy cannot expand elsewhere but toward East. In the West there are clearly defined and established States...In many respects, Italy's peaceful expansion must move toward East. Fiume represents the trait d'union between Italy and the near Middle East."[27]

Mussolini wanted to pursue the political strategy of his predecessor, Giovanni Giolitti, who in mid-1921 had proposed an alliance with the United States. According to the proposal, in case of war with another European power, "Italy would give the United States control of the Mediterranean, easy access to the markets of the near East and southern Russia. Italy would gain influence and the protection of a powerful ally."[28] Even though the American government rejected the Italian proposal in open contrast to the Wilsonian principles of self-determination and coexistence, Italian leaders never gave up and did not leave any stone unturned in seeking American solidarity. However, from 1922 to 1924, Mussolini's policy of rapprochement to the United States aimed at a larger share for Italy: Italian-American solidarity in the Mediterranean should capitalize on the development of Italy's greatness.

Echoing Mussolini's foreign policy aspirations, the *Times* of London on March 3, 1923, stated that in Mussolini's view, "the most durable alliances are those which do not need advocacy but are imposed silently by a community of vital interests."[29] These aspirations appeared to Mussolini possible and farsighted. Using this terminological guise, Mussolini expressed his longrange program of foreign policy in the near Middle East. Already in April 1923, the Fascist newspaper *Impero* asserted that Italy was looking toward America as the only country that could give moral and economic support to Italy's national and international revival. America, in many circumstances, had manifested profound sympathy for Italy. Perhaps it was a special attitude, maybe a warmer attitude than the U.S. showed other European nations. The expectations of the Italian people could be met only if both countries agreed to form an economic triangle, America-Italy-Middle East, under the influence and control of America and Italy. In this way, both countries could establish a lasting influence in the Mediterranean. Now that the Italian government had proposed the plan, it was up to consular agents throughout America to work to make both sympathy and cooperation active, possible, and concrete.[30]

Mussolini sensed that if many Americans developed an image of Fascism as anti-Bolshevik and as a doctrine of law and order, then Fascism could profoundly affect relations between Italy and the United States. Therefore, Mussolini's Fascist propaganda in the United States did not aim at engaging Fascism in conspiratorial and un-American activities, but rather at enhancing sympathy among the Italian-American community and Americans at large. In this way, he might have exercised a psychological influence in pursuing American solidarity for Italy's new international course in the near Middle East.[31]

CHAPTER 4

FASCISM IN AMERICA
IN THE AFTERMATH
OF MATTEOTTI'S MURDER

In Italy during June of 1924, Socialist Deputy Giacomo Matteotti was murdered by Fascist *squadristi*. His death came after his courageous condemnation of the atmosphere of terror and grave irregularities committed by Fascists in the general elections of April 1924. Through acts of terrorism and intimidation, Fascists had secured an unexpected and strong majority in the Italian Parliament. Matteotti's slaying raised, however, a cry of indignation and horror in Italy and abroad.

Mussolini and his Ambassador Gelasio Caetani managed to survive politically in the aftermath of Matteotti's assassination. Aware of the general distrust for his regime, Mussolini rushed in, writing personal dispatches to diplomatic agents and chargés d'affaires abroad. Mussolini instructed them to spread the word that Matteotti's murder had "aggravated the domestic situation of Italy, since Fascism was faced now with more intrigues." Though the actual executors of the crime had been secured to the Italian judiciary authorities, who would certainly render full justice to the victims, Mussolini suggested that the diplomatic authorities abroad insist in pointing out the general atmosphere of uneasiness that now confronted Fascism. Furthermore, he invited them to stress that the murder had, at least for the time being, suspended the process of national reconciliation he had initiated.[1]

On June 18, Ambassador Gelasio Caetani cabled Mussolini assuring him that the American press in general had reported the Matteotti incident, without any "sharp or unfavorable direct reaction against Mussolini and the Italian government." Particularly, the *New York Times* had commented on the "incident of Matteotti," using words of respect and sympathy on behalf of Fascism, Mussolini, and the Italian government.[2] On June 21, continuing his informative reporting, Caetani briefed Mussolini on the latest developments of the Matteotti affair: with the exception of the Italian-American anti-Fascist and a few American newspapers, such as the *World* of New York City, the majority of the American press continued to maintain "an objective position, with comments of sympathy for the Italian government." Moreover, Caetani assured Mussolini that, in an interview with the Associated Press, he had carefully followed Mussolini's instructions. He had especially emphasized the deep sorrow and grief expressed by the head of the Italian government and the nation at large. Finally, he had carefully presented the three issues Mussolini had recommended (a) that the murder had been committed by vicious elements who had infiltrated the Fascist Party with the evil intention to subvert it; (b) that justice would be meted out with severity to the material executors of the cynical crime; and (c) that recent domestic events would fortify Fascism in its program of moral and national regeneration.[3] After Caetani gave Mussolini these sympathetic assurances, anti-Fascist manifestations against *Il Duce* and his repressive regime quickly followed. On June 26, following extensive press condemnation, an anti-Fascist event was held at Carnegie Hall in New York by Italian and American anti-Fascist organizations.

The chief topic was the kidnapping and slaying of Socialist Deputy Matteotti. In three hours of speeches, Mussolini, the Fascists of Italy and America, President Coolidge, and the Ku Klux Klan were all denounced. With the cry "Down with Mussolini and Fascism," the 2,500 people attending the meeting denounced Fascism, its leaders, its doctrine, its methods, and its terrorism. At a certain point, New York City Municipal Court Justice Jacob Panken shouted that the cry "Down with Mussolini and Fascism" was not enough. The cry should be "Down with Capitalism." The crowd immediately agreed. When one of the main speakers, Charles Erwin, former editor of the suspended Socialist newspaper, the *New York Call*, addressed the audience demanding the immediate resignation of Italian Ambassador Caetani, punching, kicking, shoving and yelling broke out among the crowd. Evidently Fascist elements had infiltrated the crowd to disrupt the meeting. Several policemen and the entire Bomb Squad intervened. After order had been restored, Erwin continued reading a letter addressed to President Coolidge, demanding the immediate resignation of Ambassador Caetani, who had "avowed himself a member of the Fascists." Furthermore, Erwin demanded the American Congress pass immediately a resolution denouncing Italy, because "a nation governed by such a body does not deserve recognition as a sister nation to the civilized states of the world." The spirit of Mussolini that had poisoned all of Italy had gained strength through American recognition, concluded Erwin. Another speaker, Arturo Giovanniti, proposed a permanent "state of war between the workers of the United States and the government of Fascism in Italy." Elizabeth Gurley Flynn, the third speaker, asserted that the murder of Matteotti had been approved by Mussolini because the Socialist deputy was going to uncover scandals in Mussolini's government, which "would have made the Teapot Dome scandals look sick."[4] It may be regarded as a pure coincidence, but on June 28, the *Saturday Evening Post* started publishing a series of articles by Richard Washburn Child, former American ambassador to Italy. The articles examined the nature, doctrine, structure, and goals of Fascism in Italy. The first article, "The Making of Mussolini," was a lengthy, biased, and apologetic essay on Mussolini as person, political leader, and statesman. The second article, "Open the Gates," appeared on July 12. In it, Child stressed that Fascism was a movement of youth. Like springtime, Fascism had blossomed throughout Italy from 1920 to 1922, the year of the March on Rome. The October Revolution in Italy was described as "a rainsoaked Revolution," carried out in the spirit of the Crusades and with Mussolini's idea of moderation. The series concluded, on July 26, with the article, "What Does Mussolini Mean?" According to Child, Fascism meant full power and full responsibility. Moreover, Mussolini's immediate achievements included work for the unemployed, duties set above rights, a spirit of service, and a pragmatic vision for solving Italy's problems without illusions. All these issues made Mussolini a "glutton for work."[5]

"What a propitious moment," Caetani wrote Mussolini on June 27, "for such a series." The *Saturday Evening Post*, with an overall circulation of two million, had to be considered an "important and influential paper throughout the United States." The publication of Child's series and, above all, the very fact that Caetani notified Mussolini about the forthcoming series advances some conjectures on its role and function. Given the timing, the series, written by a Fascist sympathizer, offset anti-Fascist propaganda against Mussolini in the United States, which had become extremely aggressive in the wake of Matteotti's murder. Even though the periodical's publishers cannot be charged with connivance with Fascism, nevertheless it seems that, reflecting its conservative line, the magazine expressed more approval than disapproval of Fascism. The very fact that the series appeared when Matteotti's slaying had caused indignation and horror in Italy and abroad and was written by a diplomat well known for his sympathy toward Fascism, leads one to believe that the series had been planned. Caetani rejoiced for such a series. In his dispatch to Mussolini, he commented: "By a happy event, ex-Ambassador Child has started publication of a series on Fascism in the weekly magazine, the *Saturday Evening Post*...From what has been written in the first article, I foresee a sympathetic analysis of the Fascist Revolution."[6]

Furthermore, Mussolini's strategy to present Matteotti's murder as slowing down his program of national reconciliation in Italy seemed to have captured the imagination of many American correspondents. In analyzing press coverage of the period, it emerges unequivocally that Mussolini had succeeded in producing a remarkable mystification of Matteotti's case for the American government and people. On June 29, the *New York Times* published Arthur Livingston's article, "Power of Mussolini Is Shaken by Murder." The author of the article condemned the assassination of Matteotti. However, he found enough evidence to perpetuate the newspaper's quasi-defensive attitude toward Fascism. "In the past five years," wrote Livingston, "Mussolini has accomplished wonders as a political organizer. He has worked miracles as general manager and repairer of a collapsing State. But he is still confronted by one failure that threatens at any moment to upset him. He has failed to pacify Italy. He has failed to discipline the elements to which he owes his power." Assertions of this nature supported the thesis that Matteotti's murder had to be held as the immediate consequence of the still unstable political situation reigning in Italy. Hence, Mussolini's direct responsibility in the murder of the Socialist deputy must be excluded. "The kidnapping of Matteotti, member of the Parliament," continued Livingston, "brings the Italian public face to face with the fact that it is governed not by a legal State but by a crowd of selfish politicians." Thus, Fascism faced a tremendous challenge: to bring into the mainstream of legality and order the strong concentrations of disorderly forces running rampant in Italy. Also, Livingston invited the American public to judge Mussolini's policy in the context of Italian realities. He made crude contrasts between the youthful and aggressive Fascist organizations in Italy and the peace-oriented mentality of Americans. When Italian veterans organized *Fasci di Combattimento*, they intended to save Italy from Communism and to purge the nation of Socialism, bootlegging, and blackmail. Mussolini recognized as leaders not the young, high-minded and stout-fisted Jacobins, but rather peaceful gentlemen of old and new generations. Projected against this national background, Matteotti's murder could have been explained only as a direct consequence of a somehow youthful and Jacobin temperament of Italian *squadristi*. In a national upheaval like Fascism, it was natural and inevitable that vicious elements would be swept along into power with the good. Therefore, Fascism should not have been judged by the excesses of its "lunatic fringe."[7]

The weekly magazine *Outlook* took a pro-Fascist attitude also. According to its editorials, Communists had invented the charges against Mussolini because "neither murder nor conspiracy has been proved." In connection with the disappearance of the Socialist deputy, the magazine asserted that "violently partisan accusations" had been put forth against Mussolini by his foes. Furthermore, the magazine seemed to give special credit to the version offered by Italy's ambassador in Washington. In fact, it extensively quoted Caetani's comments on the affair. In doing so, the magazine followed the identical interpretive pattern of the *New York Times*, the *New York World*, and the *Saturday Evening Post* of Philadelphia. *Outlook* glossed over the crime by ascribing the murder to criminal elements "who exist in every party no matter how respectable and in every country." Even though Fascism was, indeed, passing through a serious moment of political adjustment, nevertheless such an unfortunate and regrettable event does not justify accusations about Mussolini's integrity. On the other hand, Communists and Socialists had staged a negative campaign against Mussolini, asserting that he had inspired Matteotti's kidnapping and murder. The magazine responded to these charges by saying they had been made "in an inflamed state of mind by radicals of the extreme type" and should not be taken seriously unless and until proven. The magazine also gave credit to Mussolini's immediate and intelligent action in the political sector. In rejecting as ominous, vicious, and unfounded the accusations moved by the extremists, Mussolini continued to defend the process of national reconstruction undertaken in Italy. Therefore, with ability and skill, *Il Duce* successfully neutralized another maneuver of the opposition that tried to use the incident of Matteotti to overthrow his regime.

The story of Mussolini's extraordinary talent in reforming Italy had to be understood as counterrevolutionary. Italy continued to suffer from the dangerous and corrosive propaganda of Bolshevism and Anarchism, which had rendered all the previous governments inefficient and supine. Though Mussolini's counterrevolution sporadically produced serious violence and lawlessness, nevertheless, he deserves credit for rescuing Italy from a perilous situation. A government established through a revolutionary act was bound to guarantee sooner or later "merciless justice against the dastardly political and personal murderers" and a national state of affairs where "constitutional guarantees and thoroughgoing representative self-government" would as a result be definitely established.[8] Pursuing this philo-Fascist line, the magazine published, on August 6, an article "After the Matteotti Murder." The Rome correspondent, a special envoy of the magazine, stressed Mussolini's new program to rid Italy of those Fascist elements who chose violence for violence's sake. The article advanced for the first time, the hypothesis that the murder of the Socialist deputy might have been instigated by dissident groups in the extremist and revolutionary fringe of the Fascist Party. In fact, in denouncing the crime, Mussolini had clearly admitted the murder of Matteotti had been "worse than a crime—a blunder." The crime, however, tightened Mussolini's firm grip to reign in Fascism to normalization. Decidedly, the process of normalization would not be smooth given the reaction and opposition of Fascist *squadristi*, who would resist settling in as normal citizens. Nonetheless, Mussolini would finally triumph over his internal and external enemies. "Yet those who think that Fascism is finished commit a grave error," continued the article. "Rome itself remembers only Matteotti; but the rest of Italy remembers the Socialist regime and threat that Fascism destroyed." Under Socialist control of almost two thousand municipal governments, Italy had witnessed a period of "ceaseless strikes, of the blackmail of society, of brutal murders." After all, Fascist violence paled compared to a tally of Socialist and Communist outrages. In spite of Fascist violence, life in Italy had been safer and quieter under Fascism, concluded the article.[9]

From June to August, the American press at large concentrated on Matteotti's murder, hypothesizing on the consequences it might bear for Fascism in Italy. The *New York Herald Tribune*, the *Brooklyn Eagle*, the *Baltimore Sun*, the *Chicago Evening Post*, and the *Philadelphia Public Ledger*, all agreed that the murder might have shaken Mussolini's political position. (The crime itself had proved unmistakably that the Fascist regime in Italy was as much an opponent of democracy and parliamentary institutions as of liberty.) On the whole, the newspapers did not foresee the immediate downfall of Mussolini. They remained favorable to him as they had since the March on Rome in October 1922. Moreover, Mussolini deserved consideration for his sincere handling of the case. He had denounced immediately the murder, calling it a "diabolic crime." Furthermore, he publicly promised to eliminate from the Fascist Party those elements considered violent, vicious, and undesirable. And above all, he had secured to justice the five criminals who had conceived and carried out the crime. Therefore, in view of Mussolini's firm stand, the newspapers doubted the murder would ruin Fascism and the governmental fabric of the regime.[10]

In the aftermath of Matteotti's murder, the monthly magazine *Current History* pointed out that Mussolini appeared conciliatory toward the constitutional Opposition. In fact, he had lifted the censorship upon foreign telegrams; he had disbanded the National Militia of Rome and had given every evidence of the "most vigorous efforts to hunt down and punish the men guilty of the murder." Moreover, quoting the speech Mussolini had delivered to the Senate of the Kingdom on June 24, the review stressed Mussolini's solemn promise to carry out his program of respect for law and the pacification of the country. In so doing, he had invited the nation and the world not to be misled by anti-Fascist propaganda and subversive activities staged in the aftermath of the Matteotti murder:

"I think," Mussolini intoned, "we must not look upon the situation with too much optimism. At bottom it is no longer a question of the assassination of Matteotti. It is clear that the ultimate object of the Opposition attack is our whole regime. These men have as their purpose the destruction of every political and moral force that resulted from the October Revolution."[11]

In July, the *Nation*, a periodical which had led the way in anti-Fascist opposition among English-language periodicals, published an article titled "Why Matteotti Had To Die," by James Fuchs. It represented the first unbiased and objective presentation of the Matteotti affair to the American people. After having presented the political situation generated in Italy since the Fascist coup d'etat of October 1922, the article analyzed the motives instigating the slaying of the Socialist deputy. According to the article, Matteotti was murdered for three reasons: because he wanted to reveal the true story of the corruption and abuses committed by the Fascists in the general elections of April 1924; because he was about to incriminate the chief participants in the after-election act of terrorism; and because he would have forced judicial action against the main corruptionists in the elections. This legal action would have provided the invalidation of enough mandates to deprive Mussolini's government of its majority.

The article proved unmistakably that Matteotti's murder should not be considered, as Mussolini had affirmed, an isolated and sporadic act of criminal offense executed by *squadristi* of the left-wing fringe. On the contrary, the crime was the immediate responsibility of Mussolini himself and his entire Fascist regime. The article concluded that Matteotti had to die because he was about to prove to the civilized world that "Italy had lost its rank as a nation with a representative government." Thus, the article brought to the attention and analysis of the American nation the most tangible acknowledgment of the despotic aims of Fascism in Italy and in the whole world.[12] In mid-July, Mussolini's own words toward the Opposition seemed to become less conciliatory than in the early days after the Matteotti affair. In an article in *Il Popolo d'Italia* on July 12, he affirmed with boldness that the national and worldwide denigratory campaign aimed at subverting Fascism and his regime, had been weathered masterfully. Moreover, the exaggerated demands advanced by the Opposition would not be granted. The National Militia would not be disbanded or turned into a "grotesque royal guard." On the contrary, it would continue to be what it had been in the past: a strong paramilitary organization on which the regime had to rely. As far as the process of national normalization was concerned, Mussolini presented his personal interpretation of the matter: "If the process of normalization in Italy meant the suppression of Fascism and its methods, then our regime refuses to submit to any judgment except the judgment of history."[13]

Criticism published by the *Nation* and other anti-Fascist newspapers in the United States was insufficient to change the pattern maintained by the overwhelming majority of the American press, which continued its pro-Fascist and pro-Mussolini stance. In particular, *Literary Digest* published in August and September of 1924, a series of articles in which Matteotti's murder was assessed differently. However, each article ended with a note of praise for Mussolini's efforts in defending Italy from attacks of subversive and Communist elements: "The present parliamentary majority retains not only the right but also the duty to assume the most important responsibilities before the possible political consequences of recent grave events, especially because the oppositions are so various and discordant that Italy cannot depend upon them for any solution."[14]

Against this pro-Fascist front—including both the conservative and liberal American press—the anti-Fascist Italian-language press staged a most courageous and massive propaganda campaign. Throughout the United States, the anti-Fascist Italian press relentlessly accused and condemned Mussolini and his regime for the assassination of Matteotti. In New York City, *Il Martello, Il Proletario, La Notizia, L'Era Nuova, La Giustizia, L'Adunata dei Refrattari,* and *L'Umanita' Nuova,* and from November 1925, *Il Nuovo Mondo,* all published editorials accusing Mussolini of the slaying of Giacomo Matteotti. Their campaign, relentless, courageous, and well planned, continued until the fall of Mussolini in 1943. In particular, *Il Martello* with its impressive anti-Fascist campaign, became the vanguard of Fascist opposition in the United States. It even proclaimed, on December 5,

1925, a nationwide boycott campaign. The newspaper invited all Italian-American anti-Fascists to join it:

> Workers, comrades: the best method to defeat our common enemy is to cut off monetary assistance and profit.
> If your doctor is Fascist: boycott him. If your lawyer is Fascist: boycott him. If your tailor is Fascist: boycott him.
> If your shoemaker is Fascist: boycott him. If your retailer is Fascist: boycott him. If your grocer is Fascist: boycott him.
> If your newspaperman is Fascist: boycott him. If your druggist is Fascist: boycott him. If your barber is Fascist: boycott him. If your landlord is Fascist: boycott him.
> If you know that Banks, Movie Theatres, Drug Stores, Insurance and Travel Agencies are owned by Fascists, boycott them. Do not buy products which bear the label Made in Italy. You must boycott, wherever you are and always. In this way, we can weaken the Italian monster. It is like a horse, if it has no oats, it changes course.[15]

Articles of condemnation of Fascism and its methods of terrorism were published in *La Parola, Il Lavoratore*, and Chicago's *Daily Worker. Il Lavoratore* took a lead role. In an editorial on July 1, 1924, the newspaper accused Fascism of transforming Italy from a civilized, democratic country to "a swamp of death, assassination, and terror." On July 28, another article appeared, declaring Fascism and the Italian government "to be drowned in a sea of innocent blood." Moreover, the Black Shirts, considered in Italy heroes of the Fascist revolution, were portrayed as "black souls" of Fascist degeneration.[16] In Detroit, anti-Fascist opposition was led by *La Voce del Popolo* and *La Luce*. In Pueblo, Colorado, two newspapers, *Marsica Nuova* and *Il Pupo*, carried on relentless attacks against Mussolini and Fascism. On May 9, 1925, *Il Pupo* published an article titled, "A Strong State," by Vincenzo Vacirca, the ex-Socialist deputy expelled from Italy for his affiliation with the Socialist Party. Vacirca criticized not only the slaying of Matteotti but also the most recent aggression suffered by another Socialist, Deputy Giovanni Amendola, who had been beaten almost fatally by the *squadristi*. This attack on Amendola, according to Vacirca, proved unmistakably that the theory of the "strong State," introduced by Mussolini to defend all citizens from treacherous elements, was a legend. Fascism had adopted the doctrine of violence for violence's sake.[17] On August 24, 1924, an editorial in the (Pittsburgh) *Unione Figli D'Italia* affirmed that the body of Matteotti one day would rise to indict the assassins and vindicate himself before the tribunal of the world. However, the proletariat of the world would assign the worst sentence to Mussolini and his regime.[18]

San Francisco had both *L'Italia* and *Il Corriere del Popolo*. In an article titled "What Is the Fatherland?" *Il Corriere del Popolo* affirmed that an ideal nation can develop only in a democratic country. A dictatorial system cannot accept or believe in the concept of Fatherland. The dictator is himself the country. Therefore, people should idolize him. Consequently, the idea of nation is mere abstraction.[19]

These newspapers carried on their unhalting anti-Fascist campaign, which had intensified in the aftermath of Matteotti's murder. Significantly, these efforts extended beyond the United States; in fact they extended to Europe and to Italy in particular. According to archival material in Rome's Central State Archives, from June 1924 to July 1925, the Italian postal service seized over 20,000 copies of the above-mentioned newspapers throughout the nation. Indeed, Mussolini and the Foreign Ministry had been informed directly from America about the smuggling into Italy of anti-Fascist materials. On June 10, 1924, an Italian *squadrista* living in Pueblo, Colorado, sent Mussolini a lengthy memorandum containing a list of addresses of people in Italy who received "subversive propaganda."[20] Mussolini and Emilio DeBono sent confidential dispatches to Provincial Post-masters instructing them to seize all "subversive newspapers, literature, and propaganda materials aimed at introducing radical and subversive ideas in Italy." All newspapers arriving from the United States received special attention.[21] This indicates that Matteotti's murder not only raised a cry of indignation and protest, but also symbolized the turning point of a worldwide anti-Fascist campaign conducted in communal spirit by American, French, English, Canadian, Mexican, and Latin-American anti-Fascists.

The course of anti-Fascism in America seems to have developed in various directions. As we have seen, the Matteotti affair raised protest and indignation even in the United States. However, the press had dissociated Mussolini from responsibility for the material execution of the crime. The superficial resolution of the case had created problems for Italian-American radicals, Socialists, and Communists. Furthermore, the interpretations of the case drew a line of demarcation between Mussolini's sympathizers and his foes. In addition, it had divided profoundly the Italian colony in America. Americans saw Italian-Americans as divided. On the one hand were those who heartily supported Mussolini and his regime of law and order, and to these groups went the moral and spiritual support of the American majority. On the other hand were those who favored Socialism, and they appeared in the Americans' eyes as subversive, radical, revolutionary, and against law and order. To these groups went popular contempt and governmental harassment.

The June 26 event at Carnegie Hall was not the only one staged by anti-Fascists in America. In the aftermath of Matteotti's murder they intensified their activity. Meetings, rallies, and public events took place in many cities throughout the United States. Police with their bomb squads were on high alert. When these events included shouting of anti-Italian and anti-American slogans, police intervened and made arrests, and police repression inflamed some of the American public. On other occasions, the events were simply prevented on the grounds that Italian radicals had organized them.

On June 30, a letter of protest appeared in the *New York Times* from New York City resident Emanuel Aronsberg, who criticized the "turbulent and violent gathering" at Carnegie Hall. The presence of Charles Erwin, former editor of the extinct Socialist daily, the *New York Call*, garnered further protest from Aronsberg. Erwin's request for the immediate resignation of Ambassador Caetani and ominous attacks against the Fascist government of Italy had to be considered unwarranted. In fact, Erwin had never, either in the past or as editor of the Socialist *Call*, criticized or expressed concern or indignation for the continued imprisonment and execution of his Socialist friends, the Mensheviks, at the hands of Bolsheviks in Russia. According to letter-writer Aronsberg, what was good for his Russian friends would be objectionable for Mussolini:

> Such is the crabbed logic of the Socialists. They have two standards of morality and justice, and still they howl and rave when they get once in a while a taste of their own medicine from Mussolini... In these circumstances, the protest of Mr. Erwin and his Socialist friends against Mussolini sounds like rank hypocrisy, and no man or woman who believes in a single standard of legality, equality, and justice, will read it without a smile of contempt and scorn.[22]

On July 4, in Philadelphia, the police arrested seven attendees during an anti-Fascist meeting protesting Matteotti's assassination. Among the arrested were C. William Thompson, editor of the Socialist newspaper the *New Jersey Leader*, and Emedio Pistilli, chairman of the meeting and president of Local 21 United Shoe Workers of America. They were charged with inciting to riot.[23] On June 29, a massive gathering took place in Boston to commemorate the sacrifice of the Socialist martyr. *Il Lavoratore* covered the event and reported over 70,000 people gathered in Boston from Quincy, Haverhill, Lawrence, Brockton, Cambridge, East Cambridge, Roxbury, E. Weymouth, and Providence. Arturo Giovannitti, Gildo Mazzarella, Giuseppe Merenda, and Fred H. Moore delivered speeches. Anti-Fascist events also took place in Pittsburgh, Erie, Dunmore, and Plains, Pennsylvania; in Baltimore, Maryland; in Syracuse and Rochester, New York; and in Cleveland, Ohio. In Detroit over 500 workers attended a meeting in mid-July sponsored by Michigan anti-Fascist groups, where Luigi Ceccoli, Romolo Bobba, and Nicola Di Gaetano spoke. In Chicago, the gathering proved a remarkable success. *Il Lavoratore,* with its editorial offices in Chicago and its wide circulation, had stirred anti-Fascist feelings among Italian-Americans there. Antonio Presi, *Il Lavoratore*'s editor, chaired the meeting. Speeches were delivered by Enea Sormenti and Alvaro Badillo. Manifestations of minor intensity took place in hundreds of towns with Italian communities.[24]

However, these protests against Fascism did not seem to interest or attract the attention of the vast majority of Americans. On the contrary, Americans considered the issue an Italian affair. Moreover, in areas like New York, Chicago, Boston, and Philadelphia, where anti-Fascist protesters managed to attract American attention, their efforts were interpreted as dangerous explosions of Anarcho-Communist-Socialist propaganda. As such, American authorities intended to observe them carefully.

Taking advantage of this paradoxical development, Ambassador Caetani went to Rome to confer with Mussolini on the situation of Fascism in America and the reaction of Americans to the Matteotti case. The Italian premier expressed his personal satisfaction for conduct surrounding the Matteotti affair and warmly received the news that the American press and public opinion at large, with very rare exceptions, still maintained perfect equanimity in judging Mussolini, Fascism, and its methods from the standpoint of domestic Italian events.[25] On November 21, Mussolini had another chance to persuade himself that Americans nurtured great sympathy for Fascism. Carlo Vinti, editor of a New York pro-Fascist paper, visited Mussolini, and expressed the devotion of the Italian-American colony and of American Fascists as well. Mussolini charged him to convey his warm greetings to the members of the Fascist Party of America.[26] The overall American reaction to Matteotti's case implies that Mussolini did not lose popularity among Americans. During the Matteotti affair things had seemed to surge in the opposite direction, but afterward a general atmosphere of normalcy prevailed. So, Mussolini had won the Matteotti case by using prudent strategy. To complete the scenario, on January 11, 1925, Mrs. John Adams Drake, president of the American Free Milk and Relief for Italy Society, met Mussolini in a special audience in Rome. She expressed such a deep sympathy and enthusiasm for *Il Duce* that Mussolini authorized her appointment as the first American woman Fascist.[27]

The years 1924–1925 saw the Waterloo of Italian-American anti-Fascism; police persecution, governmental harassment, and popular ostracism made life and activities of anti-Fascists unpleasant and dangerous. The Tresca affair and its prosecution, as we will see in later chapters, was inspired by the Italian ambassador. Tresca had been the architect of all anti-Fascist gatherings organized in New York City and throughout the state, and police and legal authorities knew him well. It is impossible, however, to assess how much Tresca's anti-Fascist activism weighed in his sentencing on November 23, 1924. The Circuit Court of Appeal in New York City condemned Tresca to a year and a day in the Atlanta Penitentiary. Dominant in the profile of Carlo Tresca is his determination to carry out courageously and with dedication the struggle against Fascism—even though he faced the prospect of deportation to Italy, since he had never requested American citizenship. Neither a jail term nor deportation, he said, would stop his anti-Fascist struggle or force his head to bow. In spite of Tresca's courage and dedication to Italian democracy, Fascism became more appealing to the American public.

Influenced by lenient, pro-Fascist media propaganda, a pro-Fascist acceptance, particularly in New York City, settled over the populace between 1924 and 1925. The philo-Fascist Italian-American press, represented by *Il Progresso Italo-Americano*, *Il Corriere d'America*, *Il Carroccio*, and many minor local newspapers serving the Italian-American community helped the cause of Fascism in America. However, some imprudent actions staged by anti-Fascists contributed to the image of Fascism as victim of a Socialist-Communist-Radical conspiracy.

Il Progresso Italo-Americano played a leading role in the philo-Fascist Italian-American press, especially between 1924 and 1925 when it ran a series of pro-Fascist editorials. By December 1923, the newspaper had already asked for answers from political parties representing the constitutional Opposition in Italy. Among other things, it asked them about their intentions regarding Fascism, and if they approved of Mussolini's program of national pacification. At the end of December, the newspaper examined Fascist ideology from the March on Rome to the period of the Fascist government's stabilization. The article, "Political and Social Doctrine of Mussolini's Fascism," covered the period during which Fascism had regenerated Italian prestige, economy, and industry, and Fascism was considered vital and irreplaceable in the life of the nation. On July 5, 1924, in the aftermath of Matteotti's murder, an editorial proclaimed that, regardless of the crime, Fascism would never abandon Italy to the Opposition. By no means, continued the article, did the Matteotti incident justify the Opposition's demand that Mussolini relinquish his power and step down. Such a move would generate an atmosphere of chaos and would yield power to Bolshevism. On July 6, the paper printed an interview with Professor Vincenzo Giuffrida of the University of Rome, "Italo-American Relations," on the future prospect of Italo-American economic cooperation. This possibility was still considered feasible, since Italy showed sufficient guarantees of economic prosperity and political stability. On July 13, the paper published a sentimental portrayal of *Il Duce*, by Nancy McCormack, "When Mussolini Poses." She describes him as impressive, strong, and fascinating. On July 16, the newspaper examined in depth the nature of the political crisis produced by the Matteotti incident, ascribing the unrest to those extremist groups that had infiltrated the Fascist Party. The article recalled that Fascism was born as a heterogeneous movement and that Mussolini had successfully blended together different groups with divergent aims. In so doing, *Il Duce* had exhibited the skill and talent of a statesman. In two articles, one on July 26, "From Achilles to Lychaon," and another on August 5, "The Council of Fascism vs. Revisionism and Militarism," the newspaper appealed to party factions to set aside their ideological differences and proceed toward the realization of goals of the Fascist revolution. National regeneration and pacification should be the primary objectives of Fascism.[28]

In addition to this widely circulated newspaper, an extended network of local philo-Fascist newspapers disseminated throughout America, provided a propaganda marathon for Fascism. *Il Corriere del Bronx,* edited by Bernardino D'Onofrio, defined Mussolini as the "apostle of liberty and justice." In New Haven, Connecticut, Antonio Pisani edited *Le Forche Caudine*. He maintained that Fascism had wiped out feudalism in Italy. In Chicago, *La Tribuna* praised Mussolini not only for his program of national regeneration but also because he had returned dignity and national pride to Italian workers abroad and made them more respected human beings. Another Chicago newspaper, *L'Italia*, praised Fascism and Mussolini because he had restored the destiny of Imperial Rome. *La Gazzetta del Massachusetts*, published in Boston, advised America to suppress the Volstead Law and adopt, for those who did not agree on the issue of prohibition, the Fascist remedies of castor oil and truncheons. *La Stella d'Italia* of Greensburg, Pennsylvania, affirmed Fascism as the ideology of the future for Italy and the world. *La Tribune* of Portland, Oregon, defended Mussolini and his philosophy of national regeneration and pacification. *Il Vaglio* of Wilkes-Barre, Pennsylvania, praised Mussolini's strong methods for restoring law and order in Italy. Pro-Fascist newspaper *Il Corriere di Syracuse* (New York), edited by Luigi Falco, had endorsed Fascism and its methods of government from its first issue (1922). *La Stampa Unita* of Rochester, New York, was edited by C. G. Lanni. Though he did not personally endorse Mussolini and Fascism, the paper extensively published pro-Fascist articles by his contributing editors Matteo Teresi and Pasquale De Masi. On June 15, 1923, in an article, "Mussolini Has Cold Blood," De Biasi defended Mussolini as the second savior of Italy. While Garibaldi, asserted De Biasi, had saved Italy with his Red Shirts, Mussolini had done it with his Black Shirts. On July 27, 1923, De Biasi called Mussolini's international policy "quid medium" between international goals pursued by France and those pursued by England, implying Mussolini was the third power between the two contestants. On July 18, 1924, at a Rochester, New York, event commemorating the Italian martyr Matteotti, Davis Salomon spoke at the Amalgamated Hall of Rochester. He averred that "the act of killing Matteotti had kindled fires or rage in a million hearts. Nothing will satisfy us, or quench these fires, until every ounce of this martyr's blood has been paid for in restitution." To Matteo Teresi of *La Stampa Unita,* these radical expressions inflamed Americans against Italians. Continuing in its relentless pro-Fascist campaign, *La Stampa Unita,* on May 15, 1925, reprinted an article, which had appeared earlier in another Rochester newspaper, the Rochester *Journal-Post Express.* The article, "What Butterflies Do We Seek?" analyzed Mussolini's achievements in Italy since 1922: "Mussolini today, ruler of Italy, is one of the most powerful men produced by modern history, or ancient history, either. In his Fascist black shirts, he rallies his legions...Mussolini is a man of strong words and of strong action. Of late, the murder of Matteotti, attributed to the Fascists, appeared to shake Mussolini's hold on the people. But Mussolini did not dodge that issue. He has never dodged any...Mussolini is powerful. Force is a great thing. But his real power is mental courage."[29]

The philo-Fascist propaganda of these newspapers was of moderate tone and, therefore, effective, incisive, and well planned for the American mentality. On the contrary, anti-Fascist propaganda was torn. On one hand it could allow Fascist principles to show their evil colors—and let it destroy democracy and freedom as it had done in Italy—and on the other it favored anti-Fascist ideological interests expressed in the anticapitalist style of Marxist-Leninist doctrine. In fact, Tresca's *Il Martello,* Giovannitti's *Il Veltro,* and Presi's *Il Lavoratore* interpreted their anti-Fascist opposition and struggle in terms of Marxist-Leninist strategy and doctrine. Not only did they advocate an alliance of all anti-Fascist forces in the U.S., Canada, and Mexico to form an anti-Fascist popular front, but also they advocated Bolshevism as the only alternative to Fascism. In an article published in *Il Lavoratore* on October 25, 1924, entitled "Neither Fascism nor Liberalism, but Bolshevism," the Opposition maintained that the capitalist bourgeoisie of the world had reached the highest stage of reaction against the working classes. Capitalism was using and hiring Fascist henchmen to perpetuate its program of exploitation and repression. Fascism, under the mien of the henchmen of capitalism, represented the most perverse and abject form of capitalism. Therefore, the alternative was not only Democracy versus Fascism, but also Bolshevism versus capitalism.[30]

This sort of propaganda, mixed with a chain of public events that police often interpreted as mobs staged by Italian radical and Communist groups, inflamed popular opinion against Italian-American anti-Fascism. On October 1, 1925, the Italian Delegation to the Washington Parliamentary Conference was attacked in New York. The incident culminated in the wounding of two Fascist delegates by Italian Communists who were residents of New York City. The occasion furthered the cause of Fascism in Italy and abroad. The Fascist press waxed indignantly.[31]

On October 28, four hundred anti-Fascists "rioted" in front of the Hotel Pennsylvania, making "several attempts to break through a police cordon." Inside, Fascists celebrated the third anniversary of the March on Rome. The celebration also honored Captain Paul C. Grening, of the *President Harding*, who had rescued in mid-Atlantic the crew of the Italian freighter *Ignazio Florio*. Guests of honor included Alessandro Sardi, former Italian minister of Public Works; Consul General of New York, Emilio Exerio; and General Mastro Mattei. Dr. Giuseppe Previtale, vice president of the *Fasci* of North America, chaired the celebration. Carlo Tresca and Pietro Allegra led the so-called anti-Fascist mob. The situation required police reinforcement. The rioters, with their cries of "Down with the Fascists," intended to go inside the hotel. The anti-Fascists' behavior led to a general protest in New York; the *New York Times*, in an editorial the following day entitled "They Should Go Home For Fighting," announced that the "newcomers," in stretching Americans' hospitality, had manifested "bad manners by attempting to fight out quarrels of their home land." The article continued in its wide condemnation of anti-Fascist behavior: "As it happens to be anti-Fascists who have chosen repeatedly to break through, upon them must fall condemnation. The police hardly could have used too much severity in repressing the riotings...If any Italian in the United States thinks that things are going badly in Italy, his duty is to go back there and rearrange them. He cannot help his country by mobbing Fascists on steamship docks and in hotels here."[32]

In a letter to the *New York Times*, on November 8, Frederick F. Lily conveyed the feelings of a majority of New Yorkers on the continued riots staged by anti-Fascists. A single letter does not reflect the viewpoint of millions of the city's people, however, it can be used as a parameter to assess the kind of frustration produced by these outbursts. According to the author, many people "were getting a little bit tired of these mobbish manifestations." Since anti-Fascism appeared to play a very limited part in the outbursts, Lily saw in them "Communism camouflaged." He invited authorities to take a serious attitude toward those pseudo–anti-Fascist elements whom he considered radical disseminators of Communist propaganda.[33]

Ironically, Matteotti's murder did not undermine the position of Fascism in America. Instead, it made it stronger and elevated it by garnering, paradoxically, the support and sympathy of the vast majority of Americans. For most Americans, Mussolini had acted with courage and wisdom in refusing to yield to the illegitimate demands of the Socialists and Communists in Italy. He had sent the executors of Matteotti's murder to justice. He had discharged his duty with honor, competence, and impartiality. In the meantime, he had defended himself and his regime from attacks by the Opposition, which had tried to use Matteotti's case to overthrow Mussolini and plunge Italy into another period of political disorder and economic instability. In the eyes of Americans, Fascism appeared more than ever the innocent victim of a Socialist-Communist-Radical conspiracy in Italy and throughout the world.

CHAPTER 5

FASCISM AND FACTIONALISM

By the end of 1923, over one hundred Fascist associations thrived in the U.S. Besides New York City's powerful group, considered the pulsing heart of Fascism in America, the movement had made enthusiastic inroads in municipalities throughout the country. This became particularly evident in those areas where the presence of the Italian-American people was more relevant and politically influential.[1]

In New York State, Utica, Troy, Kingston, Concord, Buffalo, Rochester, Syracuse, and Albany all claimed Fascist associations. Though local leaders emerged, they wielded a limited range of autonomy, and the organizations remained associated with New York City. In Albany, Professor O. Neyroz directed the *Fasci*. Of the 16,000 Italian-Americans living in the state capital, almost 8,000 joined the Fascist Party. The association, however, failed to establish an autonomous political identity and lived in the shadow of the New York City group.

Things developed differently in Rochester, however. Achille Martinengo, a former captain of the Italian army who had emigrated to the United States in the early 1920s, formed a Fascist association there on March 23, 1923. According to *La Stampa Unita*, an Italian-language pro-Mussolini newspaper published in Rochester, the Italian-American colony of Rochester welcomed Fascism as "a whiff of new life for the Italian community." Moreover, it saw in Mussolini a champion of Italian prestige abroad.

Some Rochester newspapers described enthusiasm for Fascism as a "Fascist uprising" in the city; however, they did not consider it a threat to the American system of government. Such an event, according to local Fascist leaders, would not happen for several reasons. First, citizens of Italian extraction would not countenance any movement that would inflict havoc on the American government, and second, the work of Fascism was to reorganize Italian moral prestige abroad and the welfare of humanity: "Fascism was, and it is still, a great spiritual movement aiming not only toward the good and the reconstruction of Italy, but also toward the progress and welfare of humanity. Fascism, making its own the doctrine of Nationalism, has for basic principle that any individual class must be community. Fascism is more economic than political; the financial, economic, and industrial recovery of Italy is its principal object."

In Syracuse, Giulio Fulco, editor and publisher of the pro-Fascist newspaper *Il Corriere di Syracuse*, headed the Fascist association, which "flourished spontaneously" among the 30,000 Italian-Americans living in the city, according to the newspaper. In an editorial on February 16, 1923, Fulco rejoiced at the overwhelming response to Fascism in the city: "Syracuse with its 30,000 Italian-Americans could not be inferior to other cities of the United States and could not neglect such a great ideology: Syracuse welcomes Fascism."[3]

By mid-1923, Fascist propaganda and organizations had reached the suburbs, where many Fascist branches and groups were formed. To meet the consequences of increased Fascist enthusiasm, Captain Capua, Italian *émigré* and associate of Consul Gangemi, was hired to help organize Fascist propaganda and activities in Syracuse and its suburbs. From 1923 to 1930, Fulco, Capua, and Gangemi together succeeded in disseminating Fascism throughout the Syracuse area.

The newspaper thoughtfully disseminated the group's relentless and incisive propaganda.

On November 17, 1922, a few days after the March on Rome, an *Il Corriere* editorial assessed Mussolini's program of national regeneration in Italy. Presenting *Il Duce* as a champion of anti-Communism and anti-Socialism, the newspaper wrote:

> Prime Minister Nitti had invented Italian militarism and the parliamentary intrigues. Then Fascism came to power after the failures of Giolitti, Bonomi, and Facta. It represented the historical antithesis in the dialectical process of national regeneration. Because at the very beginning Fascism was a political and social catalyzer, it needed to be impetuous, overpowering and riotous. But with the conquest of the government, Fascism changed into an orderly and well disciplined force.[4]

On December 8, 1922, another editorial, *"Le Giornate Fasciste"* (Fascist Days), proclaimed Mussolini the incarnation of a universal ideology. Italy, it proposed, was becoming the cradle of another civilization. "Now the task of the Fascists was to make their ideology nationally lasting and internationally known." Hence, Italian-Americans had to become the witnesses of Fascism in the United States.[5]

On January 5, 1923, local politician Russell S. Sims, visited Italy and expressed to *Il Corriere di Syracuse* his admiration for Mussolini, whom he described as a leader "who conceives an idea, develops it and carries it out straight forward."[6]

On January 28, 1923, Guido Podrecca, a former Italian Socialist who had migrated to the United States in the 1920s, delivered a speech at the Italian Welfare Club of Schenectady. On that occasion, Podrecca called Mussolini "the liberator, the steersman, and the reconstructor of Italy." Such an enlightened statement elated *Il Corriere*'s reporter, who praised Podrecca for his "patriotism and political maturity."[7]

On February 24, 1924, to justify Mussolini's dissolution of the Italian Parliament and the calling of new elections, *Il Corriere* said: "Italy's national representatives had lost the sense of political reality.

The Italian political system had degenerated into factionalism, obstructionism, and filibusterism." As a direct consequence of this unbearable situation, the editorial surmised, Mussolini had wisely decided to dissolve the Italian Parliament and call for new elections. Eventually, the new parliament with a pro-Fascist majority, would represent order and political imagination and would be well disposed to work for Italy's reconstruction.[8]

Fascism in Syracuse became a patriotic and sentimental issue. Adding to the political propaganda of its local leaders and philo-Fascist press was the poetry of Giuseppe Sposato. In a propaganda technique apparently unique in the U.S., Sposato composed poems praising Mussolini and Fascism. A Calabrese war veteran, Sposato emigrated to the United States in the 1920s, and expressed, between 1927 and 1935, his lingering praise for Mussolini and Fascism in a book of poetry, *Fiamme*. The two poems considered his best compositions were "Hymn to Fiume" and "Glory to Italy."[9]

In Massachusetts, Fascist associations were numerous and vociferous. Boston's association was led by Francesco Macaluso, a lawyer; Fernando Pettinella, captain in the Italian army; Giannetto Bottero, a physician; and Ubaldo Guidi, an accountant. The official newspaper of the Boston *Fasci* was *Giovinezza* (Youth), directed by Francesco Macaluso. Ten Fascist associations were formed in the state, including Lawrence, Lowell, Worcester, Fishbury, and Portland.[10]

In Pennsylvania, Fascist associations sprang up in Erie, Pittsburgh, Plains, Dunsmore, and Altoona, with two in Philadelphia. One, headed by J. Dello Russo, an Italian war veteran, was considered intransigent in that it followed the hard line of Roberto Farinacci—an Italian *ras* (boss), who advocated revolutionary solutions. Among its many uncompromising stances, the association forbade affiliation with American citizens and aliens with a permanent resident visa. This implies that Dello Russo's association was an Italian-style Fascism reserved for Italians and a genuine Fascism transplanted in the United States.

Lieutenant C. Adamoli directed the other Philadelphia organization, in collaboration with Giuseppe Pasceri, Antonio Scarduzi, Franco di Vincenzo, and Eugenio Alessandrini, assistant district attorney of the city of Philadelphia. This association came together in December 1922. Correspondence between Adamoli and the Italian Embassy in Washington shows the Italian Bureau of Foreign *Fasci* in Rome endorsed and supported this association. On the other hand, they barely tolerated Dello Russo's association since it toed Farinacci's political line. However, it would have been unwise for Bastianini to openly condemn Dello Russo's association as subversive since Farinacci was the national secretary of the Fascist Party, the Party's second highest position after Mussolini.

In Altoona, a manufacturing city in central Pennsylvania, a majority of Italian-American workers joined the Fascist association. The local *Fasci* were said to be "veterans and workers" who welcomed Mussolini's ideology, because it represented a firm commitment to make Italy the land of "patriotism and jobs." Fascism in Altoona appeared to have made conspicuous inroads among its members. A strong Fascist directorate, which had emerged as a policy-making body not only safeguarded the interests of Fascism in Altoona, but also prevented abuses and anti-Fascist activities. By 1925 it succeeded in convincing the Italian government to remove the local consular agent, P. Sterbini, as "undesirable"; he had publicly proclaimed himself "non-committed to Mussolini's Fascism." Consequently, the directorate managed to have Sterbini dismissed on the charge that the consular agent had "misused the funds of the Italian government." He was replaced with a philo-Fascist agent.

In Pittsburgh, steel company president, C. Schisano, headed the Fascist association. Fascism's appeal was relevant, and its ideology received an enthusiastic response, especially among steel workers of Italian descent. Well-organized Fascist associations also sprang up in Erie, Plains, and Dunsmore. A significant feature of the Fascist network in Pennsylvania was the appointment of Luigi Borgo as state supervisor in 1925. Borgo's main activity was to keep the Fascists of Pennsylvania abreast of major, interesting Fascist events in the state, in the country, and in the world. Borgo fulfilled this task with passion and dedication. He founded a newspaper, *Il Maglio* (the Hammer), through which he carried out a relentless pro-Fascist campaign.[11]

In Connecticut, Fascists organized in Hartford, Bridgeport, and Naugatuck. In Hartford, wealthy banker A. Andretta was appointed chairman of the local Fascist association. Unlike other Fascist associations throughout the state of Connecticut, Hartford's chapter had an aristocratic composition. Fascism as embraced by the Hartford members reflected less a political ideology and focused more on a philosophy of courage and Mussolini's theories of strength, masculinity, and boldness.[12]

In New Jersey, Fascism also had a strong following. In fact, Fascists had not only disseminated Mussolini's credo throughout the state, but also they had authorized credentials to Fascism through a Certificate of Incorporation of the Central Council of Fascisti in New Jersey. The certificate, which made Fascism a legal organization in the state, was filed at Trenton on February 16, 1924. In an explanatory memo attached to a copy, Frank S. Brunelli disclosed to Mussolini the objectives of Fascists in New Jersey. According to Brunelli, the process of incorporation blended "Fascism and Americanism." Brunelli, however, went even further; he told Mussolini that Fascism, in its true historical mission, originated in the state of New Jersey in 1900, in the city of Newark. In the aftermath of King Umberto's assassination, Italians and Italian-Americans of Newark and Paterson had organized the Society First Battalion of Italy (1905–1907). The Society had as its primary intent fighting subversivism and revolutionism in Paterson, where Gaetano Bresci, who killed the Italian king on July 29, 1900, in Monza (Italy), had received radical indoctrination.[13] Newark and Atlantic City had their own Fascist associations. In Newark, Pasquale Matullo, editor and publisher of *L'Ora* (the Hour) led the Fascists. The newspaper enjoyed a wide circulation among Italian-Americans of Newark and the entire state of New Jersey, estimated at over a half million people. In Atlantic City, the Fascist association's efficiency was probably due to A. Ruffo, a wealthy millionaire and banker who controlled the local association as well as many other groups formed in the suburban areas of Atlantic City.[14]

In Maryland, Fascist associations were reported in Baltimore and surrounding suburbs. In the city, the Fascists were headed by Oreste

Fallica and Generoso Pavese, with the latter acting as chairman of the State Fascist Directorate. The Baltimore Fascists appeared courageous and daring, since they paraded in the city streets wearing Black Shirts and Fascist emblems.[15]

Professor V. Oppedisano led the Fascist association of Chicago. Fascist appeal seemed quite robust and responsive in that city. However, Fascism in Chicago faced an aggressive anti-Fascist newspaper, *Il Lavoratore*, which published sophisticated anti-Fascist propaganda. Fascism in midwestern Chicago never made the inroad it made in the eastern United States. A dispatch to Rome from the Italian Embassy in Washington in early 1925 said the *Fasci* in Chicago appeared "to have gone through several crises since their constitution." The Italian consul in Chicago, Leopoldo Zunini, had always acted as the leading figure of Fascist propaganda there. According to the document, a strong directorate whose members were thought to be in contact with the *Unione Siciliana* (Sicilian Union)—regarded by many as the cradle of organized crime in Chicago (Mafia and Black Hand)—controlled the Fascist association. Moreover, G. Rossi, Chicago correspondent for *Il Progresso Italo-Americano,* and A. Ferrari, editor of the newspaper *L'Idea*, were connected with *Unione Siciliana*.[16]

In the state of Ohio, Cleveland and Youngstown both had Fascist associations. Professor S. Tamburella headed the local Cleveland *Fasci* where he succeeded in blending the *Fasci* with the local branch of the Sons of Italy. This unity gave Fascists of Cleveland an edge on anti-Fascists, who nevertheless maintained a relentless and courageous propaganda campaign. In fact, Cleveland's *Fasci* and Order of the Sons of Italy proved one of the strongest pro-Mussolini fronts in the United States. Their propaganda and proselytizing effectively reached Cleveland's Italian-Americans.

Youngstown's *Fasci* were in "total harmony" with the local association of Italian war veterans. June 1925, saw a confrontation between *Fasci* and the Italian Embassy in Washington. The matter concerned the appointment of A. Rosapepe, a physician, as consular agent of Youngstown. The local Fascist directorate opposed the nomination and accused Rosapepe of deserting the Italian army, delinquency in purchasing payments, and conniving with local "vicious bosses" who represented illegal interests. The directorate managed to have Rosapepe's appointment suspended *sine die* by the Italian Foreign Ministry.[17]

In Detroit, A. Colandrea led the *Fasci*, and since Colandrea was also the president of the Italian war veterans association, he managed to blend Fascists and war veterans in "full harmony." Because the local Fascists were numerous and efficient, Colandrea transferred the association headquarters to a downtown commercial section. He boasted that the association displayed the symbol of Italian *Fasci*, Lictor's Fasces, on the building's facade.[18]

In Des Moines, Iowa, R. Simonini, editor of *Il Risveglio* (the Awakening), chaired the local *Fasci* organization and preached Fascism to both Italians and Americans through his newspaper. In particular, Italians praised Simonini's dedication to the cause of Italian patriotism and identity in the United States.[19]

In Milwaukee, Wisconsin, the Fascist association was established in early 1923 by Federico Reale di Basilio, a young Sicilian *squadrista* who had emigrated to the United States from Messina, Sicily. As we shall see later, the *Fasci* of Milwaukee became the most controversial association in the United States after other Italians in Milwaukee accused the association of conspiracy and connivance with organized crime. Fascist associations were also reported in Kenosha, Wisconsin. As in Milwaukee, a Sicilian émigré led *Fasci* in Kenosha. Raffaele La Macchia, a physician, had settled in the area from Catania. Unlike all other Fascist associations in the U.S., the Wisconsin *Fasci* diverged from Mussolini's main tenet and endorsed Sicilian identity rather than Italian national identity. This unique situation spurred protests and resentments from many other Italians living in the state. Eventually, this melee contributed to making the Milwaukee *Fasci* the most factional and controversial in the United States.[20]

Wealthy industrialist Ottavio Bachechi headed the Fascist association of Albuquerque, New Mexico, whose goal was to neutralize the offensive of anti-Fascists in New Mexico. In fact, the latter deliberately spread false information that the Italian economy under Mussolini verged on total collapse. According to Bachechi, this vicious propaganda not only did harm to Italy's good name and prestige abroad, but also harmed the legitimate interests of millions of Italian-Americans living in the country. In fact, they were viewed with contempt and suspicion by their fellow Americans. Furthermore, if this obnoxious propaganda went unchecked, it would create unbearable consequences in Italy. Italians living in America would refrain from sending their regular remittances home for fear the Italian government would seize the funds for public use.[21]

Successful Fascist associations were also formed in California, with associations in Los Angeles and San Francisco where local news media supported their propaganda activity. The *Monitor*, the *San Francisco Chronicle*, the Dante Alighieri Society, the Italian war veterans association, *La Voce del Popolo*, and *Il Popolo d'Italia* all disseminated philo-Fascist propaganda from 1922 to 1940. These sources saw Mussolini as the wisest political leader in Europe, and his Fascist ideology as having restored respect for the Italian Constitution and patriotism and loyalty for Italy at home and abroad. Moreover, Amadeo Peter Giannini, who admired Mussolini's talent and charisma made an important contribution. Mussolini, on his part, repaid Giannini's praise, congratulating him for his many decades of effective service in fostering trade relations between the United States and Italy.[22]

Strong Fascist associations were formed also in Texas, Nevada, Colorado, and in Washington, D.C., emerging primarily where Italian-American numbers thrived and their community role relevant.[23]

As Bastianini repeatedly reported to the Grand Council of Fascism in Rome, Fascism in America had made impressive strides among Italian-American communities and Americans at large. According to Bastianini, American sympathy toward Fascism was motivated both by its performance at home and abroad. At home, Fascism had restored law, order, and respect for the government. Abroad, Fascists respected laws and traditions of hosting countries. Moreover, they refrained from interfering with the local political structure of host countries. Finally, Fascists acted honorably; they avoided quarreling and jealousy and promoted unity of intent and action.[24]

Was this, in reality, truly the status of Fascism in America? Was Bastianini's scenario accurate? An analysis of Fascist factionalism and feuds supports the opposite conclusion. Marred by internal factionalism, feuds, and personal interests, Fascism in America, instead of uniting Italian-American people, further divided them. Not only did Fascism create within its framework a network of personal confrontations, but also it divided Italians into two forces: Fascists and anti-Fascists. Due to the nature and background of their leaders—most were ex-*arditi*, war veterans, and Fascist militiamen who emigrated in the aftermath of the Fascist March on Rome in search of new adventures and thrills abroad—Fascist associations in America became arenas for political confrontations and pastures for personal emergence.

From 1922 to 1930, factionalism eroded the tissue of Fascism in America. Associations in New York, Boston, and Milwaukee saw internecine struggles. In New York, besides the Longo-Menicucci confrontation, which required Mussolini's personal intervention, another split took place in 1925. Giacomo Caldora, one New York City's leading figures of the Fascist movement, dissociated himself from the main association and founded the Fascist alliance *Il Duce*, Inc., with headquarters at 583 East 187th Street. Caldora's decision was motivated by political differences. According to him, Fascism in America needed to become a committed and politically relevant ideology. Moreover, he insisted, Fascism ought to conduct a free-for-all assault on anti-Fascism.[25]

But a major dispute among New York's Fascists arose in mid-1926. A Fascist committee involving prominent Italian-Americans such as P. Riccio and A. Stella had investigated the possibility of publishing a monthly English-language magazine in New York City. The magazine, to be called the *Italian Digest*, would "rectify all false news spread in America about Fascism and Italy." An ad hoc committee, headed by Count Ignazio Thaon di Revel, looked at a possible format of the future magazine. The headquarters of the committee, *Italian Digest and News, Inc.*, was located at 253 Broadway, in the heart of the city.

The magazine would become a highly sophisticated instrument of Fascist propaganda in the United States. Moreover, the participation of prominent intellectuals as collaborators represented an advantage for any publication and meant Fascism would be defended by capable and qualified individuals. Italian Ambassador Giacomo De Martino, did not hesitate to notify Mussolini about the plan.

However, unknown to the Ambassador, news of the English-language magazine had already created controversy and hostile reactions from De Biasi, *Il Carroccio*'s editor, and from the Italy-America Society. The latter had planned its own magazine, which was in the process of being introduced to the market.

Mussolini had been well informed about the Society's plan. *Il Duce* faced a dilemma; De Biasi threatened to publish an anti-Fascist magazine immediately or become the director of *Il Nuovo Mondo*, an anti-Fascist paper, if Mussolini gave the go ahead to the *Italian Digest*. The Italy-America Society would be insulted and perhaps even turn anti-Fascist. Consequently, Mussolini refused to endorse the publication of the magazine and so avoided more troubles for the already faltering Fascist association of New York.[26]

Internal factionalism in Boston's Fascist association undermined the very essence of Fascism in America. On October 13, 1923, Ambassador Caetani sent Mussolini a documented record of the activities of the Boston *Fascio*. The record included a confidential letter written by A. Ferrante, Italian consul in Boston, heralding a "serious crisis the Fascio of Boston was experiencing." According to Ferrante's account, the crisis resulted from personal confrontations between Macaluso's group (Macaluso, Pettinella, Bottero, and Guidi) and the War Veterans Association, headed by P. Cartoni. The latter accused Macaluso and company of using their Fascist affiliations and roles within the association to improve their economic situations. Moreover, the accusers made additional charges against the four:

- Macaluso, a former Socialist and Republican, had embraced Fascism for political and personal opportunism. He had no specific job and never worked steadily. He tried to rely, with expedients, on Fascism and the fortune of his newspaper, *Giovinezza* (Youth).

- Pettinella, a person without any political qualifications, was a vagrant worker and a skillful opportunist who misused funds of the local Fascist association.
- Bottero was an antimonarchy army deserter, and his political sentiments were not fully pro-Fascist.
- Guidi was an Italian emigrant with a record of army desertion and blackmailing in Italy. In fact, he was still sought by the Court House of Lucca (Italy) for extortion.

These four, whose social, political, and moral standard was highly suspect, according to their accusers, had been entrusted with the high honor of representing the prestige of Italy and running the *Fascio* of Boston. According to Ferrante, a gang of thieves should not be running the *Fasci* in the state of Massachusetts, with its large Italian-American community. At stake was not only the prestige of Fascism but also the honor and interests of the Italian-American community that had pledged its support to Mussolini as the expression of newly found Italian national identity.[27]

Another controversy, which nearly ended in a legal suit, exploded in Boston on March 16, 1926. Giuseppe Covino, head of the Fascist association of Boston, dismissed Silvio Vitale, a well-reputed Fascist member, on charges of "indiscipline and personal indignity." The controversy entered public domain when the local news media covered it. For more than two weeks, the *Gazzetta del Massachusetts* sold out every issue.

At the suggestion of Carlo Grilli, lawyer and state coordinator of Fascist activities in Massachusetts, Vitale appealed to the Grievance Committee in New York City. In the meantime, he issued a statement in the *Gazzetta* requesting Covino's public apology for what he called unfounded and slanderous charges against him. If the apology were not made in a matter of seven days, Vitale contended, Grilli would initiate legal action against Covino and the local Fascist directorate. The incident called for the immediate intervention of Thoan

Di Revel, who reinstated Silvio Vitale and dismissed Covino as head of the Boston *Fasci*.

The following day, Boston Consul Ferrante sent two highly informative memoranda to Giacomo DeMartino in Washington. The documents, totaling several pages, comprise the most impressive and enlightening documentation on the situation of Fascism in the United States and in Boston, specifically. In a rare and acute interpretation, Ferrante presented the motives beneath the factionalism that had eroded the connective tissue of Fascism in America. He presented Fascism in America as the prototype of Italian Fascism, whose keynote was heterogeneity. Fascism lacked unity, he said, because it was an aggregation of negative forces, without any clear identification and political commitment. As such, Fascism in America could not unify the Italian-American element and spur patriotic and national identity.[28]

On January 13, 1923, Italian consul in Chicago, Leopoldo Zunini, divulged to Italian Ambassador Caetani in Washington the precarious situation of the Milwaukee *Fascio*. According to the denunciation, four persons of "dubious background and suspicious credentials" had formed a Fascist movement called the Fascists and Patriots Association. The four were Federico Reale, Domenico M. Giuli, Joseph Giuli, his son, and Antonio Bellante. In forming the movement they intended to challenge Milwaukee's existing Fascist association, headed by Federico Reale di Basilio. They also intended to challenge the authority of Consular Agent Angelo Cerminara. The moral standard of the four individuals was more than dubious and questionable.

- Reale, a Sicilian, was sought for illegal practices and abandonment of his wife.
- Giuli had recently settled in Milwaukee from Philadelphia, where he had been indicted for fraudulent bankruptcy.
- Joseph Giuli had been condemned by a grand jury for larceny against the Italian Mutual Savings Bank of Milwaukee.
- Bellante had a record of arrests in California for larceny and other crimes.

According to Zunini's document, Fascism in Milwaukee, and to a certain extent in all America, had become a playground for personal ambitions and political opportunism. Self-proclaimed and self-styled Fascists, whose moral and legal records were quite often questionable and embarrassing, had taken control of the movement. They intended either to use Fascism for personal gain or to make it the protective shield for their criminal activities.[29]

From the onset, Mussolini and Bastianini had envisaged Fascism in the United States as a driving force to pursue national identity and prestige among Italian-Americans. However, a peculiar nature of Fascism proved to be factionalism; Fascism in America never became a unified movement. On the surface, it appeared as a network of associations tied together in a seamless system. Beneath this apparent cohesion, factionalism, personal conflicts, and animosities incubated. Due to this internal factionalism, Fascism never became a unique driving force with a nationwide program of concerted action. The American public as well as federal authorities interpreted these open struggles among factions and groups as "frictions between citizens of Italian origins in this country. Therefore, they contributed to generate more contempt and distrust for the Italian element."[30]

Finally, besides these negative features, Fascism never emerged as a political ideology capable of creating a valid alternative to American Democracy; Fascism never became a major issue in this country. Nor, for that matter was Fascism an immediate danger. Factionalism, which eroded most Fascist associations, represents further proof that Fascism could not have emerged as a movement with conspiratorial and anti-American goals. The good sense of Americans and the majority of Italian-Americans did not allow Fascism to transform America into a political colony of Italy.

CHAPTER 6

FASCISM IN AMERICA AND THE BASTIANINI-CAETANI CONFLICT

Confrontations between Fascist Black Shirts and the Socialist and Communist Reds were not the only manifestations of Fascism in New York City and throughout America. Though early Fascism seemed motivated by the "exaltation of Italian patriotism in America and the legal and non-legal protection of all Italians,"[1] internal strife marred the Fascist Association of New York City. In a telegram sent to Mussolini on February 2, 1923, Ambassador Caetani delineated the precarious situation of the Fascist Association of New York City. According to the document, Bastianini had authorized former Italian Lieutenant Longo to form another Fascist Association in New York City. In the meantime, on December 19, 1922, Bastianini had addressed a letter to Menicucci, giving him instructions and guidelines for running the Fascist Association of New York City. Was not this, Caetani remarked, proof that two Fascist associations would exist in the City, each in open conflict and antagonism with the other? What, indeed, were Bastianini's goals? Why had the entire operation been conducted without previous consultations with the embassy? Was not Bastianini looking for trouble between the American and Italian governments and among members of the Italian colony at large?[2]

In a relentless series of charges and accusations against Bastianini, Caetani sent Mussolini another telegram on February 6, stressing, among other things, that the anti-Fascist propaganda had intensified its campaign, and now, due to the ominous situation in New York City, it accused Fascism of "spreading violence and disorder in America among the Italian community."[3] As for the existence of two challenging associations in New York City, Caetani asked for a final decision directly from Mussolini "on which of the two should be accepted as the legitimate and sole emanation of Italian Fascism."[4]

In a telegram to Caetani on February 24, he approved without reservation the decision made by the Ambassador in demanding that the Fascists in the U.S. act honorably and refrain from quarrelling and jealousy. Also, they should promote unity and represent a driving force for the coordination of the Italian community abroad. As for the Longo-Menicucci case, Mussolini promised Caetani to look carefully into the matter before reaching a final decision.[5] Mussolini's decision came on March 3, after a thorough evaluation of the situation of Fascism in the United States and in New York City in particular. Quite plainly Bastianini's strategy of two Fascist Associations of New York City had been conducted unknown to Mussolini. However, he had been kept abreast by Caetani through memos and decoded telegrams.[6]

Furthermore, it appears Bastianini had not sufficiently informed Mussolini of the appointment of two leaders to organize Fascist Associations in New York City. Indeed, had Mussolini known of such a decision, he would have informed the Italian Ambassador and sought his advice. At least, at this point, Mussolini trusted Caetani and relied on his competence and knowledge of the American mentality. However, diplomatic records available show no traces of exchange of views or inquiries on the matter. It must be inferred that very likely

Bastianini had not briefed Mussolini. As far as the Ambassador was concerned, we have already seen his reaction: dismay and surprise at Bastianini's behavior.

What about Bastianini himself? It appears that Barone Russo, head of the Cabinet of the Minister of Foreign Affairs, constantly kept Bastianini informed of the content of memos and decoded telegrams sent to Mussolini from the Italian Embassy in Washington. Therefore, the entire matter seems veiled in intrigue and subtlety. However, to keep the situation from deteriorating even more, on February 25, Mussolini mandated Russo to ask Bastianini "what decision he had reached on the issue of the two Fascist Associations in New York City, which required an urgent and careful handling to prevent sharp divisions among the Italian-Americans."[7] Two days later, Bastianini notified Russo of the following decision:

> On the issue of the two dissident Fascist associations organized in New York City, I have reached the following decision, which I would like to see notified to the Italian Ambassador in Washington through your office. The association founded by Lieutenant Longo will be dissolved, because it has been previously directed by Colonel Passamonte, indicted for burglary.
>
> Moreover, it will be recommended that Longo's Fascists merge into Menicucci's association since the latter has been appointed and recognized as the only leader of the North American Fascist Organization (N.A.F.O.).[8]

On March 3, Mussolini gave his version: "Longo's Fascio must be immediately dissolved. Its members must join Menicucci's association; which represents the only one to be recognized by the Executive Council of the Italian *Fasci*. The Ambassador in Washington is authorized to implement this decision."[9]

Why did Mussolini procrastinate in solving the dispute? To summarize the situation, we should note again that the ominous situation of the *Fasci* in New York City had been created by Bastianini. However, questions remain. Why did Bastianini give permission both to Longo and Menicucci to form Fascist associations? Two Fascist associations to what end? Did Bastianini have specific goals in mind? If so, did the decision in fact lead only to ignoble confrontations between Fascist factions in New York? Diplomatic documents available show unmistakably that Bastianini approved of Fascist associations in the United States under the direct control of the Central Bureau of Italian *Fasci* in Foreign Countries, of which he was secretary general. Evidently, he saw in the realization and development of a Fascist network abroad the possibility of emerging as a leader in the national and international arena. Indeed, Bastianini desired power. Furthermore, he saw in the appointment of personal friends, like Longo, the possibility of maintaining command of the organizations. He tried to boycott Menicucci, because ex-*ardito* Menicucci appeared naive, intransigent, and extremist. Bastianini would have trouble receiving total allegiance from such a person.

Ambassador Caetani disclosed in a memorandum to Mussolini on November 26, 1923, that Bastianini planned to form a network of Fascist organizations in the United States. The memorandum is worth quoting in its most peculiar points:

> The Central Bureau of Italian Fasci in Foreign Countries led by Bastianini endorses the idea of organizing Fascist Associations in the United States. This intention is expressly manifested in the telegram sent to this Embassy in Washington, on August 10, 1923.
>
> The Bureau has also decided that the American Fasci must be controlled and directed by Bastianini, and through him supervised by the Grand Council of Fascism. This point is clearly stated in the memorandum sent on July 31, 1923, and bearing Bastianini's signature.
>
> As far as Bastianini's intention to take under control the whole Fascist apparatus in the United States, the same memorandum states that the Fasci abroad must be considered sections of an International of Fascism.
>
> While apparently it must be stressed that Fascism abroad is not a manifestation and emanation of Italian Fascism, nevertheless it is understood that the Secretary General of the Central Bureau of Italian Fasci in Foreign Countries is a

member of the Executive Council and the Grand Council of Fascism. Therefore, the political function, the office and the responsibilities he bears by no means must become known to the American public. This confidential memorandum must be disclosed only to those faithful Fascists who are trustworthy. To the latter, and only to them, the peculiar nature and goals of Fascism abroad may be disclosed. It is understood that Fascism in the United States is an emanation of Italian Fascism.[10]

As far as Bastianini's intention to take under control of the Fascist apparatus in the United States, the same memorandum states that the *Fasci* abroad must be considered part of an international Fascism.

Caetani's reaction was harsh and immediate. He cautioned Mussolini that American public opinion and the government would strongly condemn and oppose formation of political associations controlled by foreign governments. Moreover, such a decision would further unite the Italian Federation of Labor with American Radicals, Socialists, and Communists. Hence, the opposition to Fascism in America would become a nationwide affair.

Even though Caetani seemed to seek Mussolini's advice on such an important and controversial matter, nevertheless, he offered Mussolini three alternatives for Fascism in America. None of the alternatives, however, contained a recommendation for continuing to pursue a network of Fascist associations in America under the direct and immediate control of Bastianini. Rather, the alternatives stressed that Fascism must abandon Bastianini's aims and strategy and move in a different direction. To avoid American reaction and resentment, Caetani advanced the following recommendations:

- Fascism in America could not be dependent on Rome. Naturalized Italian-Americans should not be forced to become members of the *Fasci*. Italian consular agencies should not serve the goals of the *Fasci*. The future of Fascism in the United States should not be politically oriented, otherwise its life and duration would be limited.

- If Fascism continued to pursue Bastianini's goals, then, sooner or later it would be outlawed by the American authorities. Therefore, Fascism would face a long period of suspension. A future revival would be impossible because American sympathy toward it would never be fully restored.
- The *Fasci* should be changed into a different kind of organization named "Organizations Pro-Italy," with no political goals whatsoever. Their program might still maintain some Fascist postulates, like opposing anti-Fascist and antinational propaganda spread in the United States by radicals and Bolsheviks. Above all, the organizations should implement the objectives of the Grand Council of Fascism, that is to say, promote intellectual, ethical, and social activities on behalf of the Italian-American community. Thus the movement would get the support of all Italians in America and could be endorsed by the Embassy too.[11]

In presenting these valid alternatives, Caetani seemed well aware of the situation of Fascism in America and its future prospects. After all, the Ambassador was the person who could monitor, more than anybody else in Italy, the reaction of Americans toward Fascism. He only could weigh the extent of accusations moved against Fascism by Radicals, Socialists, and Communists, who presented Fascism as an un-American ideology. He knew that many Americans looked upon Fascism sympathetically. The liberal press, led by the *New York Times*, continued to publish editorials and articles by special correspondents extolling the progress Italy had made under Mussolini. Caetani also knew that his presence in the United States as Italy's ambassador was viewed sympathetically by Americans who considered him an academic product of the United States. In fact, he was accepted as particularly qualified "to interpret one people to the other because he knows both America and Italy from the ground up."[12] Not only his skill in the draining of the Pontine Marshes but also his suggestions to blow off the top of a peak in the Alps, which had impeded the progress of the troops in World War I, were attributed to the professional "feats he got in America, where he studied in the Colorado School of Mines and worked as a miner, lumberman and mill hand in Colorado, Alaska, and Idaho."[13] Furthermore, Caetani's decision to support cultural exchange between Italian and American universities had been welcomed with enthusiasm in both countries. In January 1923, the *New York Times* rejoiced in announcing that one hundred Italian graduates of technical schools would annually come "to acquire engineering experience in America." Some would go to the Ford plant in Detroit, some to Westinghouse, and others to General Electric. The purpose was to distribute Italian engineers and "illustrate the best that Italy has to send." At the same time, summer art courses for American students continued to be conducted by the Royal University of Roma, in cooperation with the Italy-America Society. These courses, open to students and teachers, included the study of Italian art, literature, and archaeology, and were supplemented by lectures on different phases of Italian life.[14]

In its pro-Ambassador Caetani campaign, the *New York Times*, on March 20, 1924, published an impressive editorial in which the personality and the role of the Ambassador were described as, among other attributes, highly qualified. Also, according to the editorial, his persuasive personality reflected "the manner and the language of an engineer who discusses the Mussolini period," and he had many things to say in politics, in economics, and in technical problems. He was, indeed, the most complete person who might have represented Italy in the United States. His assurances about Mussolini, the role of Fascism in America, and the economic recovery of Italy could be accepted as trustworthy.

On March 19, 1924, he assured New York's Italian Chamber of Commerce that Italy's economic status had improved under Mussolini. Strikes had been reduced by seventy-five percent, and unemployment by thirty percent; many new industries had been established; national savings were such that Italy had no need for foreign currency for national investments; circulation of paper money had been reduced; the lira had reached stability; and discipline, law, and order had been restored to the country. For all these achievements, the *Times* gave credit to Fascism. The outlook was promising, and Americans were ready to support the ambassador in his continued drives to improve the image of Italy in America and share the hopes of the eminent engineer on the rosier future of Italy.[15]

This analysis of the ambassador's public image reflected the high esteem and sympathy for Italy and Mussolini he had aroused in Americans. Therefore, the return of Gelasio Caetani to America as ambassador of Italy had been fundamental to the fortune of Fascism and Mussolini himself in the United States. Now that Fascism had reached a certain degree of popularity among Americans, Caetani tried, with careful handling, to preserve the status quo. However, in the long run, Caetani paid personally for his sincerity when he cautioned Mussolini on directing American Fascist activities from Rome.

As early as April 3, 1923, unfavorable reactions had been expressed against Caetani. In a letter to Mussolini from the Fascists of New York, the behavior of the ambassador fell under attack. To the great surprise of true Fascists, diplomatic and consular agents had expressed their disapproval of the organization of Fascist associations in New York City and throughout the United States. According to the letter, the Embassy did not do enough to spread Fascist ideology among Italian-Americans. The ambassador's absenteeism needed to be denounced. Fascists in America could no longer tolerate the fact that radical, Socialist, and Communist anti-Fascist propaganda ran rampant among the Italian community. It was requested that Mussolini and his Fascist collaborators in Rome intervene to end "this surprisingly incredible apathy of the Italian Ambassador."[16]

On April 6, 1923, another memorandum from New York reached Mussolini. It declared great confusion in the United States on how to organize Fascist Associations. Fascism in America seemed a Babel. Anti-Fascists had the advantage and profited from the confusion that existed among U.S. Fascists. Not only was there a lack of leadership but also there was an absence of a sense of responsibility on the part of the diplomatic and consular authorities. In keeping themselves unengaged and neutral, they undermined Fascism's expansion among the Italian community. Moreover, in many places, like Dallas, Texas, the local consular agencies had circulated hand bills inviting Italians *not* to join Fascist associations. Because of the total absenteeism of Italian diplomatic and consular authorities, the letter invited Mussolini, "who had organized the March on Rome, to direct from the Eternal City the cause of American Fascism and bring the ideals of the new Italy within the boundaries of America."[17]

In mid-May 1923, Superintendent of Police Molossi, arrived in the United States on a special mission, *questore in missione*. In a lengthy memorandum to Mussolini on June 6, 1923, he reported that the vast majority of Italian-Americans did not wish to see Fascist associations established in America. Though their ethnic identity thrived, nevertheless, they opposed the idea of organizing Fascist groups in the United States. Molossi mentioned many causes behind the negative response of the Italian-American elements:

- Most Italian-Americans ignored what Fascism had accomplished in Italy. They were unaware of the socioeconomic change that had occurred in Italy. The Italian language press, which still presented Italy as a backward country with an intense criminal behavior, had to be called responsible for perpetuating this unfair state of ignorance about Italy.
- Since the March on Rome, the Italian press had, in an unbroken fashion, described the daily conflicts between Fascists and Reds as a civil war. Both factions were depicted as violent, revolutionary, and antidemocratic cliques.
- The absence of a Fascist leader in America, capable of presenting and disseminating the ideology among the people, had to be called responsible for the vague and superficial knowledge Americans had about Fascism.
- The absence of a leader had discouraged many Italian-Americans from engaging themselves in Fascist propaganda. Without a leader, who might defend them, pro-Fascist activities were considered risky.

- Nevertheless, among American intellectuals and financiers, there were many who expressed sympathy and enthusiasm for Fascism. For instance, Nicholas Murray Butler, Whythe Williams, Arthur Frothingham, Theodore Prince, John Chamberlin, and Julius H. Barnes had contributed to an atmosphere of benevolence toward Fascism. It was due primarily to the propaganda of these eminent American citizens that the image of Fascism as the equivalent of the Ku Klux Klan had been rejected as untrue by the vast majority of the American people.
- Gradually, national and international events showed Fascism as an ideology striving for law, order, and discipline, in a world ravaged by Bolshevik menace.
- In spite of these external manifestations of sympathy, American public opinion still considered Fascism an Italian phenomenon, applicable only to Italy's situation. In America, it was considered out of place, ominous, and unnecessary.
- Fascism in America could not become a committed and political movement under the direct control of the Italian authorities.
- With the exception of the cities of New York, Scranton, and Chicago, Fascist associations were irrelevant or numerically nonexistent.
- Where Fascist associations or nuclei existed, anti-Fascist groups had popped up. Their objectives were to stage relentless campaigns of charges and attacks on Fascism. This anti-Fascist propaganda appeared to be very efficient, well planned, and carried out through a network of Socialist and Communist newspapers.
- Only a few people among the many interviewed by Molossi expressed the feeling that Fascist activities in America should get the support of consular and diplomatic authorities. Others considered their commitment unfair.
- Very few proposed that the Italian government financially support Fascist associations in America.

- A significant weakness of American Fascism was the absence of a solid Italian-American bourgeoisie, ready to support Fascism. Italian-Americans had not yet reached a bourgeois level in America. Most were local businessmen, shop owners, retailers, local or small entrepreneurs, intellectuals, or laborers. They had not been able to create a nationwide network of economic enterprises. The laborers, who represented the overwhelming majority of Italian-Americans, would never endorse Fascism because they feared retaliatory measures from federal and state authorities.

Lastly, Molossi stressed that Fascism would never triumph among Americans as a valid and acceptable ideology. The people of the United States maintained unchanged and unchallenged traditional democratic conservativism based upon law, order, and popular representation.[18]

During Caetani's visit to Italy in July 1923, he and Bastianini never met. However, on September 28, 1923, in the process of leaving Italy for Washington, the ambassador answered a telegram sent by Bastianini. The telegram had reached Caetani on the ship *Conte Rosso*. In expressing his regret to Bastianini "for having had no occasion at all to meet him and debate matters of common interest related to Fascist activities in the United States," Caetani promised to brief him from Washington. Nevertheless, he took the opportunity to restress some basic points:

- The constitution of Fascist associations in America had to be considered an unwise political and international decision. *Fasci* were in open conflict with traditions enjoyed by Americans. Moreover, large sectors of Americans had begun looking upon Fascism with contempt and suspicion.
- Rather than disseminating national pride and intellectual heritage, Fascist groups in America were centers of discord, factions, and personal jealousies among the Italian-Americans. These personal outbursts, under the shield of pseudonationalistic

identity and pride, had diminished American sympathy toward Italian-Americans.

- The formation of new Fascist associations in America would give the demagogues new fodder to use in their arguments against Italian immigration.
- Even if not dissolved immediately, the *Fasci* should become inactive and avoid contact with Italian-Americans for a long period.
- Furthermore, the Central Bureau of the Fascist Party of Italy should refrain from engaging directly or indirectly, with or without the consent of the Embassy, in organizing Fascist associations in the United States. This ominous procedure had created serious inconveniences for the Italian-American element.
- In the interest of both countries, diplomacy, and the good relations between Italy and America, the ambassador stressed with firmness that the Embassy in Washington would never become the cradle of un-American activities. Therefore, he would never engage diplomatic apparatus in pro-Fascist propaganda. He had stressed this principle in the past and would continue to do so in the future.[19]

To circumvent criticism of his decision, Ambassador Caetani sent a copy of this memorandum to Mussolini.[20] Mussolini's reaction came immediately. He personally wrote a telegram to Pugliese, chargé in New York, instructing him that Bastianini's decision to nominate more than one person to organize Fascist associations in America should never be implemented. The telegram denounced acts of poor behavior that had occurred among the Fascists. Consular agencies throughout the U.S. should examine carefully the overall situation. If necessary, they should proceed to dissolve the *Fasci*. The Italian government could not tolerate factionalism and personal egoism among the Fascists of America.[21] Apparently, at this point, Mussolini still trusted his ambassador and considered his advice reasonable. Nevertheless, the conflict between Caetani and Bastianini did not appear to diminish.

Between February and March 1924, Caetani's uncompromising position on Fascist associations in America and Bastianini's stubborn insistence on their necessity, clashed vehemently. On February 4, 1924, Ambassador Caetani sent Mussolini another lengthy report on Fascist activities in the United States written by F. M. Bassetti. The ambassador had received it from the Seattle Consul Alberto Alfani. The document did not hesitate to point out that the basic problem of Fascism in America was not how to present it to the people, but how to avoid negative American reaction to such an alien ideology. Americans knew that one of the many goals of Fascism was the indoctrination of Italian-Americans in the Fascist creed. It was not only a matter of *Italianità* but also a matter of giving up what they had learned during their residence in the United States. Many had embraced the principles of popular democracy and representation; many had learned that respect for law and order comes as a consequence of democracy. Therefore, the Italian community in America could not be forced to accept and support a philosophy, which had become alien to this newly acquired mentality.

In Bassetti's opinion, the Italian diplomatic and consular authorities had handled the issue with competence and knowledge. Italian activities in the United States could not transcend established intellectual, linguistic, and artistic boundaries. An Italian-committed political organization would require news media propaganda, which would imply an interference in the domestic and international problems of the United States. As for civil and economic protection promised by the Fascists, Bassetti stressed that Italian-Americans needed no such protection. These protections were sufficiently guaranteed by federal and state governments. What could work well and be accepted by the Americans was an intellectual hinterland between Italy and America to develop more insight in both countries.[22]

Bastianini, evil tempered and arrogant, disapproved of Bassetti's report. In a letter to Mussolini on March 24, 1924, he accused Caetani of using tendentious reports written by unqualified individuals to undermine the real chances Fascism had to triumph in the United States. Moreover, as secretary general of the *Fasci* in foreign countries, he believed that Caetani's relentless boycott of Fascists in the United States could be tolerated no longer. Bastianini saw the strategy pursued by the ambassador as twofold. First, he was trying to boycott the diffusion of Fascism in the United States. Second, he was trying to support organizations of the Nationalists and war veterans, who resented the secondary role Fascism had attributed to them in the aftermath of the 1923 merger. Now, said Bastianini, Caetani's aims finally had been unmasked: the ambassador was a Fascist admirer, not a believer. Furthermore, in associating himself with the Nationalists, the ambassador wanted to provoke rivalries between Fascists and Nationalists in the United States. In this way, with his support and the support of his American friends, Italian Nationalists living abroad would regain the power and identity they had lost in Italy. In his relentless action of boycott, Caetani had even vetoed admission into the *Fasci* of New York City to Gold Medal Sebastiano Sciré, a respected Italian war hero. Evidently, this decision had to be interpreted as a treacherous action taken by the ambassador to prevent the New York Fascist association's gaining prestige and fame from Sciré's affiliation.

Furthermore, in confidential meetings in his Washington office, the ambassador had on many occasions slandered Bastianini's good name and reputation, calling him an "evil-tempered and unscrupulous guy." These insults, Bastianini asserted, could no longer be tolerated. Time had come to reach a decision and prevent further harassment of Fascists in America from the Italian ambassador.

As further evidence of Caetani's ill-disposed intentions against Fascism, Bastianini attached to his letter a memorandum compiled by an Italian Infantry officer, Giovanni Costa, dealing with Fascism in America. Costa had been sent to the United States as Bastianini's special envoy on a pro-Fascist propaganda tour, in early 1924. In his memorandum, Costa described the warm reception he had received in America. Above all, the widespread sympathy he had found for Fascism and Mussolini among the Americans impressed him. At several receptions he had attended in New York City, the name of Mussolini had resounded hundreds of times. Mussolini had been idolized as "the First Man in the World," and Fascism described as the "constructive reaction of a national force against a subversive opposition." Fascism, according to Costa, was recognized by Americans as "the fourth Roman civilization, which would save the world from the threat of Bolshevism." Many Americans had expressed to Costa their intention to become Fascists and to work for Mussolini's cause. For instance, he attached to the memorandum a photograph taken at the funeral of President Harding where Fascists had been given a position of honor. The Fascists, who wore the Black Shirt, were positioned between the Mayor of Washington and the father of the late president.

As for the reaction of the Italian community to Fascism, Costa emphasized that Italian-Americans expressed approval and interest in the movement. Disapproval came only from Italian anti-Fascists, who had to be considered "bribed by the Bolshevik *soldo* (money)." These degenerate sons of Italy had sold themselves to the Third International. However, because of the general climate of confidence in law and order, the vast majority of Americans harshly condemned the subversive radicals. Positive and generally warm reactions toward Fascism could be regarded as a sign that Fascism, as a law-and-order-abiding doctrine, would convert Americans. Though this general climate of sympathy existed, Costa could not explain why the Italian diplomatic and consular authorities had taken a "neutral and uncommitted stand" toward Fascism. This position seemed unwarranted. According to grievances that had reached Costa, Fascists had been instructed to disseminate discord and factionalism among the associations. On other occasions, such as in the case of Antonino Randazzo of St. Louis, Missouri, the ambassador had turned down requests to form Fascist nuclei. "Why this aversion on the part of the ambassador?" asked Costa. Though he was reluctant to get involved in the dispute, nevertheless, Costa suggested that the whole matter of Fascism in America be reviewed carefully by Mussolini. The Italian government, in the judgment of Costa, would make a serious mistake in not giving needed attention to Fascism in America. This revision needed to be made soon to take advantage of the "good dispositions of the American people toward Fascism as they exist nowadays."[23]

To what extent Costa's assessment influenced Mussolini, we cannot say. However, one thing appears clear. In the tension between Bastianini and Caetani, the latter came out the loser. Eventually, in March 1925, Caetani was replaced by Giacomo De Martino as Italian ambassador to Washington. According to an article in *Il Lavoratore*, Caetani had been replaced because "many Italian-Americans had sent letters to protest disapproving of the ambassador's conduct and because he had been unable to respond satisfactorily to the expectations of Mussolini."[24] Evidently, it was premature for the Communist newspaper to make a thorough assessment of what had happened behind diplomatic scenes.

The replacement of Gelasio Caetani with Giacomo De Martino as Italian ambassador to the United States, in March 1925, did not provide the uplift Fascism needed in America. While Caetani's ouster might have satisfied Bastianini's ambition, certainly it did not cure the endemic malady Fascism had suffered since the very moment of its existence in the United States. American Fascism was born heterogeneous and without a peculiar program of action. Though Fascist associations tried to appear patriotic in scope and to represent a newly found form of national identity, the overwhelming majority fell to internal factionalism, which inspired outbursts and feuds among their members. Given the nature and background of the leaders of American Fascist groups—ex-*arditi*, war veterans, and Mussolini's militiamen—the associations became breeding grounds for strife.

CHAPTER 7

ANTI-FASCIST OPPOSITION
OF THE
ITALIAN CHAMBER OF LABOR
OF AMERICA

As of July 1923, over one hundred Fascist associations had been organized throughout the United States. The New York City association, the center of U.S. Fascist activities, had been founded in late 1922 by World War I *ardito*, Umberto Menicucci. By 1923, the association had 10,000 members and was the largest group of its kind in America. The New York association had a double task to accomplish: it had to neutralize anti-Fascist propaganda of Carlo Tresca and Arturo Giovannitti, described "as degenerate sons of Italy and undeserving guests of America," and in the meantime, it had to regenerate Italian prestige among Italian-Americans.[1]

Anti-Fascist opposition led by Tresca, leader of the local International Workers of the World (I.W.W.) and editor of the radical

Italian newspaper, *Il Martello* (the Hammer), staged anti-Fascist campaigns and organized anti-Fascist activities in New York. Tresca held Fascism responsible for destruction and bloodshed in Italy and for violent confrontations that had occurred in the United States. On the day Fascists dedicated their headquarters in New York, Socialists, Communists, and labor radicals organized a protest at the headquarters of *Circolo di Cultura*. Though Tresca did not admit it, he knew full well the inevitability of violence between Fascists and anti-Fascists in New York City.

In mid-March of 1923, violent confrontations between Fascist and anti-Fascist elements had already occurred in north Philadelphia and in Lawrence, Massachusetts. In north Philadelphia, radical elements had interrupted a Fascist meeting, creating such an uproar that police intervened and closed the hall to restore order. In Lawrence, Fascists had invaded a radical meeting, and a free-for-all fight ensued in which one Fascist was shot. Commenting on the events, the newspaper *Il Popolo d'Italia* said: "Remember that nobody insults Fascism and goes unpunished, not even in New York. Therefore, if he expects to deliver to the Inspector of the Cemetery his carcass untouched, let him behave."[2]

The war between Italy's Fascists and Carlo Tresca was nothing new (New York City's Fascist Association secretary acknowledged this on March 23, 1923). Tresca's animosity toward Fascists stemmed from resentments formed after the defeat of Italian Socialists and Communists at the hand of Fascists. Menicucci insisted that the Fascists of North America had no political mission whatsoever. Furthermore, he averred, Fascists in America were not organized to make war on radicals or on any other group in the United States. Fascist intervention in Lawrence had been motivated by the radical cry "Down with America and down with Italy." Any good citizen and patriot would have resented that insult; a deeply rooted sense of patriotism and Nationalism had motivated the Fascists' behavior.

According to Menicucci, nothing in the U.S. Fascist movement threatened American life or institutions, and Fascism's ultimate goal was to make Fascists better American citizens. Fascism wanted

Americans to accept and respect Italian-Americans as contributing, worthwhile individuals rather than "the humorous and picturesque 'wop' with a grind organ or a banana cart."[3]

A few days after Menicucci's comments on the nature and goals of Fascism in America, the executive board of the International Ladies' Garment Workers' Union (I.L.G.W.U.) announced the adoption of a resolution denouncing Fascist activities in Italy and America:

> When it is universally known that the Fascist reaction in Italy has wantonly and traitorously murdered thousands of men, women, and children of working classes;
> Resolved, that we call upon the president and the executive council of the American Federation of Labor to take immediate and adequate steps in order that the Fascist infamy not only be kept out of the United States but with the direct assistance of labor be also blotted out of Italy and the world;
> Resolved, that the International Ladies' Garment Workers' Union grant the fullest moral and material support to the Italian Chamber of Labor of New York in its present unremitting campaign against the Fascist menace, while we urge all other labor organizations to do likewise without stint or delay.[4]

Confrontations and denunciations followed. On March 22, Tresca warned U.S. authorities that Mussolini had cabled the Fascists of Chicago "to take orders from the New York headquarters." Joseph Di Silvestro, supreme chief of the Order of Sons of Italy, in an attempt to swing the 300,000 Sons of Italy into the Fascist organization, had made a propaganda tour of Brooklyn, Bridgeport, Philadelphia, and other industrial centers of the East.[5] The Sons, however, refused to have anything to do with the movement and New York State Senator Salvatore Cotillo warned Di Silvestro to keep Fascism out of the Sons of Italy. This ominous situation led Senator Cotillo to deliver a bitter attack on Fascism. In speeches delivered in upstate New York, he warned against transforming the Sons of Italy into an apparatus for Fascist propaganda in the United States. The senator called the Sons of Italy "all American," and said there was no room for Fascism in the order, "because the United States is not on the verge of bankruptcy or in the hands of Bolsheviks. Fascism is all right in its place, but not in America."[6]

However, pro-Fascist sympathy kept apace in New York. In January 1923, the *New York Times* had published its apologetic editorial on Gelasio Caetani, then Italian ambassador to Washington, describing him as "one of the most engaging figures among those sent in recent years to represent Europe in America," and the *Literary Digest* appeared deeply impressed with the anti-Red trend of Fascism in New York City.[7] The *Literary Digest* (April 7, 1923) quoted pro-Fascist newspaper *Il Carroccio*, directed and published by Agostino De Biasi, as saying Fascism in America "will be called upon to repeat here in the United States among the unions the battles that Fascism won in Italy, breaking the backbone of Bolshevism." Comments in *L'Opinione* of Philadelphia viewed Fascism as "a moral force, and as such the Italians throughout the world will make it their creed, their law, their gospel. It was Fascism that successfully crushed the onward march of Leninism and Communism, which for a while imperiled Western Civilization. We heartily approve, therefore, the warning to all Reds, Anarchists, Socialists, and Communists." Fascists in America, according to *Il Carroccio*, must "renew here the battle that Fascism won in Italy breaking the spinal column of Bolshevism; these are the pillars on which are built the linking between America and Italy." Further, quoting *Il Popolo* of New York, the *Literary Digest* said "as for the radicals and malefactors bearing Italian names, the American police are quite sufficient to subdue them." Finally, examining the content of an article that had appeared in the *Detroit Free Press*, the review pointed out that Fascism had done great work in Italy. In saving the peninsula from "control by Communistic and Bolshevistic elements...the practices of the Fascists proved to be sound. They also had proved to be patriotic and Nationalistic."[8]

The consistent apologetic view taken by *New York Times*, the *Literary Digest, Il Popolo, Il Corriere d'America, Il Carroccio, and Il Progresso Italo-Americano* on behalf of Fascism in Italy and in the U.S. spurred a strong reaction on the part of the Italian Chamber of Labor of New York, the Workers' Anti-Fascist Alliance of North America, the International Ladies' Garment Workers' Union, and several other philo-Socialist organizations. In mid-April 1923, these organizations issued the first anti-Fascist manifesto. Historians consider the manifesto the first official denunciation of Fascism by anti-Fascist organizations in the United States.

A short preamble containing formal greetings and acknowledgment of political solidarity with all workers of North America introduced the Manifesto's three parts. The first section reviewed Italy's political situation since Mussolini's ascendancy into power. The document says a savage "orgy of criminals, hoodlums and mercenaries" had seized control of the government with the acquiescence of the civilized world. Fascism had reduced the Italian people to the lowest form of slavery. Centuries of civilization had been destroyed, and generations of democratic process had been prostrated "under the inverted thumb of Benito Mussolini." Though Fascism currently reigned in Italy, the unstoppable forces of history were about "to hurl Fascism back to the abyss of the past whence it had emerged." The universal quest for individual liberty, humanity's instinctive search for a better and democratic life and inborn common sense would inevitably defeat Fascism. Moreover, the irrepressible and inevitable process of class struggle would strike the finishing blow against Fascism. Therefore, the final and decisive struggle against Fascism ought to be staged and conducted by the workers of America and the world. Since Italian workers could not stage a mass revolt against Mussolini and his Fascist clique, workers abroad had a moral responsibility to support them in the struggle for freedom and redemption. To this end, the first section of the manifesto advocates:

- an insistent and unflagging campaign of publicity to enlighten American public opinion on the nature and goals of Fascism in Italy and America
- that the 150,000 Italian trade unionists of the United States charge Mussolini with crimes of high treason, perjury, murder,

arson, burglary, rape and continued violence upon the body
and the property of all the workers of Italy
- a widespread campaign against Mussolini, who had sacked
and razed to the ground hundreds of private buildings, suppressed all the press of the opposition, divested the National
Assembly of every power, seized municipal administrations
of more than two thousand cities, ruled out of the law and
protection every political party of the workers, disbanded by
force of arms all labor organizations, arrested without charge
more than sixty thousand men and women

In addition to this incomplete list of Mussolini's many crimes,
Fascism had abolished the state police and substituted hordes of militia gunmen. The Italian bourgeoisie, the lowest of all the predatory
classes, had permitted all these indignities to be heaped upon the
people and the entire nation. It was against the continuation of this
illegal and immoral situation that the Italian Chamber of Labor of
New York addressed this appeal to all Italian workers of the United
States and Canada to come to the aid of the working class of Italy
before it became socially extinct.

Part two of the manifesto warns the American people not to allow
"the Fascist octopus to extend its tentacles across the Ocean and
to bring to America the Gospel of the torch, the bomb and the sti-
letto." To safeguard the interest of Americans it was necessary to
exercise rigid control over Fascist organizations in the United States,
because:

> already Fascist contingents had been organized in the various
> States of the Union; already the Black Shirts, decorated with
> the death symbol of piracy, had made their public appearance
> in New York and Philadelphia and openly disavowed, but
> secretly encouraged by the diplomatic and consular henchmen
> of Mussolini, these first Fascist vanguards of criminals,
> pillagers, and freebooters had already hurled their challenge to
> organized labor in America.

The third section of the manifesto deals with the immediate goals of Fascism in this country. According to the document, the traditions of freedom and democracy in America were endangered; Fascist organizations were conspiring against the labor movement and trying to associate with and link their criminal and repressive actions to those of the Ku Klux Klan. Their final objective was to weaken and destroy the American Labor Movement, to blast at the foundations of the workers' defense, and to act as strikebreakers and gunmen of reactionary American employers as they had acted in Italy, Mexico, and Bavaria. To prevent the monster of Fascism from bringing fire, destruction, and repression to America, the workers of America must fight tirelessly and unabatedly to wipe away the shame of Fascism from Italy. Thus the manifesto concludes by summoning all labor unions of the United States to begin at once an energetic campaign against Fascism in Italy and America.[9]

On July 28, 1923, Tresca's paper *Il Martello* was suspended from the mails pending an examination of the paper by the solicitor of the U.S. Postal Service in Washington. According to reliable sources, Italian authorities had requested suspension of the paper on the grounds that the newspaper was a subversive influence. On November 27, a federal court found Tresca guilty of sending obscene literature (a newspaper advertisement for birth control) through the mail. He was summarily sentenced to serve a year and a day in the Atlanta Penitentiary. However, on February 16, 1925, President Coolidge reduced Tresca's sentence to a third of the original sentence. After carefully following the case, Representative Fiorella LaGuardia asked the U.S. State Department point blank if the Italian Embassy had started the charge against Tresca. The State Department maintained that it would not be in the public interest to answer this specific question, and the Department did not intend to disclose the source of the complaint. Tresca affirmed, however, his prosecution had been inspired by the Italian ambassador.[10]

Tresca's case stirred strong and immediate reaction by Socialists in the U.S. The *New Leader*, a weekly Socialist newspaper published in New York, engaged in a campaign of criticism directed at federal and local authorities, charging them with silently permitting Mussolini's clammy hand to touch the United States. In an editorial on February 2, 1924, the newspaper disclosed that the Italian ambassador had requested Tresca's investigation. The newspaper could neither explain nor justify why the federal authorities had remained silent on a case "where an acknowledged foreign dictatorship directed the activities of American public officials." According to the editorial, American workers' organizations were entitled to know whether the United States had become a colony of "the freak Napoleon" who governed Italy with clubs and castor oil. In demanding the immediate release of Tresca, the Socialist paper warned American authorities that continuing these methods might well place in jeopardy the liberty of many workers fighting Mussolini's thugs in this country.[11] Despite sufficient evidence that the Italian ambassador had instigated the action of federal authorities, Tresca entered jail in December 1924.

Declaring the Italian radical a victim of Fascist influence in the United States, the American Civil Liberties Union (ACLU) forwarded a request for executive clemency for Carlo Tresca to the attorney general. The ACLU asked for clemency on the ground that the sentence was disproportionate to the offense and that it was the first prison sentence ever imposed in the United States under the statute penalizing the advertising of matter on birth control. Previous cases had resulted either in acquittals or small fines. Even under state laws the maximum sentence imposed for the crime was six months.

Moreover, the ACLU contended, the real reason for Tresca's conviction was not his birth control advertisement but his anti-Fascist activities. The ACLU also alleged the Italian Ambassador, Gelasio Caetani, had raised the charges on behalf of the Italian government. The ACLU traced in a detailed and documented statement the political interference of the Italian ambassador:

> At a dinner of welcome in July 1923, to Judge Gary, who is an honorary member of the Fascists, the Italian Ambassador suggested that a certain Italian paper in New York ought to be

suppressed. The government's attention to *Il Martello* began immediately thereafter. The July 21st issue of the paper was held up in the mails without warning and specific charges. On August 10, Tresca was arrested for an article, then three months old, criticizing the Italian Monarchy. On August 18, he was ordered to delete from his paper the announcement of a raffle, although two other papers carried the same notice unmolested. The September 8 issue of *Il Martello* was held up for containing a twoline advertisement of a birth control book. Although the advertisement was deleted and the paper allowed to pass through the mail, Tresca was indicted for this a month later. Even after the indictment, the government continued to harass the paper. On October 27, Tresca was forced to reprint an entire edition of the paper omitting an account of how the Fascists forced a woman to take castor oil.[12]

The Tresca incident seemed to have enhanced Mussolini's credibility in the eye of federal authorities. In fact, Fascist leaders in Italy and America tried to present Fascism as a doctrine aimed at making Italians abroad better citizens and proud of their Fatherland. Mussolini not only continued to stress that *Fasci* abroad should maintain national discipline, but also he recommended that Fascists abstain from any act or word offensive to diplomatic representatives.

In the meantime, Ambassador Caetani, in a farewell address to the Italian Chamber of Commerce in New York, on January 17, 1925, denounced Mussolini's foes in Italy and the United States and condemned false propaganda against Fascism. In his address Caetani said, Fascism was not born to fight Communism, though "that is still its principal aim." Communism, he said, had begun in Italy. Since Communism represented an antinational ideology and was the first obstacle on the way toward national regeneration, Fascism ought to get rid of it. "What would the American public think and do if tomorrow a large part of the American press should publish the deliberately false news of popular revolt in some of the States, thereby throwing the whole country into alarm for a few hours?" the ambassador asked. Inevitably, he said, the people of the United States would revolt and react violently against such an infamous press. According to Ambassador Caetani, the Italian government had been forced to muzzle the Italian anti-Fascist press because Opposition papers had staged a propaganda campaign of false charges and slanders against Fascism: "This is why the Fascist government was obliged to act harshly against certain papers that by spreading false and seditious news were putting in danger the laws and the economic prosperity of the country."[13] Because seditious riffraff of heterogeneous elements with different political and economic programs comprised the Opposition, Mussolini had also developed a doctrine of disrespect for parliament.

Tresca's prosecution only seemed to encourage the Black Shirts of New York, New Jersey, and Pennsylvania to clash with American and Italian-American radicals. An occasion to prove their patriotism arrived for the Black Shirts on the Fourth of July, 1925. Black Shirt warriors displayed their heralded bravado by parading outside the Garibaldi Pantheon in Rosebank, Staten Island. In the afternoon, they completed their mission by attacking an 82-year-old Garibaldean, Giuseppe Genovese, on 14th Street and Second Avenue in New York. The Black Shirts had announced the parade in the Fascist *Il Grido della Stirpe* (the Cry of the Race) several days before the holiday:

> We will be there the Fourth of July, we Black Shirts have no fear. We will go there tempered, ready for all events.[14]

The Fascist provocation of the Fourth of July was promptly condemned by the Italian Chamber of Labor of America. In an editorial in the *New Leader* of July 11, 1925, the Chamber called for the attention of local and Federal authorities. The article said:

> It is about time that the Police Department considered the activities of these understudies of Mussolini...Here is something demanding the attention of the department. Men who openly parade and carry clubs, men who have used these clubs in attacking people constitute a provocative organization that should be driven from the streets. No organization can parade without a police permit and we presume Mussolini's cowards

obtained a permit for their parade last week...The Police Department knows who the Fascists are. It knows what they have done. Are these armed bullies to be allowed to assault men and women whose crime is that they do not agree to government by castor oil and education by the club?[15]

In mid-August the Italian Chamber of Labor made headlines again. This time it protested the arrest of Vincenzo Vacirca, a member of the Italian Socialist Federation, who had been picked up in New York City on a bench warrant charging him with brawling and being a fugitive from justice in Italy. In reality, Vacirca was a political refugee who had managed to escape Mussolini's persecution in Europe and had reached America.

The Italian Chamber of Labor of America, backed by the Socialist movement, gave the following explanation of Vacirca's arrest:

> That at the behest of the American Fascists the prosecuting attorney of Essex County, New Jersey, had caused the apprehension and imprisonment of Vincenzo Vacirca.
>
> That the charge against Vacirca was that he was wanted in Italy as a fugitive of justice. However, his "crime" in Italy was a consequence of his political opposition to Mussolini.
>
> That the Fascist League of North America was carrying on a feverish campaign, working overtime and with an apparently large supply of money, to have Vacirca extradited to Italy.
>
> Counsel for Vacirca, retained by the Italian Chamber of Labor, asked Magistrate Goodman to fix bail at $500. The Essex County Prosecutor repeated his tale of Vacirca's "crime" in Italy. He asked bail to be fixed at $50,000. Goodman made it $50,000.
>
> The Chief of the Police Department had informed the Italian Chamber of Labor that Vacirca was wanted in Italy for the same thing he had been pulling here: Social stuff, radical meetings and riots.[16]

The Italian Chamber of Labor and the Socialist movement in general saw the long arm of Mussolini reaching the United States in Tresca's prosecution, Vacirca's arrest, and Fascist crime in Rosebank and New York. They expressed concern that the paranoiac who ruled Italy had U.S. authorities and others in the U.S. doing his dirty work for him. In their estimation, it was time for a thorough investigation into how and why Mussolini's agents engaged in violence in the U.S. and how the courts were used against their victims: "Meanwhile, we urge the organized working class to protest and watch that Vacirca and other anti-Fascists were not turned over to Mussolini and his assassins."[17]

On January 10, 1926, Wisconsin Socialist Congressman Victor L. Berger urged President Coolidge to inform Mussolini and the representatives of the Fascist party in Italy "the people of the United States view with concern and alarm the tyrannical methods employed in Italy and in the United States by Fascists." Following Berger's requests, thousands of Italian workers in the United States renounced their Italian citizenship. While acknowledging natural affection for their native land, nevertheless they felt "ashamed of being citizens with the murderers of Matteotti, with the Black Shirts…We are now not proud to have been born there, where murderers like Mussolini can head the government."[18] Arturo Giovannitti, Luigi Antonini, Gioacchino Artone, Giuseppe Genovese, Carlo Tresca, Girolamo Valenti, Giovanni Cannata, Vincenzo Vacirca, and many more signed the statement of renunciation of Italian citizenship.

Following the declaration of renunciation, the Anti-Fascist Alliance of New York City on March 24, 1926, issued the following statement:

> We, the undersigned, were born in Italy and it is natural for us to harbor a deep, passionate love for the country that gave birth to Bruno, Galileo, Masaniello, Bandiera, Pisacane, Pellico and Matteotti. In Italy, on our mothers' knees, we learned to speak the language of Dante; in Italy we left our parents, friends, schoolmates and childhood companions; in Italy we received our education and had our individual conscience shaped. To Italy our thoughts turn with filial devotion. We cannot, however, forget that in that very Italy we were taught by our parents, who had almost witnessed the heroic deeds of the Risorgimento, that the Savoy tyrants first

persecuted and then exploited two giants, Giuseppe Mazzini and Giuseppe Garibaldi, the former advocating a spirit of brotherly love among all the people of the world, the latter being always ready to fight for liberty in every land...As long as Italy marched together with all the civilized countries, we considered it an honor to be one of its citizens. But today we feel ashamed to be the countrymen of Giacomo Matteotti's murderers. A land controlled by a band of brigands; a land where all liberties are denied, where all rights and the very existence of the people are dependent on the will of professional murderers; a land whose judiciary is the servant of the tyrant smeared with the blood of so many martyrs of an idea; a land where so large is the number of people who have submitted to a gang of thieves; a land of this kind is a blot to all men hating selfrespect and dignity...We just say that as long as the Italian government is headed by a man like Mussolini, who has become from 1920 to this very day the hired assassin of a hungry and liberty destroying middle class, we do not know what to do with the Italian citizenship. Let all the thieves and murderers claim it. We repudiate it. We tear it into pieces in your face, brigand of Predappio. We do consider ourselves the sons of Italy, but of that Italy which waits and prepares in silence the day of liberation. The day will come when the chains will not bind Italy any longer and liberty will cease to be a "rotten goddess." We will ask, then, to be reinstated as citizens of Italy.[19]

Despite these events, the period January–July 1926 saw a strong revival of pro-Mussolini sentiment in the United States. On various occasions intellectuals and right-wing politicians expressed their sympathy and appreciation for Mussolini and Fascism. Professor William Y. Elliott of Harvard stated before the Foreign Policy Association that Italian Fascism represented an organized body "that will remain in control until the public rises." Bankers Lament and Kahn affirmed that Mussolini "holds his position and power by the overwhelmingly expressed will of the people."[20] Statements praising Benito Mussolini were made by Nicholas Murray Butler, president of Columbia University, at the dedication ceremony of the Italian House.[21]

These and many more homages to Mussolini from American intellectuals and businessmen stirred the reaction of Italian and American Socialists. Editorials in the *New Leader* condemned sternly the glorification of Mussolini by Americans. "It is significant that our American leaders pay this homage to Mussolini," reported the newspaper on January 30, 1926. "They give us an index of their mind. The men who can give their blessing to this dictator are no better than the thugs they embrace."[22]

On July 29, 1926, a federal judge in Philadelphia reportedly said "to have respect for the laws we should have a dictator, a Mussolini, here. I am serious about that."[23] The Socialist reaction was immediate and strong. In an editorial titled "Mussolini" on July 31, 1926, the *New Leader* called upon the American public to be seriously concerned about the Philadelphia judge who lauded Fascist methods. Fascists rule in the U.S. would mean the end of labor organizations, trade unions, cooperative organizations, and workers' rights and freedom. Moreover, the article went on, Fascism in America would mean the end of democracy for Americans and a long period of political and economic "vacuum."[24]

In the midst of these heated feelings and events the North America Anti-Fascist Alliance released its historic manifesto on August 26, 1926. The August Manifesto came in the wake of two previous manifestoes drafted in Italy: one by Fascist intellectuals, led by philosopher Giovanni Gentile, and the other by anti-Fascist intellectuals led by philosopher-historian Benedetto Croce. Both manifestoes had appeared in early 1925. The manifestoes published in Italy focused on philosophical and verbal disputes without offering any practical or programmatic commitment for the future of Italy. The U.S. August Manifesto represented a concrete denunciation of Fascism and its methods. Moreover, it predicted Fascism's fall as soon as socioeconomic conditions grew unbearable and the struggle between capital and labor renewed in earnest. On the ashes of Fascism a new dawn of liberty would rise for Italy.

On April 21, 1925, in connection with the celebration of the 2,878th anniversary of the founding of Rome, the Italian Fascist party issued a manifesto. Composed by philosopher Giovanni Gentile, the document was signed by some 250 Fascist intellectuals. The manifesto reviewed Fascism and its achievements from a political and intellectual point of view and described Fascism as the moral, political, and intellectual renascence of Italy.

In reality, the manifesto was issued in Bologna at the conclusion of the "First Fascist Cultural Symposium," sponsored by Italian Fascist Intellectuals and led by Giovanni Gentile. The manifesto itself is known as Gentile's Manifesto, and it closely reflects Gentile's philosophy of Fascism. The Gentile Manifesto asserts that the word *liberty* always had "the most elastic significance," even in the most democratic countries. Before reaching the state where liberty will have its truest meaning and highest realization, it must go through a series of dialectical manifestations of discipline and individual self-effacement. These stages are necessary, since the individual and spiritual values are transient, while the State remains immanent. One of Fascism's greatest aims derives from this postulate: to work out a system of true cooperation between the State and labor unions, with the former acting as the juridical adjuster of labor's problems.[25]

On May 1, 1925, the Italian anti-Fascist intellectuals, led by Benedetto Croce, published the *Manifesto degli Antifascisti*, which appeared in the newspaper *Il Mondo*. The document recalled that even German intellectuals, on the eve of World War I, had issued a manifesto of such a nature to the intellectuals of the world, and that, instead of approval, they had raised worldwide disapproval. Moreover, the Fascist intellectuals, in addressing their manifesto to the intellectuals of the world in defense of Fascism in Italy, had demonstrated vileness in bringing to the attention of the world Italy's internal political crisis. Croce's *Manifesto* rejected as antihistorical the affirmation that the "progress of a country is achieved through a relentless opposition." Furthermore, a doctrine stressing the submission of the "individual to the whole" ought to be rejected as abominable. On the issue of cooperation between the State and the labor unions, Croce charged Gentile of seriously misunderstanding labor unions, "which are economic institutions," and the State, "which is an ethical institution." Such a cooperation, if realized, would bring "reciprocal limitations and neutralization between the two institutions." Finally, Fascism was envisaged as a dialectical antithesis Italy had to pass through before achieving lasting democracy and freedom.[26]

Gentile's and Croce's manifestoes focused on philosophical and verbal disputes without offering any practical and programmatic solution to Italy's problems. Not until August 26, 1926, did a programmatic manifesto appear, and it was issued by the North American Anti-Fascist Alliance and published in New York.

In 1926, while Benito Mussolini worked toward completing the *Fascistization* of the Italian state, in the United States the North American Anti-Fascist Alliance drafted its manifesto addressed to "All workers of the United States, Canada, and Mexico; to all people of the world concerned about Italy's constitutional and civil liberties."[27] (A copy of the document was found among the author's family papers in Italy [see Appendix V].)

The August Manifesto resulted from a Communist-Socialist-Social Democrat collaboration and was the common denominator of those leftist political forces whose primary task was to overthrow Italy's Fascist regime. Significantly, it openly condemned antidemocratic Fascist trends in Italy as well as underground activities in the United States by the North American Fascist League.

The following organizations, union leaders, and newspaper editors signed and endorsed the August Manifesto: Joseph Catalanotti, vice president, Amalgamated Workers of America; Arturo Giovannitti, secretary-general, Italian Chamber of Labor; Joseph Altieri, secretary, Veterans Association "G. Pilati"; Michele Sala, president, Club of Modern Culture; Raffaele Rende, editor, *La Giustizia*; Enea Sormenti, editor, *Il Lavoratore*; Carlo Tresca, director, *Il Martello;* Luigi Antonini, vice president, I.L.G.W.U., and secretary-general, Local 89, I.L.G.W.U.; Paul Graditi, secretary, Italian Trade Union Progressive Center; Benito Mazzoti, editor, *La Scopa*; and Frank Bellanca, editor, *Il Lavoro* and *Il Nuovo Mondo.* Moreover, it was fully endorsed by the Italian Communist Party of America; the Italian Socialist Party of America; the Italian Republican Party of

America; and the Society G. B. Odierna, presided over by Giuseppe Lupis, an Italian Social Democrat and a *fuoruscito* in the eyes of the Fascists.

Historically, the August Manifesto was the very first common attempt by anti-Fascist forces aimed at the condemnation of Fascism, its ideology, and its tactics. Ample evidence tells us that the document, issued in collaboration with Communists, Socialists, Social Democrats, and Republicans in exile, was the first organized united front in the struggle against Fascism. The document proves unmistakably that the first anti-Fascist organized sanctuary and the first anti-Fascist campaign in the Western world were organized in the U.S. by Americans and Italian-Americans. In fact, the August Manifesto represents the turning point of the Alliance organized in 1923 by the aforementioned political forces. Surprisingly, not until 1936 did Italian Communists and Socialists exiled in France agree to promote a common anti-Fascist front similar to the French *Front Populaire.*

The very fact that the first alliance of anti-Fascist and leftist forces occurred in the United States seems to have re-energized Mussolini once more—through his ambassador in Washington, Caetani—to exert pressure on State Department officials. He urged them either to expel or to keep under surveillance anti-Fascists who had sought asylum in the United States. In fact, the moment advantaged Fascist propaganda. Americans had reacted positively to widespread pro-Fascist activities carried out by the North American Fascist League. Many Americans and Italian-Americans were fascinated with the myth of *Il Duce.* At the same time, Fascists endeavored to discredit the courageous attacks of the anti-Fascist opposition.

But the North American Anti-Fascist Alliance intentionally restricted its activities to the framework of the labor movement, where any unfavorable reaction could be easily appeased and where more support could be found, especially among Liberals and Progressives. Moreover, people in the Alliance wanted to avoid the glare of public opinion, which was captivated by Mussolini's charisma and bombastic explosions, because they feared governmental harassment.

Furthermore, this strategy explains the nature, structure, and style of the Manifesto. Though drafted in Marxist-oriented tones, it was intended as an appeal to the civil conscience of the workers of the United States, Canada, and Mexico.

Finally, the August Manifesto, in condemning Victor Emmanuel III, king of Italy, for his acquiescence to the *Fascistization* of Italy, put in place the historical foundations of the June 1946 national referendum and the proclamation of the Republic.

Interestingly, publication of the August Manifesto did not bridge differences dividing Socialists and Communists in America, and Communist tactics led to the rupture of the North American Anti-Fascist Alliance. For about a year the Socialists and trade unionists had tolerated the campaign of Communist slander. But in late August 1926, the Socialists severed their connections with the Communists of the Anti-Fascist Alliance. Socialists charged the Communists with trying to capture and control the Alliance by creating delegates from fictitious organizations and steamrolling the proceedings. In meetings held in the first half of 1926, the Socialists, the Italian Chamber of Labor, and various Italian trade unions were outnumbered by the delegates of fictitious Communist organizations.

Moreover, men like Ninfo and Antonini of the I.L.G.W.U.; Bellanca, Artoni, and Procopio of the Amalgamated Clothing Workers of America; Valenti, of the Shoe Workers Protective Union; and Romualdi, editor of the Italian Socialist paper *La Parola del Popolo* (Word of the People), had been assailed in the Communist press and at meetings of the Anti-Fascist Alliance.[28]

On August 14, 1926, the International Anti-Fascist League for the Freedom of Italy replaced the North America Anti-Fascist Alliance. The League sought immediate affiliation with the newly founded Anti-Fascist International with headquarters in Vienna. By the end of August, the League had appointed Eugene V. Debs honorary chairman, and John Vaccaro, of the Cigar Makers' Union, temporary secretary.[29]

The new International Anti-Fascist League for the Freedom of Italy immediately started a national propaganda drive to sway

American public opinion against the oppressors of the Italian people. The leaders of the League contended that American sympathy had helped enslave the people of Italy, and had it not been for Wall Street loans to Mussolini's government, the Italian people would have freed themselves and Mussolini would have sunk into oblivion.

The League also declared that it had nothing whatsoever to do with the Anti-Fascist Alliance of North America, an organization from which the Socialists and trade unionists had seceded because of Communist infiltrators' "boring from within tactics." The leaders of the new anti-Fascist League emphatically declared that they could not and would not be confused with an anti-Fascist group that embraced Communists, the advocates of another form of dictatorship. "One could not be against the dictatorship of Black Shirts, and at the same time approve, as Communists did, the Bolshevist dictatorship in Russia."[30]

So ended the North American Anti-Fascist Alliance. Launched in 1924 by the Italian Chamber of Labor of New York City immediately after the murder of Giacomo Matteotti, the Alliance combated Fascist infiltration of Italian communities in the U.S. and helped the cause of enslaved Italians by exposing Fascist brutalities. Nearly all the Italian labor unions and radical parties rallied around the program of the Alliance. When the Communists tried to change the program of united front to that of united spirit, the Alliance had to suspend its activities. The Alliance had a clear program: defeat Fascism for the triumph of democracy. The Communists, on the other hand, wanted the fall of Fascism to make a mockery of democracy. Communists stood for dictatorship, violence, and rule of the minority. The Socialists of the Chamber of Labor stood for democracy of the free majority.[31]

CHAPTER 8

ANTI-FASCIST OPPOSITION AND THE DISBANDING OF THE FASCIST LEAGUE OF NORTH AMERICA

The history of Fascism in America cannot be separated from that of anti-Fascism. The existence of Fascist associations spurred anti-Fascist opposition and campaigns throughout the United States. That the presence of Fascist associations had created a network of anti-Fascist organizations or groups was admitted by Ambassador Caetani in dispatches and memoranda sent to Italy from 1923 to 1925. Local Fascist associations continually informed consular agencies and the Italian Embassy in Washington of relentless anti-Fascist activities conducted by Italian-American Communists, Socialists, and Radicals organized in the Anti-Fascist Alliance of North America (AFANA).

A well-organized, active anti-Fascist network opposed the Fascist network. As two Italian-American doctors, Anthony Castruccio and Joseph Ceraso, co-wrote in a memorandum in May 1924 about Fascism in New York and Chicago: the Communist opposition was strong, tenacious, and supported by international anti-Fascist organizations. Italian-American anti-Fascists had the support of national and international movements and could penetrate and proselytize other ethnic groups.[1]

Antagonism between Fascists and anti-Fascists in New York was not the exception. Throughout America, wherever Fascist associations formed, anti-Fascist movements sprang up. Frequently, confrontations between the rival groups turned into assaults and even destruction or burning of headquarters. As early as June 30, 1922, even before Fascism had achieved control of the Italian government, Sebastiano Bonfiglio, one of the best-known Italian Socialists in the U.S., was assassinated by Fascists in his home town in Sicily. The assassination of Bonfiglio spurred protests in America. Leonardo Frisina, national organizer of the Italian Socialist Federation of America, spoke in New York, condemning the event as a sample of Fascist repression in the world.[2] From 1923 to 1930, struggles between Fascists and anti-Fascists were not limited to verbal or journalistic disputes. On the contrary, destruction of property, physical assault, and even murders and open war took place between the two opposing factions.

On November 10, 1923, anti-Fascists invaded the headquarters of the Fascist League of North America (FLNA) led by Count Ignazio Thaon di Revel. Furniture was destroyed and the files of the League burned.[3] On November 20, members of the Fascist League tried to hire henchmen from the New York underworld to destroy and burn the New York office of the Communist paper *Il Lavoratore*. The Fascists promised them a "considerable sum of money." Reporting on the attempt, *Il Lavoratore* pointed out that the Fascists of America applied the same methods to subdue opponents as Mussolini did in Italy. He hired henchmen and gangsters to carry out criminal plans against his opponents, promising them "money and protection from legal punishment."[4]

Anti-Fascist activities and propaganda intensified in mid-1924. On July 17, 1924, the AFANA issued its first strong condemnation of Fascist activities in the United States. The pretext had been the deportation to Italy of the Italian-American syndicalist, A. Tori, sought by Italian Fascists. The Anti-Fascist Alliance launched a national appeal through the newspaper *Alba Nuova* (New Dawn) to American authorities to stop this form of connivance with Italian henchmen. They followed the appeal immediately with an open invitation to all anti-Fascists living in the United States to form an international movement to protect the right of political asylum in the U.S. Above all, the organization wanted to engage all anti-Fascist forces in the country to carry out a relentless and courageous struggle against Fascism. Enthusiasm and cheers greeted the project in San Francisco, Los Angeles, Seattle, New York, Philadelphia, Baltimore, and many other cities. The murder of Matteotti, still fresh in the minds of many Italian-Americans, emphasized the necessity of such an organization.

The immediate goals of the League would be not only to condemn all political crimes committed by Fascism in Italy and abroad, but also to point out to Americans and to the world that politics and persecution motivated the deportations of anti-Fascists to Italy. Moreover, deportations appeared to be closely connected with Fascist and capitalist repressive connivance. Since this repressive campaign had a worldwide range and was conducted in the East as well as in the West, in America as well as in Europe, reaching violence in Spain, Yugoslavia, Portugal, France, Germany, Poland, Finland, Rumania and Bulgaria, then Fascism, considered an international threat, ought to be fought internationally. Only through an International Anti-Fascist League could Fascism be destroyed.

In the U.S., more than anywhere else, anti-Fascist opposition needed to organize for worldwide effect. In fact, 18 million workers of European descent had arrived in the U.S. from countries where Fascism ran rampant. A cohesive union of U.S. workers and European anti-Fascists would produce a formidable front not only against Fascism and the Ku Klux Klan in the U.S. but also against international Fascism. All democratic American labor groups founded on the principles of liberty and justice were invited to join the League. The League would soon implement these immediate objectives:

1. Appointment of a directorate formed from all labor movements in the United States
2. Initiation of contacts with all workers movements in the world to gain international status and recognition
3. An immediate program aimed at helping all anti-Fascist political prisoners and émigrés from Fascist countries
4. Sponsorship of a massive anti-Fascist campaign in America and abroad
5. Establishment of a monetary fund to help the families of the victims of Fascist repression
6. Establishment of a press office to publish anti-Fascist literature and circulate it in the U.S. and abroad.[5]

Il Lavoratore of Chicago immediately responded to the appeal of the Anti-Fascist Alliance. On July 18, the newspaper's executive board launched a campaign in the columns of the paper, setting up the following guidelines for all anti-Fascists associated with U.S. labor movements:

> For a period of three months, all workers of the Labor Federations of America will pledge a weekly contribution of 35 cents for the improvement of the newspaper *Il Lavoratore*. In the meantime, the workers would provide distribution of the paper among all Italian-American and American workers.
> Each Federation will appoint a correspondent to the newspaper editorial board.
> All workers will contribute the net income of a day's work to the cause of the campaign.
> Each Federation will send workers every two weeks to collect grievances of anti-Fascist workers and to instruct the masses on the nature and goals of Fascism.
> All members of each Federation will be divided into "activist squads." Each squad will be assigned a section or a street. Therefore, they will distribute personally the newspaper among the members of the Federation and convince those nonaffiliated to join it and make a subscription.

All workers engaged in this kind of propaganda would carry it out with dedication, patience, spirit of proselytism, and constant sacrifice. In this way, they would contribute to make scores of American and Italian-American workers aware of the nature and goals of Fascism.[6]

The idea to collect grievances against Fascist organizations in America seemed to produce positive results. In fact, between July and October 1924, over 150 grievances against Fascist activities in the United States were collected. In Pennsylvania there were 39, in New York 30, in Ohio 18, in Illinois 12, in Michigan 7, in New Jersey 6, in Indiana 5, in Massachusetts 4, in Connecticut 2, in Montana 2, and 1 each in Maryland, California, Virginia, and West Virginia. Cities registering the highest number of protests were: New York (10), Chicago (8), Yonkers (8), Plains (8), and Detroit (7).[7]

Once the mechanism of anti-Fascist opposition began to roll, it seemed that nobody could stop it. On July 28, 1924, *Il Lavoratore* printed an appeal to the Communist Party of America charging workers who did not collaborate in the struggle against Fascism with the crime of treason. According to the appeal, indolents, cowards, waverers, egoists, and passive slaves never triumphed, rather, the courageous, strong, and bold always achieved victory. The Communist Party would assemble only people endowed with determination and courage. Only through constant and incisive propaganda could the workers of America defeat Fascism and its relentless, long-armed press. The appeal addressed all workers, inviting them to collaborate in creating a strong unified front to defeat Fascism in America and in the world.[8]

On October 9 and 10, 1924, *Il Lavoratore* published two editorials by Giacinto Menotti Serrati. According to the author, Fascism was declining and its end was near. Even the bourgeois capitalist press was showing a diminished interest in Mussolini and his doctrines. In the eyes of most people, Mussolini was no longer champion of law and order but now appeared as a common criminal and bombastic politician. Fascism, which had been presented as the only ideology capable of uniting workers, middle classes, and capitalists, had subjugated Italian workers to the whims of capitalism. Rather than national regeneration and domestic socioeconomic reconstruction, Fascism had further divided the Italian nation. However, the middle classes, disappointed and frustrated, were moving toward the left and abandoning Fascism. It was now up to the middle class and the workers to hasten the death of Fascism.[9]

On November 12, 1924, the Italian Confederation of the Workers Party of America issued a brief manifesto declaring an open war on Fascism by the Italian proletariat. Though this action would cost sacrifice in human lives, nevertheless, the struggle would hasten the fall of Fascism. "The hour of the fall of Fascism is near and the Italian people ready to revolt against the assassins. The dawn of freedom is rising again on the horizon of Italy," announced the manifesto. Since the Fascists of America and Mussolini's consular henchmen had requested American federal authorities suppress *Il Lavoratore*, the editorial board asked American and Italian-American workers to be alert and avoid the suppression of their newspaper. The manifesto ended by inviting workers to stage mass protests, to support *Il Lavoratore* more than ever, and to double their efforts against Fascism in the U.S. and in the world.[10]

Anti-Fascist opposition continued throughout the United States in 1924. In Baltimore, the anti-Fascist association headed by Vincent Betro staged a march against local Fascism with the cry "Down with the Fascist assassins." Confrontations with the Fascist groups led by Generoso Pavese, head of Baltimore's Fascist directorate, occurred throughout the city, and city streets became the theater of Fascist and anti-Fascist clashes. According to Paride Perrone, many Fascists dared to walk downtown wearing the Black Shirts and the emblems of Fascism. Moreover, he deplored that the Baltimore anti-Fascists did not conduct a massive and courageous campaign against local Fascists. Instead of verbal confrontations, the anti-Fascists should engage their foes in clashes and fights. Such action, he said, would have prevented Fascists from marching unmolested in their Fascist uniforms.[11]

In Cleveland, Fernando Pascoli organized anti-Fascist activities, and in a speech on July 16, 1924, entitled, "Why Fascism Will Die," he explained to Italian-Americans of Cleveland the nature and the structure of the Fascist state. He defined Mussolini as an "Italian brigand" who had destroyed Italian liberties and democracy. More-over, he invited Italian-American workers to unite and create a strong front against Fascism in Italy and in the United States.[12]

In Plains, Dunmore, and Pittsburgh, Pennsylvania, anti-Fascist groups also staged protests against Fascism. In Plains, the United Mine Workers of America joined in the protests against Fascism in Italy and in America. They approved a resolution condemning Mussolini's ideology and his methods of government. Moreover, their document stressed the absolute necessity that all labor organizations in the world cooperate to prevent the Fascist octopus from extending its tentacles to the United States. The resolution continued:

> Resolved, that Mussolini must be retained responsible for all atrocious crimes committed against Italian workers; We pro-test against Fascism for its bold repression of all liberties, political, ideological, and personal, enjoyed by the Italian peo-ple before the advent of Fascism.
>
> We, therefore, express our solidarity with the Italian Proletar-iat and invite it to continue in its struggle to defeat Mussolini's shameful regime.[13]

In Dunmore, anti-Fascist events took place from July to October 1924. Socialist A. Pippan, anarchist P. Zonchiello, and mine workers led by F. Di Vincenzo organized over a thousand workers in anti-Fascist groups.[14] In Pittsburgh, the Italian Socialist Party organized meetings and conferences to denounce Mussolini and his ideology to American and Italian-American workers. A. Pippan and E. Clemente kept the Italian-American community of Pennsylvania abreast of events occurring in Italy under Mussolini. In a meeting held at Kings Hall in Pittsburgh, on July 20, 1924, clashes erupted between Fas-cists and anti-Fascists. Cries of "Down with Fascism and Mussolini" and "Long live Fascism in Italy and America," were shouted.[15] During October and November 1924, the anti-Fascist organization of Philadelphia presented the documentary film, "The Beauty and the Bolshevik," to raise money for the Anti-Fascist League. Screenings of the film also took place in Rochester and Buffalo, New York. Moreover, in Rochester, an anti-Fascist group led by Oberdan Rizzo organized "The International Grand Dance," in the Genenimo Hall, on October 25, 1924, to raise money for the Anti-Fascist League.

Life for Fascism was no rosier in Syracuse than in any other city in the U.S. thanks to Nicole De Pietro, who led the city's anti-Fascist opposition. In *Il Lavoratore*, which covered Syracuse-area news, local anti-Fascists denounced Fascist abuses daily.[16] Consul Gangemi's habits were under continued censure. On July 24, 1924, anti-Fascists accused Gangemi of illegally overcharging Italian-Americans who sent money back home while he was Italian consular agent. While all Syracuse banks charged only $9.00 as a service and delivery charge on a $200.00 remittance (4.5 percent), the Italian consular agency charged $9.50. For Power of Attorney, usually written by Italian consuls, Gangemi charged $5.00, while Italian regulations and ordinances authorized only $2.66. According to the anti-Fascist group, Gangemi exploited his position of Italian consul, connived with local Fascist leaders, and used his office for personal gain. Gangemi had little education and had been a bottom-saw in a New York tailor shop before volunteering in World War I. He went back to Italy in 1915 and emerged from the Fascist Revolution with the stripes of captain in the Italian Militia. In becoming Mussolini's agent, he had requested duty in the United States to serve the cause of Fascism. Since Gangemi was Menicucci's protégé, the New York organization directly controlled the Syracuse *Fasci*. In the eyes of Syracuse's anti-Fascists, the connivance between the two *Fasci* proved once again that Mussolini's henchmen in America had created a Camorralike organization to exploit Italian-Americans and their deeply felt sentiments of *Italianitá*.[17]

At Naugatuck, Connecticut, anti-Fascist opposition exploded during a public religious festival. At the Fiesta of the Virgin of Mount Carmel, on July 16, 1924, a local band performed the "Italian Royal March" to honor Mussolini and Italy. The anti-Fascist opposition, led by Joseph Borgnis, asked the band to play the "Workers' March." When the Fiesta's Committee refused, a scuffle between Fascist and anti-Fascists erupted. A second religious event, this one in Syracuse, ended with the performance of the "Royal March." However, the anti-Fascists then forced the director of the band to perform the "Workers' March," at the shouts of "Down with Mussolini and the King."[18]

In Jersey City, the anti-Fascist opposition called for a statewide boycott. Gaetano Turchi, editor of *Il Piccone* (the Pickaxe) programmed and directed the boycott activities. Anti-Fascists boycotted the Express Travel Agency, run by owners C. Ocone and C. Vignone, both members of the Fascist Party.[19]

In Wilmington, Delaware, on October 5, 1924, the Sons of Labor protested the deportation of Pietro Nigra, a Socialist sought by Italian Fascists, to Secretary of Labor James J. Davis. The Detroit branch of the International Women's League "Peace and Liberty," staged a similar protest to prevent the deportation of many political prisoners, including Aldo Nigra, of the International Workers of the World (IWW), a professed anti-Fascist. On October 23, 1924, the local chapter of the Communist Party staged another anti-Fascist event. This time continued delays in the trial of Luigi Ceccoli, indicted for aggression against Mussolini's envoy, Zopito Valentini, motivated the protest. The alleged aggression occurred in Detroit following Matteotti's assassination in Italy. However, Ceccoli was acquitted."[20]

In Chicago, the anti-Fascist campaign was carried on by *Il Lavoratore* with its relentless attack on Fascism in Italy and the United States. In November 1924, the newspaper engaged in a violent campaign against the Italian consul in Chicago, Leopoldo Zunini. He had become the mountebank of Fascism and Mussolini in the state of Illinois, delivering speeches at the Italian Chamber of Commerce of Chicago and defending Mussolini and his regime. According to Zunini, Mussolini "was to be regarded as the leader who had carried on the historical revolution that had changed Italy." *Il Lavoratore*'s reaction was immediate and solemn. In two editorials on

November 20 and 22, 1924, the newspaper rejected as unfounded the claims of the Italian consul, affirming among other issues, that Zunini did not defend the legitimate interests of Italian-Americans and Italy at large in the United States, but rather operated as "the secret agent of a government which has suppressed in Italy all rights and liberties." The editorials ended by pointing out that the Italian-American anti-Fascists would continue their struggle against Fascism "to free the Italian proletariat from the yoke of the common enemy: Mussolini."[21]

In California, anti-Fascist movements were operative and aggressive. In San Francisco, Francesco Gagliasso led the anti-Fascist groups. However, the struggle in that city was quite complex, since the groups had to face not only the Italian-American Fascists united in the Dante Alighieri, but also an aggressive philo-Fascist war veterans association (*Associazione Ex Combattenti e Reduci*). Moreover, the local press had praised Mussolini since the advent of Italian Fascism in 1922—the *San Francisco Chronicle* being the most sympathetic. In editorials, the newspaper showed relentless support for Mussolini from 1922 to 1930. For instance, on November 4, 1922, the editorial "Premier Mussolini of Italy Possibly the Wisest European Statesman," praised the Italian leader for his promise to restore "private initiative and enterprise which had been throttled by previous state ownership and operation." According to the newspaper, Italy's "deplorable situation, a result of mistaken state policy of the state ownership," might offer an eloquent lesson for California. As Italy had been tempted in the past, so was California tempted "to yield to the lure of State Socialism." Though the newspaper did not advocate another Mussolini for California, nevertheless, it suggested a form of government which could keep "the parasitic Socialist flies" away from the state apparatus.[22]

In Los Angeles, in addition to the anti-Fascist groups, which fought against Fascism and the activities of the Italian consulate, the American Friends of Italian Freedom, organized "to combat the misrepresentations of Fascist propaganda in America and to aid in the struggle for political liberty in Italy," staged many protests against the Italian consular agency. The most famous was addressed to U.S. Secretary of State Henry L. Stimson, on May 3, 1929. The matter concerned the attempt made by the Italian consul in Los Angeles to prevent Gaetano Salvemini, a *fuoruscito* in the eyes of Fascists, from addressing anti-Fascist meetings scheduled for April 1929, in Los Angeles and elsewhere in the state. According to the document, the Italian consul had organized Italian-American Fascists to discourage and even prevent the meetings from taking place. Moreover, Vice-Consul Conte Buzzi di Gradenigo had summoned to his office a number of American citizens of Italian extraction and urged them to boycott the meetings and prevent other Italians from attending them. Consequently, the American Friends of Italian Liberties requested that the U.S. State Department ask the Italian government to recall its vice-consul "who had disregarded basic principles of the American Constitution and overstepped the bounds allowed by International Law." However, the American authorities rejected the request on the basis that "the allegations did not furnish grounds for such an action."[23]

Significantly, several non-Communist organizations took part in this protest campaign staged by leftist groups against Fascism. Though their influence was limited, since they lacked nationwide organizations, nevertheless, their voice was strong and efficient. For instance, on June 4, 1929, an article on the front page of the *Christian Science Monitor*, "Fascist Activities in the United States Cause Complaints by Italians," motivated the first severe scrutiny on the part of the federal authorities. The investigation involved J. Edgar Hoover, director of the Justice Department; William R. Castle, Jr., assistant secretary of state; and N. C. Bannerman, of the Division of Current Information. The results of the investigation found "nothing specific that has happened in the last year that would clearly be found objectionable by this government and at the same time be proven as instigated by the Fascisti."[24]

On November 19, 1929, an article in the *New York Herald Tribune*, "Dr. Fama Urges Congressional Fascist Inquiry," spurred the reaction of the Italian ambassador in Washington, Giacomo de Martino.

Dr. Charles A. Fama, identified in the article as president of the Defenders of the Constitution Society, requested a congressional investigation of the Fascist League of North America, based on the charge that the League had forced many American citizens of Italian extraction "to maintain allegiance to this country and serve the Fascist party at the same time." Among the charges, Dr. Fama contended that Fascists had levied "taxes on bachelors of Italian origin, even on those who had become naturalized American citizens;" that in many states the League had "established schools to instill the spirit of Fascism among the Italian and the Italian-American children;" and that in Bridgeport, Connecticut, "The Fascist Popular University," had been established to teach Fascism at the university level. Moreover, libraries had been established in many cities and towns to allow people to become acquainted with the doctrine of Fascism. Finally, the article denounced the intimidation and boycotting of many shop owners throughout the country by Fascists.[25]

Fama requested that the American government investigate Mussolini's activities in the U.S. carried out by his consular agents, controlled and directed by Thaon di Revel, president of the Fascist League of North America. According to Fama, Count di Revel had more power in the United States than the Italian ambassador, and in his propaganda campaign he was assisted by Giovanni Di Silvestro, head of the Sons of Italy. The latter had led a pilgrimage of hundreds of Italians and Italian-Americans to Rome to pay tribute to Mussolini in the summer of 1929. Finally, the document protested Mussolini's attempt to organize, among Italian residents in the United States, strong Fascist groups to transform America into a colony of Italian Fascism.

The Italian ambassador reacted immediately to Fama's article. The same day the article appeared (November 19, 1929), the ambassador made a private visit to the secretary of state in Washington. According to a document revealing the conversation, both diplomats analyzed carefully the matter and the charges moved against Mussolini and Fascism by Fama. Though De Martino held the League responsible for "exceeding the proprieties of its position," nevertheless he rejected

Fama's charges against the Fascists of America as unfounded, unfair, and coming from a "bad man." The secretary of state, in a marginal note, agreed with the Italian ambassador ("He is, I think, correct.").[26]

From November 10 to December 15, 1929, the Fascist League of North America, Mussolini's consular agents, and all Fascist associations in America fell under severe scrutiny by federal authorities. Articles by Fama in the *New York Herald Tribune* and Marcus Duffield in *Harper's Magazine* (November 1929) assisted in soliciting governmental investigation. However, memoranda from the U.S. embassy in Rome, on December 7, and from the secretary of state on December 13, 1929, shed new light on the reaction of the American authorities to Fama's and Duffield's charges against Fascism and its activities in the United States. A careful examination of the documents proves that the American investigating committee reached conclusions contrary to Fama's and Duffield's. The thesis of Fascism as a movement aimed at undermining American constitutional rights and liberties of Americans, at creating a network of Fascist or pro-Fascist colonies in America, and taking revenge upon those Italians or Italian-Americans unwilling to submit to alien domination were dismissed as unfounded and arbitrary:

> The investigations of the incidents referred to in Duffield's and Fama's articles have indicated that most of them were completely unfounded, frivolous, or merely indicated friction between citizens of Italian origin in this country. It would seem therefore perfectly appropriate for you (the Secretary of State) to inform the Italian Ambassador, as well as the press, that the investigation completed by the State Department has indicated no activities of inhabitants of this country of Italian origin or descent directed against this government.[27]

However, the Department of State must have been gratified when the furor against Fascism and its alleged un-American activities did bring about the disbanding of the Fascist League of North America by Mussolini in December 1929. Were these publications instrumental in the decision? It seems very likely that Mussolini had made the

decision to disband the League long before the events of December
1929. Three major events undoubtedly convinced Mussolini to disband the League.

First, the relentless and well-organized anti-Fascist campaign by
Italian and Italian-American Socialists, Communists, and Radicals
took its toll. Indeed, the incessant badgering fragmented and neutralized Fascist chances in the United States. Second, continued warn-
ings by Ambassador Caetani from 1923 to 1925, to avoid Fascist
interference in domestic issues in the U.S. had made an impression
on Mussolini. Third, events that occurred in New York City in June
1926, and May 1927, created resentments in both Italy and the U.S.
Another event may have had an influence, though it later proved
unfounded: the crash of the City Trust Company, a bank owned by
Francesco M. Ferrari, on February 11, 1929. The latter event nearly
created an international scandal in which Fascism seemed to be
directly involved.

On June 2, 1926, the Italian Foreign Office complained to
American authorities of an alleged attack on three Fascist sailors on
the *S. S. Conte Biancamano*, docked in New York City. According
to the complaint, an anti-Fascist gang of Italian-Americans living
in New York City attacked the three Fascist sailors. The victims,
Severino Carosso, Edoardo Berlinghieri, and Cesare Musso were
seriously injured; Mussolini requested that the U.S. Embassy in
Rome inform the Department of State in Washington, urging that
more efficient steps be taken in New York for the protection of Italian
Fascist sailors against anti-Fascist attacks and retaliations. Even
though security measures at the Port of New York were tightened
to prevent the recurrence of such attacks, and the New York Police
Department assured the protection on Italian vessels, the incident
seemed to have convinced Mussolini that New York had become a
strong operational field and pulsing heart of anti-Fascist activities.[28]

On May 31, 1927, two Fascists were found slain on the doorsteps of
New York's Times Square. Anti-Fascists had shot and stabbed Joseph
Carisi, 39, and Nicholas Amoroso, 22, on their way to join a detach-
ment of 400 brethren of the Black Shirts to march in Manhattan's

Memorial Day parade. President of the Fascist League of North America, Count di Revel, called the killing of Carisi and Amoroso an episode of "simple murder," rather than acknowledging the crime as the direct consequence of a heightened status of hatred and animosity in New York City between Fascists and anti-Fascists. While Dr. Charles Fama, interviewed about the killing, linked the murders to anti-Fascist opposition to Mussolini's propaganda in the U.S., Count di Revel played down this link. Undoubtedly, Revel's interpretation was aimed at preventing American authorities disbanding the League to prevent further acts of violence. However, a few days following the New York killing, Mussolini commented in *Il Popolo d'Italia*. According to the article, the double assassination had been perpetrated by the "refuse of Italy who have come to New York." Mussolini advocated open war against all "the renegades" who were living in foreign countries engaged in criminal propaganda against Italy.[29]

Though Mussolini exploded bombastically against the Italian-American anti-Fascists of New York, nevertheless, W. R. Castle, of the U. S. State Department, took a different tact. In an opinion to Ambassador De Martino, Castle made clear that American authorities and people in general were "strongly opposed to the banding together of the Fascisti in public parades, wearing uniforms which make them the representatives of an Italian institution." Confirming his opinion that the May killings resulted from political hatred between Fascists and anti-Fascists, Castle continued: "There seems to be no doubt that, so long as the Fascisti insist in parading in New York City in uniforms as an organized body, there are going to be murders and vicious assaults." Finally, the American diplomat insisted that Fascists in America not only stop parading but that they also handle their organizations differently, "making it clear they would not interfere with American institutions and would keep themselves as foreigners in the background."[30]

The final straw was the crash of the City Trust Company in New York, owned and directed by Francesco M. Ferrari. Ferrari died 10 days before Joseph A. Broderick, state banking superintendent, made the announcement on April 11, 1929. European and American newspapers of the day make it possible to fashion a fairly accurate picture of the circumstances that brought about the $7,000,000 failure of the City Trust Company. Ferrari, the story goes, had connections with drug traffic and had used international transatlantic Italian vessels for such trafficking purposes since 1924. Fascists had discovered the drug traffic and exploited this knowledge by blackmailing Ferrari. They managed to wrest substantial sums for the Fascist League of North America from the banker. While investigating Ferrari's drug trafficking, Alvin McK. Sylvester, the assistant United States attorney, uncovered information indicating that a great deal of money had been extorted from the banker by individuals who knew of his criminal activity. Much of this blackmail money, maintained Sylvester, appeared to have gone to Italian Fascism. Federal authorities estimated that the money wrested from Ferrari ran into the millions.[31]

However, on May 18, 1929, United States Attorney Charles H. Tuttle, wrote the following note to the *Herald Tribune*:

> This office has no evidence whatever that Fascism had any connection with the City Trust Company or any one associated with it, and this office has no evidence that any funds of the City Trust Company or of any one associated with it went to the cause of Fascism. We have no evidence that there was any blackmailing of any one in the interests of Fascism or that any Fascists engaged in any blackmailing. [32]

Even though Tuttle denied any connection between the bank's crash and the Fascists' blackmailing of Ferrari, Fascism's tarnished image transcended the boundaries of the United States. In fact, *Italia*, a fortnightly bulletin published in France by the Socialist leader Filippo Turati, retold the details of the scandal on the front page under large headlines.[33] Public opinion in America, under a constant deluge of anti-Fascist propaganda, continued to grow more suspicious of the League in the United States. This must have influenced Mussolini in his decision that the time had come to disband the League to avoid further confrontations between the two governments, which would inevitably lead to diplomatic hostilities.

CHAPTER 9

MODIGLIANI'S VISIT
TO THE UNITED STATES
AND THE
AMERICAN LABOR PARTY

On November 27, 1934, Giuseppe Emanuele Modigliani, Italian Socialist hero and renowned leader of world Socialism, arrived in the United States accompanied by his wife, Vera. The Modiglianis had been invited to this country by Local 89 of the International Ladies' Garment Workers' Union, the Italian-American dressmakers, who constituted the largest single local union in the United States. The Union sent the invitation for the celebration of the group's fifteenth anniversary. Upon their arrival, thousands of Socialists and trade unionists greeted the Modiglianis with cheers, red flags, and music. At the anniversary celebration at Madison Square Garden, the chorus of the Metropolitan Opera House, 110 members strong, performed the stirring Italian Socialist anthem.[1]

In her book *Esilio* (Exile), Vera Modigliani recalls that visit to the United States with emotion, tenderness, and excitement:

> How wonderful it is to recall among the many memories the trip to the United States. It lasted four months. It was an exciting experience. It drew together thousands of persons of different political ideologies. It enhanced, indeed, confidence in the principles of freedom and democracy. It reaffirmed the spirit of international brotherhood and solidarity among the American Socialists and workers at large. In calling for a struggle to a finish against Fascism, my husband reinforced in the Italian-Americans the determination to continue their fight for the liberation of Italy from the tyranny of Fascism. Blessed that trip![2]

A close friend of Morris Hillquit, who spoke of him with tenderness and love, Modigliani was well known in the Socialist circles of America as the last survivor of the "holy trinity" of Italian Socialism, Modigliani, Filippo Turati, and Claudio Treves. The latter two died in exile in France in 1932 and 1933, respectively. An enemy of war, a member of the Executive of Labor and Socialist International, Modigliani had lived in Paris since 1925 as the active head of the International Anti-Fascist Movement. A man of lionlike courage, he dared to fight Mussolini to the very last and shouted in the Italian Chamber of Deputies, completely dominated by Mussolini's Black Shirts armed with loaded guns, "Long Live Socialism." From his exile in France, Modigliani wrote several articles on the origins and nature of Fascism for the American Socialist weekly, the *New Leader*.[3]

The reason for Modigliani's trip to the United States was twofold. He participated in the celebration of the fifteenth anniversary of the Local 89, I.L.G.W.U., and stirred Italian and American workers against Fascism. The celebration, held on November 28, 1934, took place at Madison Square Garden in the presence of 25,000 members representing the Union's 45,000 members. A closer reading of the *New Leader* coverage, however, makes clear that more than usual in his anti-Fascist routine, Modigliani spoke of the need for cooperation among all labor movements in the United States to promote a united front against Fascism and capitalism under the direction of Socialist forces. He called upon American labor not only to unite and fight against Fascism but also to organize an independent political party of workers in the United States. This idea thrilled the 25,000 persons who crowded Madison Square Garden.[4]

Modigliani began his speech by recalling that over 2,000 people died from October 1922 to October 1926 in Italy during the Fascist regime. He invited the workers of America to remember the sacrifice of the Italian martyrs and to speak in their memory. He praised Local 89 as one of the best labor unions in the United States. He invited the members of the Union to remain faithful to American tradition and to reclaim the right to be free: free to organize themselves, free to be equally educated, and free to pursue workers' emancipation through political participation. He cautioned the workers of America not to view freedom as a mere nationalistic affair. Rather, he asked that American labor forces send a warning and rallying cry throughout the world that people must be free, respected, and the masters of their own destinies. Accordingly, Modigliani assigned to the American labor forces the task of leading the struggle for the restoration of freedom and democracy in the world, saying:

> But I would not remain the Socialist that I am, should I fail to add that the Italians under the yoke of Fascism and those facing the harshness of political exile are not expecting from you material help only. Yes, that is very much needed and urgent, not for the sake of charity, but for the necessity of the struggle. But the Italians for whom I speak ask you and expect from you above anything else that you take here, and from here all over the world, the place which it is your duty to take in the struggle for the emancipation of the workers not only from the Fascist threat but also from capitalist exploitation.[5]

Since capitalism and its foul offspring, Fascism and Nazism, had defeated the armies of labor and Socialism in some European countries, he admonished, it was imperative that workers from the land of Washington and Lincoln, Debs, and Sacco and Vanzetti, march at the head of a new army of labor to restore freedom and justice in the world. According to Modigliani, American labor possessed all the rights and all the qualities to become the vanguard of the true New Deal of American civilization at home and abroad. Modigliani believed that effects of the Great Depression of 1929 had thereafter allowed the workers of the United States to take their place in politics. He maintained that the New Deal under President Roosevelt was not a step in the direction of Fascism because it was founded upon the preservation of democracy and civil liberties. The logical outcome of the New Deal, with the development of a powerful labor movement in this country, would be a Socialist transformation of the United States:

> Already there are symptoms that the economic crisis is pushing American workers towards an orientation of a marked political nature, which until yesterday was less understood...The time has come, then, to advance toward the political orientation of the organized strength of the American working class. I mean that the time has come for the American labor unions to decide to organize a Labor Party.[6]

As one of the foremost spokesmen of international Socialism who had waged a gallant war against capitalism and Fascism, Modigliani became the champion of workers' rights. He relentlessly asserted the principle that the workers of the world should not limit themselves to trade unions but should also march in the political arena to exercise their influence and control over political institutions of their respective countries. Through this form of political participation, workers would achieve class consciousness. From achievement to achievement in the political field, a new era of human redemption would take place. In developing a political character, workers would easily defeat Fascism, considered the most atrocious instrument of the capitalist class against workers' rights and aspirations. The unity of all workers represented the stepping stone for the redemption of all men. Moreover, it would be the decisive moment in workers' struggle for justice and security in the internal relations and for more enduring successes in the international front. Once this new atmosphere of international collaboration had been achieved, workers of the world would triumph over capitalism and its Fascist and Nazi reactions. Then, the labor movement would become the active force for the defense of liberty and for the achievement of a world in which the exploitation of man would change into a common struggle for the satisfaction of the needs of all.[7]

Modigliani's message to U.S. workers was delivered in the wake of increasing intrigues in America by Mussolini when capitalist reaction against labor forces had reached an alarming point.

According to weekly reports in the *New Leader* by A. N. Kruger, in 1934 the Italian-American Fascists resumed antiworking-class campaigns in collaboration with the Nazis. Various Fascist and philo-Fascist groups reorganized to keep Fascist propaganda and activities in high gear. Very prominent among them was the *Littorio* Federation, which had replaced the Fascist League of North America, disbanded in 1930. The tasks of the Fascist and Nazi groups consisted in "unifying Americans for the elimination of parasitical, unassailable and antinational elements, through force, if necessary."[8] Antinational elements meant, of course, Socialists and anticapitalists. Fascism and Nazism in America both aimed at defending the establishment from attacks of international Socialism.[9]

In addition to this strong resurgence of Fascist activities and propaganda, American workers became victims of a concatenation of antiunion efforts staged by American capitalists. Company-hired special police squads murdered workers in Kholer, Wisconsin, during an August 1934 strike. In Portland, Oregon, Socialists and workers faced Fascist bands organized by capitalist and banking elements. The bands intended "to wage a campaign against radical and subversive elements." Meanwhile, the Oregon Supreme Court passed an antisyndicalism act, deciding that "mere membership in a party which advocates mass action and violence was sufficient to sustain a conviction of any member of such a party." In San Francisco, as soon as longshoremen launched a strike in August 1934, they were faced with Fascist and Nazi-like intimidation by the Chamber of

Commerce and the Industrial Association. Philo-Fascist propaganda slogans like "What we need is a Mussolini" were published in business circles.[10]

By 1934, the Khaki Shirts of America, founded by General Art J. Smith and incorporated in the District of Columbia in August 1932, had made great headway. The movement's objectives were outlined in the founding charter: "To maintain universal respect for the U.S. Constitution and diligent opposition to the spread of subversive propaganda and doctrines aimed at the overthrow of constitutional government." The methods employed by the movement in recruiting members were evident from tactics used in West Virginia, New York, and Pennsylvania. In West Virginia, the Khaki Shirts approached the Ku Klux Klan, the Daughters of the American Revolution, and the headquarters of two capitalist parties of Charleston.[11]

In New York, Khaki Shirts' activities became controversial and highly suspicious in the Terzani case. Athos Terzani, a young anti-Fascist, indicted on August 3, 1933, was charged with murdering Antonio Fierro. The latter was killed by a shot fired in a fight, which broke up a meeting of Khaki Shirts of America, in Astoria on July 14. During the trial, however, evidence emerged that Fierro had been killed by Frank Moffer of Philadelphia, a former Khaki Shirts' member. Consequently, Terzani was acquitted on December 13, 1933. Commenting on the verdict, Norman Thomas, head of Terzani's defense committee, wrote that the Terzani case was not only a further proof of the Fascist activities in the United States but also blatant proof that "the administration of criminal law in America was rotten to the core." It allowed, continued Thomas, scores of guilty to escape, especially if they were well connected. Thomas concluded that if the district attorney of Queens County had properly investigated the case, General Smith would have been indicted as an accomplice in the murder. Norman Thomas invited all Socialists and labor men to use the Terzani case as specific evidence of the way in which "an innocent can be framed by direct and diabolic collusion" as subversive and criminal, while those responsible escape punishment.[12]

In Philadelphia, serious riots occurred between Khaki Shirts and Socialists. Among the backers of the Khaki Shirts was R. G. Morgan, Philadelphia open-shop furniture manufacturer, who was rewarded for his support of the movement with a Khaki Shirts generalship that placed him second in command after Art J. Smith. It was in Philadelphia that the worst confrontation between Khaki Shirts and Socialists occurred in June 1933. Over 150 Khaki Shirts attacked a Socialist meeting, and more than a dozen were injured in the knifing and clubbing fray that ensued. Dominic Sica, a Khaki Shirt, was stabbed several times in the stomach and eventually died.[13] Besides West Virginia, New York, and Pennsylvania, Khaki Shirts' movements were reported in California, Utah, New Mexico, Texas, Missouri, Iowa, Illinois, and Louisiana. The Khaki Shirts' movement throughout the United States claimed a membership of 6,000,000. Moreover, Art J. Smith estimated that by July 4th, the tentative date "for taking over the Government of the United States," the total enrollment would be 10,000,000.[14]

These and many more philo-Fascist activities in the United States spurred the immediate reaction of American workers. During the month of October 1934, documents were distributed by the American Federation of Labor in California inviting workers to intensify the fight against every form of Fascism. Condemning the antiworkers as reactionary forces, Francis Gorman, vice president of the United Textile Workers, revealed that in every strike "American workers were faced with the whole great combination of reactionary forces."[15] On October 24, 1934, New York organized labor launched a massive campaign against Fascism, Nazism, and their capitalist supporters, calling for an "immediate, determined fight against the terrorism and despotism of Fascist tyranny in America and abroad."[16]

On November 24, 1934, the *New Leader* commanded newspaper headlines. That day's editorial warned American workers that a Fascist march on Washington had been organized by a group of Wall Street multimillionaires. According to the editorial, General Smedley D. Butler had revealed the plan of the coup before a committee of the House of Representatives. Butler had revealed that members

of Wall Street firms met with him on August 22 at the Bellevue
Stratford Hotel in Philadelphia and invited him to recruit 500,000
men for the march on Washington:

> The upshot of the proposition was that I was to head a soldier
> organization of half a million men, that this group would
> assemble probably a year from now in Washington, and that
> within a few days it could take over the functions of the gov-
> ernment. To be perfectly fair to McGuire (the person who had
> conducted the negotiation), he did not seem bloodthirsty. He
> felt that such a show of force in Washington would probably
> result in a peaceful overturn of the government. He suggested
> that we might even go along with Roosevelt and do with him
> what Mussolini did with the King of Italy.[17]

It was in the midst of these domestic events that Giuseppe
Emanuele Modigliani arrived in the United States and was enthusi-
astically welcomed by Socialists and trade unionists from New York
and nearby cities. Indeed, Italian, American, Polish, German, Jewish
Socialists, and workers welcomed Modigliani. Accepted as an international ambassador of freedom against the tyranny of Fascism,
Nazism, and capitalism, Modigliani toured the U.S. after the anniversary celebration in New York City. His tour took him as far as the
Pacific Ocean. A heavy schedule kept Modigliani moving from city
to city: from November 28 to December 21, he rallied the masses
of New York City; on December 22, he delivered a speech at the
Polish People's Home in Passaic, New Jersey; from December 31
to January 8, 1935, he spoke at rallies in Paterson, Vineland, and
Hammonton, New Jersey, in Providence, Rhode Island, and in
Boston, Massachusetts; on January 10, he delivered speeches in
Washington, D.C.; on January 13, he was in Pittsburgh and on the
14th in Cincinnati. On January 15, he arrived in St. Louis, and on
the 17th in Chicago. From Chicago, Modigliani went to Milwaukee,
Minneapolis, and Seattle, down the Pacific Coast, returning to the
East Coast via Denver, Kansas City, Detroit, and Cleveland.[18]

Modigliani delivered his speeches in Italian or German, depend-
ing on the audience, and they were translated into English by Serafino

Romualdi, a representative of the American Federation of Labor, who accompanied the Socialist leader. According to Romualdi's reports in the *New Leader* of March 23 and 30, 1935, Modigliani's meetings with American people were triumphant. Though the Fascist consuls of Detroit, Seattle, and Portland tried to prevent the meetings, Modigliani was welcomed everywhere with enthusiasm and sympathy. Indeed, the temperamental attitudes of Fascist consuls against the Socialist leader did much to draw a greater American audience to hear Modigliani condemn Mussolini's policy in Italy and his activities in the United States. In many cities where labor movements had seldom staged anti-Fascist demonstrations, the Modiglianis' presence served to fuel anti-Fascist sentiments and protests. Elsewhere, the protests became a "large-scale enterprise with the labor forces taking the lead and bringing the struggle to faraway localities where never before an opponent of Mussolini had had the opportunity to speak for the labor and Socialist movement in the face of poisonous propaganda."[19]

Everywhere, Modigliani's presence was nothing short of triumphant among workers of many different nationalities. In some instances Italian workers were in the minority. They flocked to hear the message of the lovable and inspiring apostle of Italian Socialism and learn from him the lesson of the Italian tragedy. Yet, according to Romualdi, Modigliani never confined himself to the chronological presentation of events, which led to the advent of Fascism in Italy. He discussed the political and psychological reasons that made Mussolini's coup d'état possible. In Modigliani's view, when the government of a country is left in the exclusive hands of political elites who lean toward dictatorial principles, democratic institutions will perish. Using the tragic circumstances of Italy, Modigliani delivered a warning message to Americans. If they wanted to preserve the democratic institutions of their country, the working forces ought to enter the political arena under the colors of a Labor Party. Modigliani invited American labor and Union leaders to rally the working masses around a well-defined political party. With this message, Modigliani left to return to Paris. A farewell banquet was held on March 14, 1935, at Roseff's restaurant in New York City.[20]

Modigliani's contacts with Socialist and union leaders of America continued more consistently and articulately in the aftermath of his visit. In September 1935, Luigi Antonini, New York City's first vice president of the International Ladies' Garment Workers' Union, (I.L.G.W.U.) attended the International Anti-Fascist Congress in Brussels.[21]

On July 22, 1936, the People's Party, headed by Louis Waldman, and Labor's Non-Partisan League, led by Antonini, agreed to merge and form a new political party. At the meeting Antonini promised to build an American Labor party as a permanent organization representative of the program and aspirations of organized labor. He also announced that the official name of the new party would be the American Labor Party (ALP).[22]

Although Modigliani's name was not mentioned as the pioneer of this idea, nevertheless, on August 8, the *New Leader* disclosed an important detail. Under the title "Modigliani Called for the Labor Party," the article released details of two letters (July 7 and 10, 1936), one from Modigliani to Romualdi and a second from Pietro Nenni, secretary of the Italian Socialists in exile, to Antonini. Modigliani's letter was of special interest. His 1934 extended tour of the United States had particularly qualified him to understand the situation of Socialism in the U.S. Examining labor's Non-Partisan League, he wrote: "Were I an American, I should have exerted all my influence to induce the Labor Non-Partisan League to declare openly that it considers itself the nucleus of a future Labor Party. However, the important thing is to have an army. When the army exists and goes on into battle according to the tactics that suit the movement, no one has a right to find fault."[23]

Nenni's letter to Antonini dealt with the role American Socialists ought to play in supporting the re-election of President Roosevelt: "I am following with great interest the political development in the United States. While I do not as yet possess sufficient information to express a positive opinion as to the attitude of the Socialist Party in your country, it appears to me certain that today Roosevelt represents progress as against reaction. Everything possible ought to be done to assure his re-election."[24]

On August 10, 1936, the committee of the newly formed American Labor Party issued a manifesto: "American Labor Party—Why?" The major points of the document, published in the August 15 issue of the *New Leader,* are worth reviewing here:

> Organized and backed by the trade unions, the American Labor Party, known to thousands of socially conscious citizens as the "ALP", is the New York affiliate of Labor's Non-Partisan League. Our immediate enemy is the combination of antisocial and antilabor forces which handpicked Governor Alf Landon as their mouthpiece; our immediate objective is the re-election of President Roosevelt and Governor Lehman.
>
> The issues of this campaign are not "campaign issues." They are part of the very social and economic fabric of the country. Wage earners, salaried people, professionals—all know that their working standards, the happiness of their families, the education of their children, the very substance and spirit of their lives are at issue. Social forces of such magnitude must be harnessed permanently if they are to be directed into the channels of progress. In the heat of this campaign we must prepare for the next. That is why we have created a permanent organization.
>
> That permanent organization in New York State is the ALP. It has been formed to add the ballot to the picket line as a direct weapon of labor. Just as the unions have economic front, so the ALP will make that power felt on the political front. Built on the strength of the unionists and their families, supported by those forthright elements in the community disgusted with the inhumanity of the money changers and the dishonesty of grab politics, the ALP is labor's instrument for independent political action. It mobilizes the political power of labor and the progressive forces of the people in our state on a platform dedicated to freedom as against reaction, for economic democracy as against exploitation and oppression, for security and happiness of the broad masses of the population.[25]

On August, 29, 1936, in an article entitled "Roosevelt—Candidate of Organized Labor," Louis Waldman explained the motives behind the American Labor Party's support of President Roosevelt. Waldman called upon Socialists to campaign to keep Roosevelt in the White House, because the president represented the forces of progress against those of reaction. Moreover, for the first time in the history of the United States, a president had proclaimed the philosophy that unless millions of people who constituted the backbone of the country were prosperous and secure, there could be no worthwhile prosperity for the nation. Roosevelt, according to Waldman, had placed the welfare of labor and the social and economic well-being of the masses of America as a permanent aim of the government. Further, in little more than three years, the president had restored the faith of millions of people, in America and the world over, in democracy as a means of bringing about "progress through law."[26]

A comparison of the two documents shows a striking similarity between the program of the American Labor Party and the issues Modigliani had presented to the workers of America. The issues of justice, emancipation, freedom, and opposition to all forms of tyranny formed the living gospel of Modigliani's Socialism. But mostly, he presented the workers of America the idea of organizing an independent political party in the United States to educate and channel workers toward a marked political orientation.

CHAPTER 10

ITALIAN-AMERICANS
AND THE ETHIOPIAN CRISIS

On October 2, 1935, Mussolini broadcast a bombastic address to Italians, and it ended with his ordering a march on Ethiopia. "At the end of the World War," said Mussolini, "only crumbs of colonial booty were left for Italy." He added that twenty million Italians were gathered in the squares of Italy: "Twenty million: One heart, one will, one decision!" What motives induced the Italian dictator to attack Ethiopia thousands of miles away? Mussolini cynically declared that his attack was inspired by the desire for spoils of war, which Italy had failed to get at the end of the First World War.

Whatever Mussolini's intentions, the Ethiopian campaign stirred Italian-Americans in the U.S. "into a state of Nationalistic frenzy."[1] Since July 1935, pro-Fascist newspapers in the United States had expressed their full support and approval of Mussolini's plans to invade Ethiopia. In editorials, articles, and news columns they unanimously supported Italy's need for a colonial outlet. The press insisted that Mussolini's conquest of Ethiopia was necessary because excess population in Italy required overseas colonies. According to Robert Gale Woolbert of the *New York Times*, Mussolini intended to colonize Ethiopia with hundreds of thousands, if not millions, of Italy's surplus population. Also, the press portrayed Mussolini as a new-style Caesar who wanted to introduce civilization to barbarous Ethiopia.

In a concerted choir in July 1935, the *Italian Echo* of Providence, *La Voce Coloniale* of New Orleans, *La Libera Parola* of Philadelphia, *La Tribuna Italiana* of Dallas, *La Capitale* of Sacramento, and *La Stampa Unita* of Rochester all stressed the appropriateness of Italy's colonizing mission because Italy represented a highly evolved civilization and the virtue of the Italian people: "The main proposition is whether civilization shall take a backward or forward step. It is our firm belief that civilization must ever step forward, and that when progress ceases then civilization ends."[2]

While the press lauded this civilizing mission on the part of Mussolini, they leveled criticism against blacks in America for supporting Ethiopia. According to William Dubois, black men in the United States came together at the outset of the Ethiopian crisis as they had never done before. Mass meetings and attempts to recruit volunteers took place in Harlem. The issue at stake was more than Italy's aggression toward Ethiopia: "The Black world knows this is the last effort of white man and white Europe to secure the subjection of Black men." In his analysis, Dubois saw in the black outcry for Ethiopia an increase of racial confrontation between blacks and whites in the world: "Italy has forced the world into a position where, whether or not she wins, race hate will increase; while if she loses, the prestige of the white world will receive a check comparable to that involved in the defeat of Russia by Japan."[3]

The Italian-American press reacted quickly and forcefully. Editorials in *L'Opinione* of Philadelphia (February 1935), *La Capitale* of Sacramento (June 1935), and *La Stampa Unita* of Rochester (July 1935) rejected the outcry as unjustified and groundless. The newspapers asked why U.S. blacks had suddenly become inflamed against Italy when they had never railed against England, France,

Spain, Portugal, and other European countries who carried out major imperialistic colonial campaigns in Africa. According to *La Stampa Unita*, the whole truth about the Italian-Ethiopian affair had not come out. Moreover, the paper continued, blacks in the U.S. should know that what the Italians "are doing in Ethiopia is nothing worse than what other nations have done in the past. And that Italy may do so much good for civilization as countries have done in the past." Therefore, American blacks owed Italy a debt of gratitude for civilizing their African brothers.[4]

On July 3, 1935, Haile Selassie sent a note to the American chargé d'affaires at Addis Ababa requesting that the United States enforce the Kellogg-Briand Pact. The Pact, to which Italy, among many other nations, had agreed, pledged the signers to renounce war as an instrument of national policy and to solve their disputes by pacific means. The note practically invoked American intervention in the dispute. Even though the Roosevelt administration stayed noncommittal in its reply, nevertheless, the Italian-American press made clear that the slightest moral gesture in defense of Ethiopia would signify an initiative against Italy.[5] Selassie's note definitely spurred a revival of *Italianitá* among Italian-Americans. In New York the formation of two new groups headquartered at Rockefeller Center was announced: the *Lega Americana Pro-Italia* (American League Pro-Italy), presided over by Luigi Criscuolo; and *L'Unione Italiana d'America* (Italian Union of America), presided over by Ugo D'Annunzio.[6] In September many Italian-American organizations from New York and Rhode Island assembled in Providence. They approved a resolution calling Italian expansion in Ethiopia "the final act" of a policy initiated a century before. The resolution closed with an appeal to the American press at large to use "traditional and customary freedom of opinion and unbiased judgment in dealing with the Ethiopian affair."[7]

When the League of Nations Council opened its session on September 4, 1935, the members received their first official memorandum on the Italo-Ethiopian crisis. On September 18, the Committee of Five submitted a plan to use as a basis for negotiations.

Mussolini, however, rejected the plan, insisting that the dispute with Ethiopia was a "colonial and local matter." On October 3, 1935, he ordered Italian troops to invade Ethiopia.

A few days later, the League's Council charged Italy with committing an act of aggression, saying that the Italian government had blatantly violated the League's covenant. On October 11, the Assembly voted sanctions against Italy. The United States, not being a member of the League, did not participate in the sanctions. However, two days after the outbreak of hostilities between Italy and Ethiopia, President Roosevelt invoked the Neutrality Act, approved by the American Congress in August 1935. Moreover, the president declared an embargo of arms for both Italy and Ethiopia and warned American citizens against traveling on ships of the belligerent countries. In effect, the president asked Americans to stop doing business with Italy. (In fact, the U.S. exported very few goods to Ethiopia; the overwhelming volume of activity happened to be with Italy.) By invoking the Neutrality Act, Roosevelt put in motion the machine of the Italian-American press. It initiated a campaign of criticism against the president of the United States, accusing him of "nourishing sentiments of antipathy for Italy."[8] *La Libera Parola* of Philadelphia accused the president of applying sanctions against Italy even before England had. Word was spread that the presidential decision had been influenced by England, since the latter feared that an Italian victory in Ethiopia would endanger English control of the Mediterranean. Henceforth, the newspaper invited businessmen in this country to fight England's desire to punish Italy.[9] The strongest reaction appeared in *Il Progresso Italo-Americano* on October 27, 1935. Under the title "For the Neutrality of the United States," Generoso Pope published a letter he had sent to President Roosevelt on October 17. The letter is worth reprinting in full:

> Dear Mr. President:
> The avowed sentiment of an overwhelming majority of the American people has long opposed entanglement in foreign dealings and relationships. Especially has there been strong resistance to memberships of our country in the League of

Nations, which, from its inception, has ardently sought the affiliation of the United States. The wars-carred history of Europe has always served as a warning to us of the consequence of affinity with the nations of that continent, and our people have feared that our participation in European affairs would again enmesh us in international conflict.

At the present time, under the respectable cloak of high morality and the human good, sanctions are being voted against a nation which is pursuing a policy which has not only been looked upon favorably by the other nations of the world, but has been the means of attainment of power by the very members of the League who are most prominent in the imposition of these penalties. The cry of "the white man's burden" was first raised and idealized by the very nation which now seeks to thwart the proper and peaceful expansion of another country.

I do not desire, of course, to discuss or question the rights of Italy or Ethiopia. I do believe, however, and I believe it strongly, that the peace of the world will be promoted if our country is not drawn into the European storm, and if we refuse to be deluded by the pretentious phrases, which conceal their true motives, of the nations which are taking a stand, not for Ethiopia but against Italy. The fear of any nation that another may expand and assume a position of influence and prominence should not deceive us. Our policy should be one of neutrality.

Sincerely,
Generoso Pope

The month of November saw Italian-Americans throughout the country engaged in a relentless campaign of protest against the U.S. administration. Hundreds of meetings, speeches, and conferences took place. The Italian-American press offered its facilities and published articles, letters of protest, and appeals to support Mussolini up to the final victory. On November 5, 7, and 14, *La Stampa Unita* published three appeals: "In This Solemn Hour;" "It Is Our Duty;" and "The Italian-Americans Must Be Vigilant." The appeals invited American citizens of Italian extraction to keep intact the sacred sentiments of *Italianitá* and to defend in that historical moment the prestige and the rights of the Fatherland: "Indeed, it is impossible to be good American citizens if we have not the courage to defend the country where we came from. It is to Italy—whose genius has given us modern sculpture and art, whose painters and their exquisite works will live until time is no more, whose scholars were liberators of human thought, and whose soldiers have fought the most memorable battles in history—that we owe the debt to gratitude."[10]

Continuing in their relentless campaign, Italian-Americans exerted political pressure in Washington. They sent chain protest letters amounting to hundreds of thousands. November and December became the months of a pro-Italy crusade. Senators, members of the House of Representatives, and political leaders of both parties were buried under an avalanche of protest letters. The letter drafted by the American Friends of Italy and disseminated through news media channels said:

> Fellow American Citizens:
> Write a separate letter to President Roosevelt, to United States Senator Robert F. Wagner, and to your local Congressman—all in Washington, D.C.—protesting against certain activities of the present administration.
>
> Make two or more copies of this entire sheet and give them to at least two other Americans having similar views.
>
> See to it that these two friends write letters at once to Washington.
>
> Everyone who protests must secure at least two others in an unending chain until all Americans sharing these views have acted.
>
> Send a card with your name and address to the Committee. This will entitle you to free literature regarding the progress of this movement.
>
> One million letters of protest are expected to reach Washington before January, when Congress meets.
>
> American Friends of Italy
> 157 East 49th Street
> New York, New York

Copy or write letters similar to the following:
Date
(Name)
Washington, D. C.

Honorable Sir:
I protest against American association with League of Nations sanctioned activities. I protest against statements of members of the present administration in Washington showing cooperation with the schemes of the British government as regards sanctions and embargoes. I protest against our government meddling with European sanctions and embargo policies.

Very respectfully,
(Signature)
(Address)[11]

On January 3, 1936, President Roosevelt stated in his message to Congress that in case of war, his administration would pursue a two-fold policy of neutrality: it would order the embargo of arms and limit the selling of American goods to belligerent countries. On the day of the message, a new Neutrality Bill, reflecting the president's ideas, was introduced in both houses of Congress by Senator Pittman and Representative Reynolds. From New York, Pennsylvania, Massachusetts, New Jersey, Connecticut, and Rhode Island, letters of protest arrived in Washington. They asked senators and congressmen to oppose the new Neutrality Bill on the grounds it granted the president unconstitutional power to regulate trade with foreign countries.[12]

The effects of the protest were effective immediately. Many senators and congressmen reacted favorably to the requests of the Italian-Americans. John P. Higgins of Massachusetts spoke in Congress on February 17:

Let us keep out of war by refraining from the policy of invoking sanctions against Italy, for such a policy will inevitably embroil us in war. We have no quarrel with Italy, but let us not fool ourselves. We cannot take sides and be neutral at the same time. We have prescribed a definite American policy on

Neutrality. This was done in a time of peace (August 1935), and for us to change the rules in wartime to accommodate the League of Nations is, in my opinion, a hostile act.[13]

Among many Italian-American prominent leaders involved, Generoso Pope led the battle. He contacted senators and congressmen, and he had conversations with Secretary of State Cordell Hull and other foreign affairs experts. He eventually had a meeting with President Roosevelt. Moreover, other prominent Italian-Americans went to Washington to push the cause of Italy. Supreme Venerable of the Order of the Sons of Italy Stefano Miele; Judge Eugene V. Alessandroni of Philadelphia; Judge Frank Leverone of Boston; Andrew Cassara, former mayor of Revere, Massachusetts; Francis Pallotti of Hartford, former secretary of state of Connecticut, and many more testified before the House Foreign Affairs Committee.[14] On January 10, 1936, Senator Thomas of Utah proposed that the 1935 Neutrality Bill be renewed for another year. The proposal received congressional approval on February 18. The Italian-American press heralded the event in headlines and editorials. Generoso Pope, quoted in *Il Progresso Italo-Americano* of February 20, 1936, pointed out that it marked the first time a movement of Italian-Americans had assumed such proportions and had received immediate satisfaction. *La Tribuna Italiana d'America* of Detroit (February 21, 1936), *Il Corriere del Connecticut* (February 21, 1936), and *L'Italia* of Chicago (April 2, 1936) opined that the Italian-American protest had succeeded in Washington due to the hundreds of thousands of letters sent to Washington. Moreover, for the first time, senators and representatives had seriously considered the electoral weight of the Italian-American constituency.

The American-Italian Union of New York shared this view. In its 1936 annual report, the Union stressed the strength of the Italian-Americans and their future potential political influence. To this end, the Union stressed the need to continue to work toward the following:

1. To achieve the unity of all Italian-Americans of Italian extraction
2. To maintain the prestige and the pride of Italy

3. To instill into the millions of Italian-Americans love for their land of origin along with their allegiance to the United States

4. To collaborate for better relations between the two governments

The Union was proud to sum up its work done in 1935: over 100 conferences and speeches organized; 150 articles written; over 300,000 pamphlets distributed; and over 250,000 notes and memos circulated.[15]

On May 9, 1936, Mussolini declared the annexation of Ethiopia and the birth of the Italian empire in Africa. Though the United States never recognized Italy's annexation of Ethiopia, nevertheless, Italian-Americans rejoiced for the victory and the empire. Echoing Italian-American feelings, Arthur Brisbane, in the May 11, 1936, editorial of the *Daily Mirror*, wrote:

> Mussolini now owns Ethiopia, and nobody is going to do anything about it. Will power counts in this world. Italy had announced that from now on she has an Empire. Some who ask, "What will Mussolini do with this gigantic new African country?" are partly answered by this picture: Mussolini ploughs up that country and makes things grow there...Any man who combines Mussolini's common sense and willpower ought to go a long way. Too bad he cannot live another hundred years. Where will Italy or all Europe find another will like him.[16]

Interestingly, the anti-Fascist reaction to the Ethiopian crisis was not as strong, organized, or consistent as one might have expected. It assumed more the aspects of an ideological dispute on the nature of Fascism as an offspring of colonialism and imperialism than of an organized campaign against Italy's rights in Africa.

As early as May 1935, the *New Leader* published anti-Fascist articles on Mussolini's adventure in Ethiopia. In an article titled, "Masses Hope for Mussolini," F. Alminati portrayed Mussolini's adventure in Ethiopia as a skillful maneuver to keep the true Fascist inferno from the world. To Alminati, Mussolini's invasion of Ethiopia further demonstrated the megalomania of European dictators.[17]

On July 13, 1935, the *New Leader* published an editorial pointing out that the invasion of Ethiopia could bring an end to Mussolini's regime in Italy. The article predicted that Mussolini's Ethiopian policy would collapse in economic disaster for Italy. International economists had made these predictions:

> "One gets the distinct impression that the bankers do not see how Mussolini can finance the Ethiopian war and that they await with misgivings the repercussions on other currencies and economics," and "They foresee monetary and commercial strain if Premier Mussolini continues his Ethiopian policy."[18]

U.S. anti-Fascists viewed the Ethiopian adventure as bad for Italy from every point of view. The predictions proved to be true. To win the Ethiopian war Mussolini spent an estimated $815,000,000. Once these figures are added to the $535,000,000 budget deficit in 1934–35, one has the overall picture of Italy's economic disaster.

On July 14, Girolamo Valenti, editor of *La Stampa Libera*, publicly denounced Mussolini's adventure in Ethiopia. In an article titled, "The Civilization Mussolini Would Impose on Ethiopia," the author points out the extent of the efforts the Fascist Italian and U.S. press engaged in to convince people that the planned invasion of Ethiopia was just, fair, and necessary. "Fascist Italy is bound to bring culture and civilization to the Ethiopian people," the Mussolini mouthpieces declared. "What kind of civilization, we may ask," argued Valenti. The Fascist dictatorship had reduced Italy to a great military field with its concentration camps, dungeons, and firing squads. So, what civilization or freedom would Mussolini export to Ethiopia? The Fascist dictatorship had made Italians slaves, soldiers, spies, and agents provocateurs of all shades and description. So, what culture would Mussolini send to Ethiopia? Valenti concluded, saying the "enslaved and despoiled Italian people cannot favor Mussolini's plan to export culture and civilization to Ethiopia when the dictator and his armed black shirt bands still deny them the civilization that was forcibly taken away from them thirteen years ago."[19]

On July 27, Arturo Giovannitti published a lengthy article in the *New Leader*, "Who Is This Man To Bring Light To The Abyssinians?" The author compared the impending Ethiopian invasion to the fable of the wolf eating the lamb: "Mussolini's hired assassins and the barefooted helpless hordes of Haile Selassie." According to Giovannitti, Mussolini's march against Ethiopia was the direct consequence of the greediness and rapacity of imperialism and its consuming passion for military glory "which gnaws at the heart of every dictator." Furthermore, continued Giovannitti, the Fascist clamor that the Ethiopian war was one of civilization against barbarism was much like "the wolf eating the lamb." Though it was still true that slavery was rife in Ethiopia, that such pious indignation "should come from Mussolini and his fellow turnkeys of the Italian people is the acme of impudence and hypocrisy."[20]

On August 10, the American Labor Movement joined the International Federation of Trade Unions and Labor and Socialist International in condemning Mussolini's aggression on Ethiopia. In a manifesto launched throughout the world, the Labor Internationals appealed to the whole world to join with one voice in the protest against Fascist Italy, "which is on the point of breaking the peace." The manifesto called on organizers of the Labor Movement and supporters of democracy and freedom "to use their combined influence on the government of their own countries to take all possible actions to obtain a peaceful solution of the conflict between Italy and Abyssinia."[21]

The *New Leader*'s editorials of August 24 and 31 continued to condemn Mussolini's madness. The articles pointed out that Mussolini's adventure in Ethiopia represented merely the prelude of imperialistic plans. His real intention was to establish "an Italian overlordship over Western democracies and all the Near East." Mussolini was portrayed as a self-styled Caesar. However, the Caesar in Mussolini was mingled with the Machiavelli, concluded the articles.[22]

On September 7, the eve of the International Congress of Labor and Socialists Internationals in Geneva, Switzerland, American and

Italian-American Socialists invited every Socialist in the country and every labor organization affiliated with the International Federation to stage colossal antiwar demonstrations "to endeavor to stay the bloody hand of the Fascist bully and to seek to prevent Mussolini from plunging two nations—and possibly the whole world—into a bloody conflict."[23]

On September 14, the *New Leader* published a front page article accusing Russia of helping Mussolini in the Ethiopian adventure. The article, "Soviet Russia Helps Mussolini's War Plan," made the most amazing revelation of the entire Ethiopian campaign. The Soviet government had continued to help Mussolini by supplying him with foodstuffs and war materials for his Ethiopian aggression. "Helping dictators to wage war on democracies," ended the article, "has thus become a tradition with the Soviet Government."[24]

Maintaining their relentless charges against Mussolini, the anti-Fascists continued to use the *New Leader* as the means to condemn Mussolini and his Fascist imperialism. On September 28, the article "Statesmen Discover Mussolini and Fascism," denounced Mussolini's megalomania and the true soul of Fascism as an offspring of imperialism. On October 3, the article "American Labor Battles Against World Fascism" alerted American workers to be vigilant against the imperialistic aims of Fascism. On October 12, the editorial "Mussolini's Blood Bath Reveals Fascism Soul" denounced Mussolini's visionary dream of Empire and control of the world.[25]

Finally, on October 12, 1935, a few days after the invasion of Ethiopia had started, the *New Leader* published an impressive editorial "And This Is Civilization." The article presented the most accurate analysis of the Ethiopian adventure: "This is the war that this Fascist chief deliberately, consciously and in cold blood, prepared to loose upon the world. This is the war that Fascism has given as its finest flower to a world that was slowly and painfully climbing out of the mire and morasses of the last great war into which it had been plunged by a crazy and cruel system."[26]

In conclusion, the Ethiopian crisis meant two different things to Italian-Americans. To the overwhelming majority, the Ethiopian crisis became an ethnic undertaking. The ordeal of the crisis convinced many Italian-Americans that Cordell Hull's attitude in the dispute was predominantly pro-British while that of the president was largely anti-Italian. Neither Fascism nor Mussolini seemed to be an issue. The zeal that the Ethiopian crisis spurred among the Italian-Americans came from their commitment to defend Italian pride and prestige in the United States. The Italian Division of the New York State Republican Committee, in its annual congress on September 10, 1936, called upon all Italian-Americans to intensify their campaign and attacks against President Roosevelt "who had demonstrated open hostility against Italy in the Ethiopian crisis. The Italian-American voters will never forget Roosevelt's enmity toward Italy."[27]

On the other hand, to the small minority of Italian-American anti-Fascists, the Ethiopian war further proved Mussolini's greediness and political megalomania. To them the Ethiopian crisis disclosed the very nature of Fascism: a dictatorship, which needed war and could not survive without it; the dictator needed victory, blood-stained victory, and the intoxication of triumph to bring the Italian people once more to his feet. The Ethiopian adventure had finally disclosed the very soul of Fascism.

CHAPTER 11

MUSSOLINI'S REACTION TO THE GIORDANO PLAN

The rejection of the Giordano Plan by Mussolini in 1939 marked the epilogue of the most bizarre attempt at Fascist propaganda in the U.S. In December 1938, Vincent Giordano, a capable Italo-American journalist in the United States, was promoted by Generoso Pope, director of the Rome office of *Il Progresso Italo-Americano* and *Il Corriere d'America*.[1] Giordano's appointment to director in charge of correspondence from Rome meant stronger relations with Italian Fascists as well as the possibility of special and favorable treatment for Pope's two New York Italian dailies. In letters to Italian authorities, Pope and Giordano expressed hope that the opening of an office in Rome signaled their intense desire "to put our Italian-American dailies at the service of the Fascist regime and Italy."[2]

In the first quarter of 1939, Giordano received a special visa to tour *L'Africa Orientale Italiana* (Italian African Colonies) and write a series of articles for *Il Progresso Italo-Americano* and *Il Corriere d'America*. Evidently, he assured Italian Fascists that his correspondence would favor Fascism and underscore the Fascists' achievements in the Italian colonies of Africa.[3]

In June, the Ministry of Communications granted Giordano special permission to use 3,000 additional words for his monthly correspondences from Rome free of charge. Moreover, due to his "particularly patriotic propaganda activity on behalf of Fascism among the Italian-American collectivity," he was also accorded secretly an additional 12,000 words a month "to carry his pro-Fascist propaganda campaign among the Italian-Americans more effectively." The Ministry of Popular Culture assumed the total cost of the additional 12,000 words used by Giordano. On July 5, 1939, in sending his earnest appreciation to the Italian authorities for the special treatment reserved to his correspondent in Rome, Generoso Pope reassured Mussolini he remained "available personally and through his newspapers" to the cause and ideals of Fascism.[4]

By the end of November, Giordano received from the Ministry of Popular Culture the exclusive right to handle the Daily Foreign Press Phono-Bulletin for the United States.[5] This appointment was of great importance because it gave Giordano the discretion to interpret "in his own Fascist way the Italian events and then transmit them to the American Press at large."

In spite of all these special considerations, the same Ministry of Popular Culture turned down, early in December, Giordano's personal request for an appointment as a member of the Superior Committee on National Economy presided over by Mussolini. The rejection was not entirely unexpected since the Committee handled sensitive matters related to Italy's fading economy, and Mussolini did not want any foreign witness to it.[6]

However, the most important event, which signified Mussolini's declining interest in U.S. Fascist propaganda, was his rejection of the Giordano Plan. The Plan, presented to Mussolini on June 19, 1939, proposed the immediate publication in the United States of a weekly English-language magazine, in the format of the *Saturday Evening Post*. The magazine would be "Fascist one hundred percent and would publish articles of collaborators carefully selected in Italy and in the United States." According to Giordano, Italian-Americans living in the United States needed a patriotic regeneration. Although Italy could count on six million Italian-Americans, nevertheless she could not run the risk of losing their future support. The two dailies, *Il Progresso Italo-Americano* and *Il Corriere d'America*, had kept alive patriotic ideals among the older generations. However, at this point, it was necessary to create new channels of communication to instill philo-Italian sentiments in the new generations. Having been brought up in an American atmosphere, they manifested signs of rejecting and disregarding their ancestors' patriotic affiliations to Italy. While the two newspapers continued to keep alive the ties with the motherland among the old generations, the new magazine would serve the purpose of instilling sentiments of interest and sympathy toward Fascism and its leader Benito Mussolini.

Besides these patriotic goals, the magazine would neutralize and counterbalance the new political trend developed in America under President Roosevelt. In Giordano's opinion, the United States was going through a very alarming and serious period. He felt that the Communists had invaded and were controlling most of the workers' unions, and they had penetrated political and academic circles. As a consequence, production, politics, and education had fallen into Communist hands. To make things worse, the press had become increasingly anti-Italian and Roosevelt a declared enemy of Italy. In fact, no Italian politician or leader had been appointed to a cabinet position. The whole Roosevelt entourage was represented by Jewish people. The publication of a magazine critical of Roosevelt's treatment and behavior toward Italian-Americans "could produce considerable impact on the results of the forthcoming presidential elections." Also, Giordano pointed out in the document that Republican presidents had been more responsive to Italian-Americans and that under their presidency "the relations between Italy and the United States had always been cordial." All these events and historical facts could be disclosed by the Italians collectively only through a magazine. In addition, anti-Italian sentiments and behavior could be openly denounced to sway public opinion. The Italian-American collectivity had come of age and, at this point, had political strength. However, Giordano pointed out that the collectivity "if organized and oriented politically could become a kind of turning point in the political spectrum of America. It could back up a candidate ready to support Mussolini's regime and acknowledge the existence of a second Italy in America."

How could this program be implemented? According to the Plan, the much-needed philo-Italian magazine had to start its publication immediately. Its circulation ought to be over 300,000 copies. Fifty thousand should be distributed by mail free to U.S. senators and representatives, governors, state senators and assemblymen, mayors, college and university professors, and industrialists and businessmen throughout the country. In addition, an intensive radio advertising campaign ought to begin. The estimated cost of this enterprise was 10 million lire, to be borne by the Italian government. However, to avoid and prevent hostile reaction on the part of the American public, Giordano suggested that the financial support be kept secret "to prevent the American people from finding out that the magazine is financed by a foreign country." To keep the whole operation a secret, Giordano suggested that Italian authorities accept that the board of directors be exclusively Americans with deep sympathy for Italy. The curator or the treasurer ought to be an American citizen of Italian extraction with experience in the political and economic affairs of both countries.[7]

The Plan was accompanied by a laudatory letter addressed to Mussolini on June 9, 1939. In the letter Giordano retraced the history of his allegiance to Mussolini since 1919. Giordano recalled that in 1919 he had launched the idea of awarding the King of Italy a gold medal on behalf of Italian-Americans of New York. He also recalled his pro-Italy propaganda activity in 1920. In fact, in January of that year, he had promoted the collection of 300,000 lire among the Italian-American community of New York to help the D'Annunzio expedition on Fiume. The money was sent to Mussolini. In 1921, Giordano spent eight months in Italy acquainting himself with Fascist philosophy. Due to this unforgettable experience, Giordano reached the conclusion that Mussolini was really "the man sent by Providence to save Italy."

The love, the admiration, and the respect that these contacts had generated convinced Giordano that he, himself, had a mission to accomplish in the United States. The mission, to spread the Fascist word among Italian-Americans, needed reliable journalists as correspondents from Rome for *Il Progresso Italo-Americano* and *Il Corriere d'America*. Hence, he was able to convince Generoso Pope to replace all the pro-Giolitti correspondents with pro-Fascists. As a consequence of this shuffle, all the articles and editorials published from 1922 on represented a constant Fascist apologia. According to Giordano's letter, this period could be considered as "the golden age of Giordano's dedication to Fascism in the United States." Finally, the letter ended with a renewed appeal to Mussolini to accept the Plan. It would, indeed, guarantee the revival of Fascism and Italianism in America.[8]

Mussolini forthrightly rejected the Plan. The available document bears Mussolini's handwriting note with a final "No."[9] Why, did Mussolini reject the Plan? At least two major motives prompted Mussolini's rejection; first, the economic conditions of Italy. The Italian treasury was drained. The budget deficit had increased to over $700,000,000, or 25 percent of the total national revenue. Moreover, Mussolini had no interest whatsoever in reorganizing Fascism in America, nor did a pro-Fascist trend exist at this time in America. Even existing associations such as the *Littorio* Federation, the National United Italian Association, the Dante Alighieri Society, the Italian World War veterans, the Italian-American Society, and all the Italian clubs in universities, colleges, and high schools had more or less lost sympathy for Mussolini and functioned as fraternal and educational associations. However, among their members existed people who exploited Fascism to sway Italians of lower income groups and collect their money by playing on their patriotism, always a successful method among less-informed Italians.[10] Mussolini knew full well the situation in the United States. He also knew of the charge brought against him by the Paris Italian-language anti-Fascist newspaper, *Giustizia e Libertá*, which accused him of giving secret orders to Fascists to fight the re-election of President Roosevelt: "Il Duce is determined to fight President Roosevelt in his own home. To do that, he had given orders to New York Fascists to promote, among the Italians living in that city, an anti-Roosevelt campaign. A large sum of money has been put at the disposal of the Italian consulate of New York for the purpose of financing the campaign."[11]

The *New Leader* brought this to the attention of Americans on April 22, 1939, in an article "Duce Orders U.S. Italian Fascists to Fight FDR." Thus, it is easy to understand Mussolini's motives when he rejected the Giordano Plan. The publication of a pro-Fascist, anti-Roosevelt magazine, as it was intended, would have proved Mussolini's culpability.[12] Second, the real intentions behind the Giordano Plan surely did not escape Mussolini's attention. In fact, in the document Giordano clearly said that 10 million lire were needed to implement the magazine. "In a year or so," he continued, "the magazine would certainly become self-supporting and would better serve the purpose of making the Italian-Americans a rising force for a new balance of power between Democrats and Republicans in the United States." Was Giordano implying that after a short period the magazine would claim independent action? Thereafter, who would control it? What kind of economic and political rewards could he guarantee the Italian government? Who would own it for the time being except Giordano?

It appears that the Giordano Plan intended to resume an accelerated process of Fascist propaganda in the United States. Indeed, it was a carefully drawn plan to use Italian money to lay down the foundations of an editorial business whose profit would have benefited only Vincenzo Giordano.

CHAPTER 12

GELASIO CAETANI:
HIS ANCESTRY,
CAREER, AND LIFE

Nobility, honors, prestige, luster, and cosmopolitanism blended together in the ancient patrician Caetani family. In fact, records indicate that the Caetani (originally Gaetani) family dates back to the 8th century A.D. In the 9th century A.D., the family joined the Christian League and played an important role in the defense of the towns of Fondi and Gaeta in the Battle of the Garigliano River against the Saracens (Muslims). From the 12th century on, several patrician families, one of which was the Caetanis, controlled the city of Fondi. Legend has it that Fondi came under siege by the Saracens in 1534 and again in 1594. During the first siege, Emperor Barbarossa and the Saracens tried to abduct the beautiful Giulia Gonzaga, widow of Vespasiano Colonna, to give her to the sultan as a special gift.[1]

With a certain degree of historical accuracy, we can say the Caetanis comprised a noble and patrician family that controlled vast areas of feudal land in the regions of Lazio and Campania. Highly regarded by the patriciate of those regions, they belonged to the Guelphs' faction, which supported the papacy against the Ghibellines, who supported the emperor.

During the 12th century, members of the Caetani family branched out and expanded their territorial possessions, with one branch settling in Gaeta, where Giovanni Caetani was born. A monk of the Abbey of Montecassino, Giovanni was made cardinal, elected pope, and took the name Gelasius II (1118–1119). Pope Gelasius faced two powerful enemies: the Frangipane family, a potent Roman baronial and feudal family with possessions in Anzio, Terracina, and Marino; and the Holy Roman Emperor and king of Germany, Henry V. The conflict with the emperor centered on the issue of the clergy's investiture. To challenge the pope, Henry endorsed the election of an antipope in the person of Maurizio Bardia, archbishop of Braga, who took the name of Pope Gregory VIII. A pope elected in violation of canonical and ecclesiastical dispositions was considered antipope under the principle: "*Ille non esset papa, sed intrusus*" ("He cannot be pope, only an intruder").[2]

Another branch of the Caetani family relocated in the area of Anagni. To this branch, perhaps, belonged Pope Boniface VIII (Benedetto Caetani), born in Anagni in 1235. An excellent canonist, Boniface VIII possessed a vast knowledge of Church law and history. His papal bull *Unam Sanctam* represented the highest moment of the doctrine of the Church of Rome in defense of her authority over the temporal power of kings. *Unam Sanctam* was incorporated into the *Corpus Iuris Canonici*.

As a consequence of this and other documents issued by Boniface VIII, the king of France, Philip IV, called "the Fair," became recalcitrant and quarreled with the pope. The quarrel escalated. The king sent Nogaret de Guillaume, a French jurist and professor at the University of Montpellier, to Anagni to kidnap the pope and bring him to France for trial. The plot, which involved Sciarra Colonna, a bitter enemy of Pope Boniface, failed. However, Philip IV's conspirators imprisoned Boniface for three days in his palace and physically abused him. The event, known as the Outrage of Anagni, includes a report that Sciarra Colonna, a member of the Colonna family "slapped the Pope in the face" (*Lo Schiaffo di Anagni*). In the end, the people of Anagni liberated the pope; Boniface VIII returned to Rome, however, only to die a few days later on October 11, 1303.

Pope Boniface left his mark, though. Among his accomplishments, he reorganized the Vatican Library and founded the University of Roma, La Sapienza.[3] The pontificate of Boniface VIII no doubt benefited the Caetani family, who received vast territories, including the coastland and surrounding territories of the Pontine Marshes, where malaria was widespread. After a drainage project initiated in 1926 by Gelasio Caetani, the cities of Aprilia, Cisterna, Latina, and Pontinia were built in that area. In addition, the family received possessions in the surrounding areas of Caserta and Naples. This incorporation of vast feudal land gave the Caetani family the clout necessary to challenge the potent Colonna family of Rome.

Around 1420, Giacomo Caetani divided his feudal possessions. The coastal territories were given to the first-born son, who took the title of Duke of Sermoneta and Prince of Teano. The territories of the Neapolitan and Casertan areas were assigned to the second-born son, Cristoforo, from whom originated the lineage of the Caetani of Aragon, Counts of Fondi, Princes of Altamura, and Piedimonte d'Alife.

In more recent times, the Caetani family continued to distinguish itself for outstanding achievements in the areas of education, politics, husbandry, and cosmopolitanism. Michelangelo Caetani (1804–1882), Duke of Sermoneta and Prince of Teano was an eminent political figure. He became governor of Rome after the Italian government occupied the Eternal City and declared it capital of Italy in 1870. Michelangelo's versatility covered many areas. He succeeded in literature, sculpture, and goldsmithing.

He became a respected commentator on Dante Alighieri and published seminal works, such as *La Materia nella Divina Commedia* and *Carteggio Dantesco*. His house became the meeting place of national and international scholars. In 1840 Michelangelo married the

Polish Countess Calixta Rzewvski; they had a son and a daughter, Onorato and Ersilia. Onorato, elected to the Italian Parliament, had a brilliant political career and was appointed foreign minister by Prime Minister Antonio Marquis di Rudini.

Onorato Caetani married Ada Booth Wilbraham of the House of Latham in England. They had five sons and a daughter: Leone, Roffredo, Livio, Giovannella, Gelasio, and Michelangelo. Leone was born in Rome in 1869. He learned Sanskrit and Arabic, graduating from the University of Rome after studying Ancient and Oriental Languages and History. He became a renowned scholar of Islamic history and published *Gli Annali dell'Islam* in 10 volumes and *Una Cronografia Generale del Bacino Mediterraneo e dell'Oriente Mussulmano.* He traveled extensively to Greece, Turkey, Iraq, Syria, Egypt, and Palestine. In 1891 he traveled to the United States and Canada and recorded his impressions of both countries. In 1901, Leone married Vittoria Colonna, a member of the Colonna family that had been, throughout the centuries, the archrival of the Caetani family. The marriage, however, did not last. In 1916, Leone met Ofelia Fabiani, daughter of a Roman engineer. They had a daughter.

After WWI, Italy's political landscape changed. Leone's feudal land estate came under attack from leftist political parties, which advocated land expropriation on behalf of the peasants. His economic fortunes dwindled, and in 1921, Leone and his family moved to Canada, where he died in 1935.

Gelasio Caetani, the fifth offspring of Onorato and Ada Wilbraham and brother of Leone, was born on August 7, 1877 in Rome. The *tabularium* of Gelasio Caetani in Rome provides the following data:

Father: Onorato.

Mother: Ada Wilbraham. Born in Rome on August 7, 1877.

Nobility Titles: Duke of Sermoneta, Roman Noble, Neapolitan Patrician and Noble of Velletri.

Residence: Caetani Palace, Via delle Botteghe Oscure 32, Rome.

Education: Laurea in Ingegneria Mineraria (Doctorate in Mining Engineering), University of Rome, 1901.

The *Dizionario Biografico Degli Italiani,* Vol. 16, 1973, and the *Columbia University Quarterly,* Vol. XXVII, no. 4, provide detailed descriptions of Gelasio Caetani's life in Italy and in the United States. After receiving his doctorate at the University of Rome with high honors, he studied at the Mining School of Liege in Belgium (1902). He then attended the School of Mining at Columbia University in New York, where in 1903 he received the degree of Engineer of Mines. He trained at several silver mines in Utah and Idaho and concentrated on ore treatment in the states of California, Mexico, and Alaska. He conducted experiments in Mexico in grinding ores and published papers with the American Institute of Mining Engineers.

In January 1910, Caetani cofounded the company Burch, Caetani, and Hershey and started two metallurgical companies in California and Colorado. On account of his reputation and expertise, the Harvard Engineering School invited Caetani to teach during the summer quarters (1912–1914). The Burch, Caetani, and Hershey Company "realizing the business value of Caetani's social relationships in the United States and abroad," decided to open an office in New York and put Caetani in charge of it.

In 1913 Gelasio Caetani returned to Italy before the start of WWI. In the winter of 1914, he joined an Italian organization which sought to assist Belgium's war victims, and he thereafter received the Cross of Leopold II. In 1915, he led a relief operation in earthquake-devastated Avezzano, Italy. In August Gelasio received an appointment as Lieutenant of the First Regiment of Suppers and Mines, assigned to the Val Cordevole in the Alps, near the Col di Lana. Because all efforts to dislodge the Austrian-Hungarian troops from the Col had failed, Caetani, with the help of two engineers, masterminded the blasting of the Col di Lana with explosives. The operation was successful and Caetani was honored with the Cross of the Military Order of Savoy.

After he conducted other military operations in Macedonia and on the Piave, his name was inscribed in the *Gran Libro della Riconoscenza Nazionale.* His honors, positions, and achievements include, among others

Royal Italian Ambassador to Washington, D.C. (1922–1925);

Honorary Royal Italian Ambassador in the Italian Ministry of
Foreign Affairs (1925–1929);

Senator of the Italian Parliament;

Member of the Italian Academy of Lynxes;

Recipient of four honorary doctoral degrees (Columbia University,
Yale University, University of Idaho, and Colorado State
University);

Financier of the G. Caetani Scholarship of the Italy American
Society;

Supporter of the Carnegie Peace Endowment to establish the Cat-
alogue of the Vatican Library.

Author of several works in the 1920s and 1930s, including the
Caietanorum Genealogia, which contains the history of the Caetani
family; from 1925–1932, the six-volume *Regesta Chartarum*, containing the most important documents of the Caetani family from
950 to 1522; and *Epistolarium Honorati Caetani*, containing the
correspondence of Onorato III, and in 1933, the *Domus Caietana* in
three volumes.

Historians consider *Domus Caietana* "the history of the Caetani
family but also the political, economic, artistic and cultural history of Rome and Latium since the Middle Ages." A collection of
speeches delivered in the United States from 1922 to 1925 as Italian Ambassador to the United States was published in Italy. In 1924
and 1934, *National Geographic Magazine* published "The Story and
Legends of the Pontine Marshes" and the "Redemption of the Pontine Marshes."

From 1926 to 1934, Gelasio Caetani concentrated on the drainage of
the Pontine Marshes to reclaim over 175,000 acres of land of the Agro
Pontino, some belonging to the Caetani family. The work led to the
restoration of the family castle of Sermoneta and Ninfa and was completed in 1934. Gelasio Caetani died in Rome on October 23, 1934.[4]

A fervent Nationalist, Gelasio Caetani took part in the March on
Rome in October 1922. In Gelasio Caetani, Mussolini recognized an

Italian who possessed all the qualities, including intellectual ability, needed to serve as an outstanding representative of the Fascist government in the United States. He appointed him Italian Ambassador to Washington in November 1922. Convinced of Caetani's capabilities, Mussolini thought the man's great experience and successful professional career in the United States could help the Fascist regime settle Italy's war debt with the United States government. In addition, Mussolini considered Gelasio Caetani the right person to neutralize negative reactions of the American people toward Fascism and its totalitarian bent. The appointment of a distinguished Italian intellectual with a long tradition of ancestral nobility, especially one already well known in the United States, would bring to America the new and bold image of the Italian Fascist nation, the image of an Italy where law and order had been restored. Italian-Americans would see in Fascism a re-emergence of the millennial glory and greatness of their fatherland. Many Italians living abroad considered Mussolini the reincarnation of the Roman Caesar; *Il Duce* became the leader and protector of all Italians at home and abroad.

As ambassador, Caetani had to cope with the problem of Fascist sectarianism, factionalism, fanaticism, and dissidence. Italian Fascism contained too many discordant voices. Jealousy, envy, opportunism, paternalism, and corruption at local and national levels permeated the Fascist *gerarchi*. Fascist *dissidentismo* (dissidence) was widespread. Mussolini was aware of it, and to minimize the impact of factional conflicts, he reserved for himself the right to dismiss, replace, and appoint his collaborators. They had to pledge unlimited obedience to him.[5]

Luigi Bastianini was one of Mussolini's *gerarchi*. Born in Perugia, he took an active part in the preparation and execution of the March on Rome. Appointed vice-secretary general of the Fascist party, he became a member of the *Gran Consiglio del Fascismo*. From 1922 to 1926, he was responsible for the organization of the *Fasci all'Estero*. Under Bastianini's leadership, the *Fasci all'Estero* spread and multiplied. He reported frequently to the Grand Council of Fascism on the success and activities of the *Fasci all'Estero*.

In October 1925, with Mussolini in attendance, the Fasces Abroad held their first international congress in Rome.

In 1923, Bastianini published the book *Rivoluzione*, in which he articulated his theory of Fascist dissemination abroad. Under the motto *Ubi Italicus, Ibi Italia* (Where there is an Italian, there is Italy), Bastianini and his collaborators launched a program to spread Fascism and its ideology to other countries by instilling solidarity and fidelity to the fatherland among the Italians living abroad. Bastianini and his collaborators believed that by spreading the doctrine of Fascism, they would lay down the ideological foundation of a worldwide National Fascist imperialism—an imperialism founded not on war and military intervention, as Napoleon had tried to do, but on ideas, principles, and actions. Italians living abroad, separated geographically from the fatherland, could be reunited to Italy through Fascist propaganda, education, and persuasion. A National Fascist imperialism would lead to a new *weltanschauung*, no longer dominated by *gens britannica* or *germanica,* but by *gens latina.* By establishing a worldwide dominance of *gens latina,* Italy would emerge as a world power with a leading role in the international arena. The world would recognize Benito Mussolini as the creator and champion of the new world order: *Aut Caesar aut nihil* (Either Caesar or nothing).

Bastianini argued that two kinds of nation-states had influenced the history of the world. Those involved in constant warfare for national pride and territorial expansion and those forced to adopt an aggressive stance driven by domestic and economic necessities to punish the "sacred egoism" of the world's wealthy nations. Italy belonged to this second group of nations. With the advent of Fascism, Italy had acquired the right to play its role in the concert of nations. Under Mussolini's leadership, the Italian nation had become a world power, one power based on a millennial civilization that had imposed recognition, respect, and admiration. For centuries, Italians abroad had been victims of exploitation, abuse, stereotyping, and xenophobia.

Bastianini attributed the responsibility of the demise of *gens italica* to the liberal-democratic governments that had ruled Italy since the Unification. During that period, Italians abroad received neither protection nor moral and spiritual assistance from the Italian government. They were abandoned to their own destiny as sheep without a shepherd. Faced with neglect on the part of the fatherland, Bastianini argued, Italians living abroad abandoned their national identity, language, culture, tradition, and religion. Left alone, they became easy prey of individualism, subjectivism, and subversivism.

Under the leadership of Benito Mussolini and his Fascist government, however, the relationship between Italians at home and Italians abroad had been restored. Fascism had fostered a spontaneous process of *Italianitá* among Italians living abroad. Fascist associations sprang up everywhere in the world. The main goal of the associations was to enhance and spread Italian national identity and achieve a *Nietzschian isothymia* on behalf of the Italian people. Mussolini's Fascism wanted recognition as equals for Italy and Italians, wherever they lived. Under Mussolini's leadership, Italy and Italians living abroad had finally gained respect; a respect, which generated into a newly found national identity. Fascist associations abroad, therefore, had a twofold function. First, spiritually reunite all Italians abroad under the banner of Fascism, restoring the respect of the nation that had been a beacon of civilization *(faro di civiltá)* throughout the world for centuries. Second, establish an *italicum imperium*, which would extend beyond the Mediterranean *(Mare Nostrum)*, giving Italy the right to seek political, economic, colonial, industrial, and commercial expansion throughout the world.[6]

Since 1918 Alfredo Rocco and Francesco Coppola had articulated Italy's post-WWI program of action in their journal *Politica*. From the Versailles Conference, Italy expected a world order based on peace, security, and a new international balance of power, which would allow the Italian nation to complete its territorial reunification, establish homeland security, and pursue unhindered worldwide access to natural resources vital to Italy's economic development. The peace that Italy expected from Versailles was not Woodrow Wilson's idealist view of democracy, humanitarianism, pacifism, and anti-imperialism. Italy's long-term foreign policy included Italian colonialism and imperialism as a legitimate aspiration of the nation.

Had not Mussolini stated, after the American Congress passed the Johnson Act in 1924, that Italy's destiny was "either to expand or explode" and in 1939, in Berlin, had he not reiterated Italy's necessity to establish a German-Italian collaboration to acquire new living space *(Lebensraum)*?

The success of this foreign policy required, however, the unity of the nation and, first and foremost, the solution of the domestic dilemma that Italy faced, Nationalism or Socialism. According to the National Fascists, Nationalism represented the regeneration of the country, Socialism its degeneration. Fascism, into which Nationalism had merged and blended in 1923, embodied the new Italy; liberal-socialist democracy represented the old Italy.

This Italian bipolar contraposition had been examined at length by the Nationalists since 1918. Francesco Coppola, Arturo Rocco, philosopher Giovanni Gentile, and Luigi Federzoni, among others, had publicly advocated the advent of a new Italy, the Italy of Vittorio Veneto. The axiom of the National Fascist state, after the March on Rome, implied the condemnation and rejection of liberalism, Socialism, and democracy—a vision of the state implying control and regulation by individual citizens. Consequently, its sovereignty had become an *extrinsic* component of the state. National Fascists, on the other hand, advocated *uno stato forte* (a strong state). Alfredo Rocco emerged as the leading nationalist of the strong state based on the "total subordination of all individual rights and interests to those of the state." Rocco had been working on his theory of the *stato forte* long before the advent of Fascism, presumably before 1918.

According to Rocco, the state was sovereign because it had its own finalities, which were superior and transcended the interests of individuals. On the contrary, the liberal-socialist-democratic conception of the state was a *solvitur in singularitates,* meaning that the interests of the state and those of individuals were identical and reciprocal. Rocco rejected the liberal-socialist-democratic view of the state, believing it led to instability and anarchy. The National Fascist state, instead, had its own distinct and separate identity, function, and will. Consequently, such a state had its own political mission, social justice, economy, ethics, and religion, which transcended individual interests: "Nothing above the state, nothing against the state, everything within the state."[7]

Commenting on Rocco's doctrine of the state and on his hard work for the completion of the reforms of the *Codice Penale* and the *Codice di Procedura Penale*, Dino Grandi praised Rocco as the "legislator of the Fascist Revolution."[8]

Significantly, Rocco served as minister of Justice (*Guardasigilli*) from 1926 to 1932, and Mussolini appointed other nationalist jurists to run that ministry, as well. Indeed, many Nationalists continued to occupy important positions in the apparatus of the Fascist hierarchy of the Italian state.

Moreover, Alfredo Rocco conceived of the state as a central power structure in which all units came together in permanent collaboration and solidarity. All conflicts, contradictions, and oppositions had to be solved by the state and solely by the state. Rocco and his nationalist collaborators injected into Fascism and its organizational structure a new geopolitical vision of the nation, the state, and the world. A *concordantia oppositorum* (concordance of opposites) comprised reality, national and international, and needed framing as a logical *unum* in which freedom could not degenerate into individual arbitrariness.[9] In the of words Giovanni Gentile, "Freedom is not a right but a duty. The citizens must be ready to give everything to their state without asking anything in return."[10]

The *Rocchismo, Gentilismo,* and *Ducismo* worked together for the transformation of the Italian liberal-democratic system into the Fascist state, a modern Leviathan based on unlimited control and supremacy of the state. This was the essence of Mussolini's totalitarianism. Gentile summarized well the essence of the Fascist state: "If the state is not strong, it is not a state. To be strong, a state must be powerful internally and externally. The strong state demonstrates its power in war and through war asserts its autonomy from other nations."[11]

Ambassador Caetani proved a clever ambassador endowed with a keen sense of political realism. He skillfully informed Benito Mussolini, through his dispatches, of the tradition, nature, and mentality of the American people. He reiterated to Mussolini and other Fascist *gerarchi* that the people of the United States abhorred any kind of totalitarianism and would not tolerate any action aimed at subverting the traditional democratic institutions of the United States, let alone any attempt at exporting Italian Fascism to the United States. The American people were deeply steeped in their political institutions founded on democracy and freedom. America did not provide fertile ground for dictatorial or totalitarian experiments, let alone Italian Fascism. Caetani assured them that what Mussolini and his collaborators considered desirable would not be possible in the United States, namely, exporting and spreading Fascist doctrine, action, and tactics.

Ambassador Caetani understood correctly that a large sector of the American public and the American press saw in Fascism an ideological movement which required alignment and conformity to Mussolini's programs. Sectors of the Italian-American community welcomed Fascism as a movement that stressed patriotism and a newly found national identity. Some embraced Fascism not only for its romantic and sentimental attachment to the myth of *Il Duce,* but also for its use as an antidote to American nativism and xenophobia and as a weapon to force Americans to relax their paranoia against the Italian-American community.

From 1922 to 1940, Fascism as a potential political and revolutionary force functioned only as mere tokenism and never assumed a conspiratorial character among the Italian-American community. A well-organized anti-Fascist movement confronted Fascism and its propaganda. The Anti-Fascist Alliance of North America prevented Fascism from establishing an efficient network to disseminate its Fascist propaganda throughout the United States. This situation produced a constant friction between the Fascists and the anti-Fascists in the United States—one which never subsided.

Faced with anti-Fascist propaganda, internal factionalism, personal feuds, and consular conflicts and differences, a beset Mussolini disbanded the Fascist League of North America in December 1929. Fascism never emerged as a political force or ideology capable of creating an alternative to American democracy.

Appendix I

Italian Foreign Fascis*

General Secretary   86 Via Agostino Depretis ROME
TO THE FASCISTI DELEGATES &
TO THE SECRETARIES OF THE FOREIGN FASCIS
TO THE ITALIANS ABROAD.

The number of Italians living far from their Mother Country is about 10 million.

Such a strength, instead of being left aside, as was the case during the past, must rather be considered as a most vital national reserve. The victorious War has proved to the Italians the patriotism, faith and capacity of the emigrates, showing moreover how it was a very great mistake in the past to abandon to their own destiny all those who, due to the necessities and contingencies of life, had to search far from their own country their own living.

Moved by a high feeling of national solidarity, Fascism intends to include, in the great strengths that give life and development to the Nation, also the strength of the Italians who live in foreign countries.

In order to reach that aim, the Great Fascisti Council has decided that also the Italians abroad constitute good Fascis in order to unite under the same badge, that is of the renewed Motherland, all the sons of Italy unforgetful of their own duty and who understand their own mission in the world.

Object of such Fascism is the gathering of all the Italians in a disciplined Block, solid with goodwill of aims and energies. This is to keep awake among them the feeling of *Italianità* and the Faith in the Motherland.

The Fascis, while they must explain the idealities of Fascism in Foreign Countries, have the duty of rectifying all those opinions that are purposely spread abroad in respect to Italy and its government, in order to depreciate the acts of the government and hide the power and intentions of Italy. They must further spread and make understood abroad the knowledge of art, culture, sciences and Italian industries, cooperating thus in the most efficient manner to form in all the Countries all over the World a public opinion favorably disposed to talk of our Country, of its beauties and its manifestations in the various fields of human activities. It is also a duty of the Fascis to inform this General Secretary of Foreign Fascis of any events that may interest him. Therefore, the Foreign Fascis will create proper Propaganda Offices and a Technical Office that study the questions interesting our Colonies abroad and the possibilities for our Country for its valorization. Offices for Assistance must also be constituted in order that Italian citizens may find all possible aid.

At the Head of such Foreign Fascis must be individuals under all respects unsuspected and unattackable, and highly understanding their own duties towards the Country of which they are guests, with whom they must have continual contact and upkeep of esteem, and cordial sympathy reciprocally. For such reason the Foreign Fascis are not allowed to interfere in questions concerning the Countries they are guests of. On the contrary, it will be the care of the Fascis to demonstrate with rigid observance of the laws, the high spirit of discipline that animates Italian citizens.

The Foreign Fascis must never forget that in foreign territory they are the expression of the New Italy and they must therefore refrain from taking any initiative that might in any way be contrary to the action of the government.

Any initiative of political character must be submitted to the approval of the General Secretary.

Among the duties that Fascists abroad have towards their Motherland, there is that: not to diminish, in carrying out their action, the authority and prestige of the Representatives and Officials of the Country that are invested with the Power of Official Representatives of our Country.

The Fascis must consider themselves helpers and efficient cooperators of the work that they will carry out with illuminated and patriotic fervor according to the instructions given them by the Minister of Foreign Affairs who is also the Chief of Fascism. It must not be allowed anyone to think of constituting Fascis in order to fight and boycotting the action of Italian Representatives abroad.

Any personal question must be abandoned in the superior interest of our Country. Unfortunately until yesterday Italian Colonies spread over the World were divided by continual fighting that were harmful (not very little) to the prestige of our Country and its valorization. Fascis must be organizations of unity and not the object of new divisions among the Italian Colonies.

To the Italians in Foreign Countries, as to those residing in Italy, it is a duty "discipline," so that Italy may be honored to have them as children. Fidelity, Love, Discipline and Work, these are the words to be impressed on the heart of all the Italians!

* This circular, enacted by the Bureau of Italian *Fasci* in Foreign Countries in 1923, was sent by Ambassador Henry P. Fletcher to the Department of State in Washington on May 9, 1924. See the Archives of the Department of State (U.S.D.S.), Fletcher to State, Rome, May 9, 1924, 811.00F/12.

Appendix II

Embassy of the
United States of America

No. 41.   Rome, May 9, 1924.
CONFIDENTIAL.
The Honorable
The Secretary of State,
Washington.

Sir:

Referring to the Department's instruction No. 344 of April 24, 1923, and my predecessor's dispatch No. 669 of May 15, 1923, with reference to the organization and activities of Fascist groups in foreign countries and especially in the United States, I have the honor to report that I met casually a few evenings ago Mr. Guido Sollazzo, Vice-Secretary General of Italian Fasci in Foreign Countries, who asked if he could call upon me and explain the progress and activities of his organization in foreign countries. I replied that I would be very glad to have him call, which he did yesterday accompanied by Prof. Alfredo Francini, of the Secretariat General of Foreign Fasci, who acted as his interpreter, as Mr. Sollazzo speaks no English or French.

Mr. Sollazzo, who is an attorney, is, under the direction of Mussolini and the General Fascist Council, the active head of the Fascist movement in foreign countries. He explained that the growth of the Fascist movement in foreign parts was entirely spontaneous and emanated from the desire of Italians living abroad, who sympathize with the Fascist movement in Italy and believe in the principles of Fascism, to form themselves into organizations which would enable them more effectively to express this sympathy and adherence. He said that the Central Committee of the Fascist party felt that it would be safer from every point of view to have some control over the activities of these organizations, and had therefore decided to set up an organization in Rome to control and direct the foreign Fascist groups. Mr. Sollazzo handed to me an English translation of a circular issued by the Secretariat General to the Italian Foreign Fasci, setting forth the ideals and objects to be pursued. I enclose a copy of this circular. Mr. Sollazzo also handed to me a copy of the certificate of incorporation of the Central Council of the Fascists of New Jersey, (copy enclosed), in order to show in what manner and for what object Fascist organizations are established in the United States. He gave me to understand that future organizations of the Fascists in the United States would follow the lines of this certificate of incorporation.

Mr. Sollazzo was emphatic in stating that foreign Fasci were enjoined to refrain from interfering or taking part in the internal politics of the country in which they were located; that they were, on the contrary, called upon to cooperate in every way in fostering the good relations between their mother country and the country of their residence; that their mission was spiritual and cultural; that they were expected to explain and defend, in case of necessity, the pure ideals and principles of Italian Fascism, but strict instructions had been issued to them to avoid controversies with those holding Bolshevist or anti-Fascist opinions. In this connection, Mr. Sollazzo referred to the collisions which had occurred between Bolshevists and Fascists in France and explained that the French situation was abnormal in that the conflicts and disorders were due to the activities of Italian Communists who, eluding their vigilance, had escaped over the border into France.

I informed Mr. Sollazzo that I was very glad to learn of the high purposes of these organizations and the facts which he had been kind enough to relate. I explained to him that I was particularly anxious to acquaint myself with foreign Fascist activities in the United States, because I felt a natural uneasiness lest the activities of this or any other organization might affect adversely the good relations which we all hoped to see firmly maintained between Italy and the United States. I explained to him the great danger to these good relations involved in any political activity of a foreign controlled and directed organization in the United States. I pointed out to him the concern which our Government, or any other government, might feel if an organization of this kind should threaten domestic order and internal peace, pointing out to him that the repression of the activities of the Bolshevists, Communists or any others holding views opposed to those held by Fascists was a matter exclusively in the hands of the national authorities. Mr. Sollazzo replied that these and similar possible dangers had been considered by the General Council, that strict instructions had and would be given on this head, and that the desire to exercise the greatest possible control in this regard was one of the principal reasons why his organization had been created. This gave me an opportunity to refer to the necessity of exercising that control in such a way as not to set up, especially in the United States, an *imperium in imperio* which, even if their activities should involve no actual violation of the laws of the United States, might yet prove to be unwelcome and undesirable from a social and political point of view.

I asked Mr. Sollazzo whether the Fascist organizations were composed of Italians in the United States who had retained their original nationality, or whether they included also American citizens of Italian origin. He replied that both were included.

I have thought it wise to establish a friendly, personal contact with the directing heads of the foreign Fascists in order to be in a position by informal conversations to try to avoid any serious effect upon United States-Italian relations arising from their excess of zeal or ignorance of the American point of view. I have been careful, of course, to refrain from expressing any endorsement or approval of their activities in the United States, and have confined myself strictly to an attitude of seeking information.

Should the activities of any of these organizations in the United States be such as to cause the Department concern I believe with the contacts established here, and especially from the fact that Mussolini is the Minister for Foreign Affairs, I shall be in a position to assist in preventing or removing these difficulties; and would suggest that in cases of this kind the Embassy be promptly informed in order that the matter can also be dealt with here.

I have the honor to be, Sir,

Your obedient servant,
Henry P. Fletcher

APPENDIX III

HYMNS

HYMN TO ITALY

Forward, Italy,
invincible and proud,
Black shirts
shall overcome.
The tricolored flag national glory
flying on the frontiers
and in the sun.
Free are you now
powerful and feared,
death cannot
prostrate you.
Disbanded and routed
your adversaries,
all traitors and swindlers
lie dejected.
Faith in you
never will fail,
you are a spark
twinkling eternally.
You are an Idea
sublime and great,
never betraying our hearts.
You are youth
strong and brave, ready to die
for your grandeur.
The Unknown Soldier
with his example,
faith and courage
in you instills.
From the Eternal City,
the Alma Rome,
your indomitable race

will some day arise.
A Great Leader,
a wise Man,
shapes and forges
your new destinies.
Only your Duce
incomparable and unsurpassable
everything he wants
only can dare.
He always acts
He never stops
He makes Italy
great and haughty

HYMN TO FIUME

City of charm
shore of warm
you suffered a lot
for all the plot
against your rights.
0 magic harbor
0 beautiful Quarnero
the Christmas' magic,
the fatal, shameful day
remember as tragic.
Of a foreign deceiver
and evil adviser
Italy's Prime Minister
abject and bolder
suddenly agreed to be follower.
Therefore the slaughter
premeditated willful murder
and execrated soon
consummated.
But a Great Soldier
to the act of betrayal indignant
and dreadful angry reacted
and soon for you intervened.
Later unvanquished

and unabated
the Great Commander to the
Alma Rome Fiume United.
And finally il Duce Italy's
glory redeemer
annexed wanted
those Italian lands
to the motherland.
And the strong cry
Fiume or death
resounded in our chests
the Alps overpassed
on the seas echoed
and the Italians over the world
of the final triumph were told.

—Giuseppe Sposato, *Fiamme*
Syracuse, New York, 1937

Appendix IV

Certificate of Incorporation of Central Council of the Fascisti of New Jersey

Under the Act of April 21st, 1908 entitled, "An Act to Incorporate Associations not for Pecuniary Profit" and the several supplements thereto and acts amendatory thereof.

FIRST: The name of the corporation shall be the CENTRAL COUNCIL OF THE FASCISTI OF NEW JERSEY:

SECOND: The Central Council of the Fascisti of New Jersey shall have power to grant charters to subordinate lodges throughout the State of New Jersey in accordance with its constitution and bylaws, and to revoke the same for causes:

THIRD, The purpose of the Grand Council and such subordinate lodges shall be a strict adherence to the principles of the constitution of the United States of America and its laws; to help aliens to become American citizens by schooling them in the meaning of the constitution of the United States; preparing them for the first and second citizenship papers:

FOURTH: By promoting the development of the economical, moral and intellectual, as well as political life of its members:

FIFTH: To act as a society for the protection of the immigrants and to cooperate with every possible legal means to the safeguarding of their rights when these rights harmonize with the American national interest:

SIXTH: To promote good-will between the laboring class and their employers:

SEVENTH: To promote the commercial ties between America and Italy and to bind closer the ties of friendship between them.

*****

The number of trustees elected for the first year are as follows:
Frank S. Brunelli
Gerardo Rita
Raffaele Campione
Giuseppe Sagarese
Domenico Ammiano
The name of the Agent and upon whom process may be served, with his address, is
Nicola Ferrara
#45 Clifton Avenue, Newark, N.J.
IN WITNESS WHEREOF, the Trustees who have associated themselves as the CENTRAL COUNCIL OF THE FASCISTI OF NEW JERSEY, have hereunto set their hands and seals this 25th day of January, A.D. 1924.

Signed, sealed, and delivered in the presence of
Peter A. Cavacchia
Frank S. Brunelli
Gerardo Rita
Guiseppe Sagarese
Domenico Ammiano

*****

STATE OF NEW JERSEY
                    : SS.
COUNTY OF ESSEX
BE IT REMEMBERED, That on this 25th day of January, A.D., 1924, before me, an Attorney at Law of New Jersey personally appeared
Frank S. Brunelli
Gerardo Rita

Raffaele Campione
Giuseppe Sagarese
Domenico Ammiano

*****

whom I am satisfied are the Trustees in the within Certificate of Incorporation: and I having first made known to them the contents thereof, they did acknowledge that they signed, sealed and delivered the same as their voluntary set and deed, for the uses and purposes therein expressed.
Peter A. Cavicchia.
Attorney at Law of New Jersey.

*****

STATE OF NEW JERSEY
DEPARTMENT OF STATE.

I, THOMAS F. MARTIN, Secretary of State of the State of New Jersey, do hereby certify that the foregoing is a true copy of the Certificate of Incorporation of CENTRAL COUNCIL OF THE FASCISTI OF NEW JERSEY, and the endorsements thereon, as the same is taken from and compared with the original filed in my office on the Sixteenth day of February, A.D. 1924, and now remaining on file and of record therein.

IN TESTIMONY WHEREOF, I have hereunto set my hand and affixed my Official Seal at Trenton, this Sixteenth day of February, A.D., 1924.

Thomas F. Martin
Secretary of State

Appendix V

Il Nuovo Mondo

August 26, 1926
North American Anti-Fascist Alliance
MANIFESTO

To all Workers of the United States, Canada, and Mexico. To Those People Concerned About Italy's Constitutional and Civil Liberties: Greetings and Brotherhood.

The supreme sacrifice of the Italian people has been fulfilled. The residual traces of the Italian constitutional and civil liberties, the heritage of generations of heroes and martyrs, have been destroyed. What centuries of barbarian invasions could not wipe out has been cancelled by a gang of Italian adventurers and cowards led by a bold, seven times unscrupulous leader of the insignia of Fascism.

In a short period of time, all Italian liberties—the heritage and conquest of our ancestors, philosophers, poets, martyrs, and apostles— have been first outraged and violated, then abolished and destroyed. The well organized plan of "fascistization" has been carried on by Mussolini with the consent of the parliament controlled by the black shirts, with the connivance of the judicial authority and the acquiescence of the Monarchy. It is against these cowards and traitors, who have destroyed the entire apparatus of the state that WE protest. We charge Fascism with the following crimes of high treason against the sovereignty and liberty of the Italian people and denounce the regime to the tribunal of the conscience of the civil nations of the world and to history:

1) Freedom of the press and of opinion have been suppressed in Italy. Opposition is no longer allowed. Political dissent and anti-Fascist opposition can no longer be voiced. Those who

dissent with the line and ideology of Fascism are persecuted, dragged before the Fascist-controlled courts and subject to disproportionate sanctions up to the point that the accused are in jeopardy of being deprived of their belongings or of being murdered.

2) Freedom of association has been completely wiped out. All civic and labor associations have been abolished. The lodges of free-masons have been dissolved and their estates, belongings, and properties have been confiscated and divided among the "Black Bands."

3) Freedom of thought has been nullified in Italy. When human thought is not free to express itself through the natural and inalienable rights of expression, then freedom of opinion is suppressed. No teacher is allowed to teach unless he proves to be a Fascist, a Catholic or the receptor of an authorization from the local Fascist section. No university professor is allowed to teach new doctrines, theories or disciplines which have not been previously selected or expurgated by the officials of the regime. No state employee is permitted to perform his duties unless he proves to be a member of the Fascist Party.

4) Freedom of worship no longer exists in Italy. The Fascist regime, interfering with the spiritual rights of the individual, had obliged all secondary school pupils—regardless of their parental religion or creed—to conform to the principles and the canons of the official state religion. The regime is going to extend these medieval impositions even to college and university students.

5) The right to hold Italian citizenship is denied to those who have abandoned the national territory and have settled abroad to escape Fascist persecutions. Moreover, those anti-Fascists still in Italy have no protection whatsoever. Safeguard of life, protection of property, and hereditary rights to family holdings are definitely subject to the whims of the black shirts. In the last two years following the murder of Giacomo Matteotti, murders, pillages, larcenies, rapes have increased. Statistics,

if made available, would prove easily that the arrogance, the arbitrariness, and the lawlessness of the Fascist *gerarchi* have been instrumental in forcing many members of the opposition parties to leave the country. The popular masses have been completely subdued.

What else can be added to what we have said? What more is needed to condemn such an unbearable and ruthless regime to the moral and civil conscience of the world? Today the Italian judicial authority is subservient to the whims of the dictator. While the members of the Fascist Party are easily acquitted or set free for many serious criminal acts, Mussolini's enemies, on the contrary, are subject to the heaviest penalties for such negligent actions as labor protest, insult to the person or image of Il Duce, and criticism of his regime. Since antinational slogans and propaganda are outlawed, capital punishment is meted out to those found responsible for these "crimes". This situation is a direct consequence of the introduction of the so-called Fascist laws, shaped by the Minister of Justice, Alfredo Rocco. The Parliament—the Chamber of Deputies and the Senate—is an illegal association of Fascist acolytes deprived of any autonomous function. Their function now is to listen to Mussolini's speeches, to applaud and receive the reward for such sycophantic services. Mussolini has solemnly declared that the Liberal state (the representative state) has withered away. The new parliament has the function of ratifying those international treaties, commercial agreements and documents for which parliamentary approval is required by international conventions.

The state police have been abolished. The royal guards have been substituted by black shirts and the Militia, whose role and power are unlimited. The persecutions by the latter have become a feature of the regime. Public and secret persecutions have been introduced to safeguard national interest. The constant moral decline of the individual and popular values are pursued as means towards the triumph of the idea of the immanent nation,

Here is where Italy stands now. While the United States is celebrating the 150th anniversary of its independence, Italy mourns the

4th anniversary of the suppression of all civil and public liberties. Paradoxically, in the United States news media reporters, philo-Fascist newspapers, secret agents, and selected propagandists have been hired to bestow high praise on the regime, for the purpose of installing it in the United States of America. The philo-Fascist propaganda is infiltrating among Italian immigrants and among the young unaware children of Italian-Americans who see in Mussolini the myth of the incarnation of Caesar.

Citizens, Workers of America:

If you concluded that American citizens should not get involved in the domestic affairs of Italy you would act like Cain who declared not to be the guardian of his brother. This would signify that Italy had no right whatsoever to demand your protest or your help to break down the chains of its tyranny. But YOU, Americans, you helped and defended Europe in World War I, YOU gave asylum to Kossuth, to Garibaldi, and Carl Schurz. Still, YOU might decide not to get involved in Italy's internal problems. If this is your answer, it is your prerogative. However, we do know that a nation cannot rid itself of a tyrant unless it relies upon its national ability, courage and strength. But when this tyranny is in the process of being transplanted onto your soil, the consciences of your workers are under constant antidemocratic pressure and the principle of popular sovereignty—that you have con-secrated in your country—is in jeopardy, then YOU can-not continue to be silent and remain indifferent. If you continue to maintain such an attitude, your Fathers' voices will rise to accuse you of cowardice and treason against the immortal ideals of your country.

Citizens, workers, Americans all: be alert!

Fascism has reached the apex in Italy, but it cannot survive unless it expands. It is trying to expand where many proselytes can be made. Moreover, Fascist leaders know that such a kind of proselytism is easily attainable in the United States of America. Therefore, Mussolini, who is not an intellectual but a shrewd politician, pursues his goals in this country. This explains why Mussolini is concentrating all his efforts on imposing the ideology of Fascism upon the will of the Americans. In fact, he has introduced a new gospel: that

Fascism is the only valid alternative to Liberalism and Bolshevism, and that it is the stronghold which is going to defend the American establishment from the assaults of the lower classes.

Citizens of America, fellow Americans, be alert!

Our common task is to condemn publicly and solemnly Fascism, its postulates, and its continuous threats on this country. Moreover, we must strongly oppose those Americans and Italian-Americans who favor the triumph of Fascism in this country.

WE ACCUSE!

We accuse the Fascist government of conducting a disruptive propaganda in this country among Americans and Italian-Americans to undermine the essence of the Declaration of Independence and destroy the ideals of equality and freedom.

We accuse the Fascist government of organizing a centre of espionage whose aims are to infiltrate among factory workers to foment strikes, unrest, disruption, and inefficiency.

We accuse the Fascist government of the continuous distribution of insignia, rewards, titles, crosses, and so on, to Americans and Italian-Americans. Through Ambassadors, Consuls, Consular Agencies, and local organizations, these insignia are distributed to judges, to central and local officials, governmental authorities, lawyers, doctors, professors, senators, congressmen, bankers, ecclesiastical dignitaries, news media reporters, artists, educators, and businessmen. Mussolini has distributed as many crosses in America as he has placed on Italian graves as a result of his persecutions.

We accuse Mussolini and his Fascist organizations of organizing sport clubs and associations in this country. These organizations carry Fascist insignia, flags, pennants, and other paraphernalia. American youths are offered Fascist indoctrination and are trained in the use of arms. On many national and civic occasions, they parade in our streets as it has already happened on the occasion of the Grand Army and the American Legion parades in New York City.

We accuse the Fascist government of controlling a well organized Fascist Embassy in Washington whose aims are not to defend the Americans' or Italian-Americans' interests, but to control and supervise the apparatus of Fascism in America.

We accuse King Victor Emmanuel III of allowing the "fascistization" of the Italian State. He has encouraged and seconded the fulfillment of the Fascist plan to turn Italy into a dictatorship. Our protest is motivated by the lack of courage and decision showed when Mussolini destroyed the constitutional and civil liberties in Italy. In so doing, the king betrayed the ideals of the Statute and violated the postulates upon which the Risorgimento was attained in Italy. Since the King has been demoted to the rank of Mussolini's puppet, we declare Victor Emmanuel III dethroned along with his family and dynasty. The right to decide on the future institutional formula belongs to the people of Italy. Moreover, in denouncing the connivance with Fascism, we consider King Victor Emmanuel III responsible for Mussolini's plans to establish a Fascist control in the United States of America.

Workers, citizens, Italian-Americans, Italians, lovers of liberty!

Three years ago the North American Anti-Fascist Alliance was formed. It was formed in this country to carry on a struggle on behalf of the inborn, inalienable human rights of the individual. To the Alliance adhered many worker parties and the Liberal Party. At that time we thought that Fascism would be a transient movement of collective madness. Today, instead, we have to affirm sadly that Fascism is still operative and aggressive, in spite of national and international condemnation. As a Black Death, it is attempting to proselytize in many European countries and in America as well. It is trying in Greece, Spain, Poland, France, England, and in the United States of America. If this monster is not strangled soon—and it should be done before it comes of age—it will undermine all liberties. To prevent these nefarious consequences, the North American Anti-Fascist Alliance is addressing this Manifesto to all workers, to all political parties, Liberal, Moderate, Radical, Communist, Socialist, Republican, to organize an opposition against Fascism. Let Fascism not triumph in the democratic countries of the world. Let America expel any Fascist or pro-Fascist element.

With these goals in sight, The North American Anti-Fascist Alliance invites all persons, regardless of their rank, affiliation, religion, to endorse the program of the Alliance. The final goal of the Alliance is to overthrow Fascism in Italy so that the whole world will be immune from the Fascist virus. The Alliance does not impose upon its supporters any political or ideological affiliation. It does not impose any religious creed or principle. It does not undermine individual freedom, and it does not try to prevent criticism and autonomy of action. Nevertheless, the historic events of our times compel the formation of a strong, common front to oppose Fascism and its ideology. The Alliance—for the prevention of partisan positions or conflicts—establishes a common canon of ethics to achieve unity within diversity.

Let all citizens and political organizations unite to carry on this noble program of anti-Fascist struggle.

Let us join together and look forward to meeting in New York at the First International Congress of the Working Forces, scheduled for September 4–6, 1926.

WORKERS OF ITALY:

Yours is the struggle, yours the defense of the heritage of your Fathers. Only this should be your war cry: to redeem Italy forever! Your friends in America, Europe, and in the whole world can help, be on your side, but they cannot free Italy without getting involved directly. Therefore, your primary task is to break your chains. All anti-Fascist forces still in Italy, and those abroad, must unite and concentrate on the struggle against Fascism. In the meantime, together we must proceed in laying down the foundation of the Republic in Italy.

On behalf of our martyrs: Long live the Republic! For our future generations: Long live the Republic! Against the Savoy Monarchy: Long live the Republic! For the honor and the glory of the Italian people:

Long live the Republic!

United let us proceed against our common tyrant: Mussolini.

/s/ Pietro Allegra, Secretary

The North American Anti-Fascist Alliance

APPENDIX VI

CORRESPONDENCE TO
THE AMBASSADOR OF ITALY

June 17, 1927.

His Excellency
Nobile Giacomo de Martino,
Ambassador of Italy.

My dear Mr. Ambassador:

You asked me a few days ago to get you, if I could, a statement as to the opinion of people in New York on the subject of parades in uniform by Fascisti organizations in New York. I have received a statement on the subject, which is substantially as follows:

"In response to your request of June 10th asking for an unofficial expression on the subject of the Fascisti parading in New York City in their black shirts, I beg to advise that this matter has been discussed with me on numerous occasions. I have heard several expressions of opinion concerning the general feeling in the community regarding these parades.

As nearly as I can ascertain from what I have heard from time to time the general sentiment of the best elements in New York is favorable to the Fascisti organizations, as there seems to be a general belief that they believe in law and order and that in an emergency they would stand by the governmental authorities of this government. The same people who feel this way, however, are also strongly opposed to the banding together of the Fascisti in public parades with uniforms on which make them the representatives of an Italian institution. They take the view that America is not the place for them to make these demonstrations and that especially in the City of New York they ought to be eliminated for the reason that there is a large element among the Italians who do not agree with Fascisti ideas, who are not Americans, have not the least loyalty to law and order or a very great respect for government officials. The result is that these elements on every occasion make as much trouble as possible for the constituted authorities by insulting their opponents, by using violence and in many ways necessitating the interference of the police and disciplinary organizations.

I know personally from expressions of city officials that, while they are not unfavorable to the Fascisti elements, they are violently opposed to the parades they carry on from time to time in their uniforms and also are strongly opposed to bringing up these purely Italian questions in America, especially in New York City with its vast foreign population. The police would much prefer to see the Fascisti elements kept within their private organizations and not make any public display on the highways. There seems to be a growing feeling that if it is wise to permit the Fascisti to parade in their black shirts, thus inevitably creating strife and disorder from time to time, there is no reason why the Ku Klux Klan, composed as it is of native-born Americans, should not at least have a similar right to the Fascisti, which is largely composed of Italians who are not yet American citizens. There seems to be no doubt that, so long as the Fascisti insist in parading in New York City in their uniforms as an organized body, there are going to be murders and vicious assaults.

Public opinion seems to be reaching the point, especially among native-born Americans, where more and more people are writing to the newspapers and asking them why they do not denounce these foreign activities in the United States. In fact, some of the newspapers have stated that they are getting letters almost daily from people demanding to know why this country is so lenient to these foreign elements.

I am satisfied that the consensus of opinion is that these elements should all have the right to organize if they want to, have any opinions they want to, as long as they do not violate our laws, but when they make a public parade of their ideals and do so in such a manner as to cause the opposition to commit acts of violence, that the whole business should be suppressed. The police feel very much like the average good citizen. They dislike to express any opinion that is unfavorable to the element that they really believe is all right. If the Italian Ambassador were to ask the police officials their opinion, it is unlikely that they would tell him the facts as I have stated them above because personally they are friendly to the Fascisti, who are thoroughly anti-Bolshevik. I am sure, however, that the facts are exactly as I have stated them. I feel also that these Fascisti parades will, in the end, do a good deal of harm since I understand that certain elements, probably of the Ku Klux Klan, outside of the City are beginning to criticize very severely the New York police, asserting that they are showing favoritism to the Fascisti and that they are acting unfairly to the native-born elements. This is of no particular interest in so far as New York City is concerned, but when such talk goes throughout the country it has a very bad effect. In fact, it will certainly have a tendency to mould public opinion outside of New York City against the Fascisti. On the other hand, there can be no doubt that if the Fascisti stop parading and handle their organizations a little differently, making it quite clear that they are not attempting in any way to interfere with American institutions and keep themselves as foreigners in the background, that they will retain the good will of the people of New York, as well as of the whole country and will be much better off."

I have quoted the above because it seems to me a very clear and frank statement of conditions.

Sincerely yours,
W. R. Castle, Jr.
A-E WRC/AB

APPENDIX VII

IL PROGRESSO ITALO-AMERICANO AND *IL CORRIERE D'AMERICA*

Office of Correspondence of Rome
Director Vincenzo Giordano   Rome, June 6, 1939
Excellency Dino Alfieri
Minister of Popular Culture
Rome

Excellency:

I came out of our first meeting with the firm conviction that you are a man of great talent and deep dedication.

As I mentioned to you, our two dailies in New York, *Il Progresso Italo-Americano* and *Il Corriere d'America*, are engaged in a relentless propaganda campaign on behalf of Fascism and are sufficient enough to keep united the old generations of Italian-Americans living in the United States.

Already much work has been done. Soon, in collaboration with the Italian Ministry of Foreign Affairs, our dailies will publish messages by Italian mayors, interviews with local Italian people, photographic accounts and reports dealing with the progress made in Italy in the last decade under Fascism. This will revive sentiments of patriotism among the Italian-Americans; it will regenerate the spirit of *Italianitá* in the entire Italian collectivity; it will prevent the Italian-Americans falling victims of the American anti-Italian propaganda. As a consequence of this relentless activity of moral and patriotic regeneration of the Italians in America, many will become eager to visit Italy and appreciate the stupendous realizations of the regime.

However, at this point in time, we are faced with the problem of the young generations of Italian-Americans.

Very recently the journalist Gayda has written: "We can rely on 10 million Italians throughout the world."

This is true. However, I reply: "We run the risk of losing them and should do everything in our power to gain their confidence in us."

In the United States there are almost 6 million Italians. Three millions are represented by Italian-Americans. While the elder people disappear, the young, brought up in an American atmosphere, start to neglect their ancestors' motherland and patriotic affiliations. Why all this? Because nothing has been done to keep them abreast of the new Italy and also because there is no Italian magazine in English language that can maintain the communications with the young generations.

The United States is going through a very alarming and serious period. The Communists have invaded and control most of the workers' unions. The Communists have made inroads into political life, schools and other areas. The press is hostile to Italy. Roosevelt is a declared enemy of Italy. There is no Italian leader or politician in his cabinet. The whole Roosevelt entourage is formed by Jewish people. We are fifteen months away from the presidential elections. We must do something and soon. The magazine could produce considerable impact on the results of the forthcoming elections.

It is well known that, when the Republican party was in power, the relations between Italy and the United States were always cordial. Even though the magazine should not appear extremely partisan, nevertheless the final goal should be: "To organize the millions of Italians in the United States." If organized and oriented politically, they could become a kind of turning point in the political spectrum of America. They could back up a candidate ready to support Mussolini's regime and acknowledge the existence of a second Italy in America.

In many American cities there are numerous competent Italian politicians. They even occupy high positions in the local political structure. However, they do not have enough support and sufficient defense against local press slurs.

There was a moment in the United States when the Italian collectivity rose up against the government. It was during the Ethiopian crisis. Throughout the crisis, Pope's two Italian dailies did everything they could. As a consequence of the relentless action of defense on behalf of Italy, the Italian collectivity disclosed courage, dedication, and a new sense of patriotism, Once the war was over, its enthusiasm disappeared. At that time an Italian magazine in English language would have been sold out every week by millions of copies. Not only the Italian-Americans but also the Americans who sympathized with Italy would have bought it. The magazine could have an important impact on the Italian-Americans, on the Americans, and on the undecided. It might have produced the defeat of Italy's worst enemy: Roosevelt. Moreover, the presence of a magazine of this nature would have created millions of sympathizers for Fascism. Millions would have become mentors of Mussolini. The Italian-Americans would have grown politically stronger. They would have convinced the American people that six million Italian-Americans, though sincere and honest citizens of America, would never give up their allegiance to their motherland. In so doing, they would constitute an army ready to defend Italy and the Italian prestige from the scurrilous attacks of her enemies.

The Italian collectivity in America is politically and economically strong. If well organized it could bring advantage to Italy directly and indirectly.

Therefore, I propose that the Italian government introduce a magazine in English language of the format of the Saturday Evening Post. The magazine will be Fascist one hundred percent and will publish articles of collaborators carefully selected in Italy and in the United States.

The magazine would underline the realizations of Italy in the fields of economy, politics, social life, and law and order, everything Fascism has realized in the last two decades and what it plans for the future. The magazine would analyze comparatively the forms of government in Italy and the United States. It would underline what has been done by the Roosevelt's government in the last six years and what has been accomplished by Mussolini in the same period. It would put in evidence that while in Italy public services are controlled by the State, in the United States they are controlled by the enemies of the State: the workers. The magazine would stress the realizations in Italy in the field of law and order, individual liberties, public and private responsibilities, the morality of political life and public offices. While doing all these things, the magazine would be the best organ of defense of Fascism and its philosophical postulates. However, it is imperative to keep secret that the magazine is financed by the Italian government. In this way American people would not find out that the magazine is financed by a foreign country. The magazine would start with an immediate circulation of over 300,000 copies. Fifty thousand would be distributed by mail and free of charge to Senators and House Representatives in Washington, to Governors, to State Senators and Assemblymen, to Mayors, to College and University Professors, to industrialists and businessmen throughout the country.

In addition, an intense advertising campaign would be carried out through radio networks throughout the country. The estimated cost of this entire operation would run to 10,000,000 lire, to be provided by the Italian government. The cost might appear extremely high. However, you have to bear in mind that the magazine has to compete with the best American published weeklies. In the long run, the profit that the magazine would accrue to Italy and the Italians in America would be of immense proportions. The 10 million lire are needed to assure the life of the magazine for one year at least. Thereafter, the magazine would become self-sufficient and would continue its own way. After this period, the magazine would become an important instrument in the political spectrum of America and eventually would make the Italian-Americans the new balance of power in the political arena of America.

The board of directors of the magazine would be formed exclusively of Americans with deep sympathy toward Italy. The curator or treasurer, instead, would be an American citizen of Italian extraction with experience in the political and economic affairs of both countries. Since you showed me a great interest in the Plan, promising you would submit it to Il Duce as soon as it was in your possession, I am sending it to you. I would like to meet Il Duce personally. Since I am leaving for the United States very soon, I could confer with him on my return to Rome within two months.

Sincerely yours,
Vincenzo Giordano

Notes

Preface

1. For a detailed analysis of Fascist organizations and nomenclature, see R. J. B. Bosworth, *Mussolini's Italy, Life Under the Fascist Dictatorship, 1915–1945*, New York, 2006. 9–149.

Chapter 1

1. E. Schuyler, "Italian Immigration Into the United States," *Political Science Quarterly* IV, Sept. 1889, 480.
2. J. J. Davis, "An American Immigration Policy," *American Federationist*, XXXI, n. 4, April 1924, 289–94. J. R. Quinn, "America and Immigration," *American Federationist*, XXXI, n. 4, April 1924, 295–99.
3. O. Handlin, *Immigration as Factor in American History* (New Jersey, 1963) 202–3. Moreover, Italian statistical data from 1908 to 1916 show that for every 100 Italians entering the United States, 412 Italians who had resided in the United States between 1 to 5 years left. This phenomenon was not restricted to the war period, since the outward trend began in 1908. Indexes as early as 1908 reported this movement: 1908 (82.6%), 1909 (80.9%), 1910 (77.8%), 1911 (78%), 1912 (72%), 1913 (67.9%), 1914 (68.9%), 1915 (81.8%), and 1916 (57.9%). Many of those who left the United States may have returned after a few months or within a couple of years. Between 1896 and 1908, about 244,236 returned to the United States. Presumably, of every five immigrants who returned to Italy, two came back to the U.S.

    According to Gino C. Speranza, Secretary of the Society for the Protection of Italian Immigrants from 1901 to 1923, the number of Italians admitted to the United States in 1920 through the Ellis Island Immigration Bureau totaled 95,145. Those departed numbered 88,909. In 1921, the number of admitted totaled 222,260, while 48,192 left. In 1923, the number of admitted totaled 40,319, while 53,651 departed, with a net loss of 13,332. See C. G. Speranza, "Correspondence and Papers, Society for Italian Immigrants, 1901–1923, Envelope, Jan.–June, 1923," New York Public Library, Manuscript Div., New York.

The *Wheeling Intelligencer* of West Virginia reported that from 1906 on many Italians departed the area, leaving employment in the Virginian mines. "Their main reason for leaving is they are afraid that the mills will be idle all winter and that hard times will be the result...At the present time, all the foreigners at New York cannot leave the country as the ships have their passenger capacity taxed to its fullest. The steamship agents hereabouts and in other towns have been informed to cease the selling of tickets, as there is no room left for the persons to be supplied with sleeping quarters on the various steamships." *Wheeling Intelligencer*, Nov. 20, 27, 1907.

4. M. T. Bennet, *American Immigration Policies*, (Washington, D.C., 1963). The author provides probably the most explicit examples of racial arguments: "The citizens of northern Italy are superior to those of southern Italy...The southern Italian is virtually an illiterate peasant. Although industrious and thrifty, he is of a culture alien to that in the United States and shows no desire to adapt himself to American culture...Immigrants from southern and eastern Europe generally are not only ignorant but their low standard of living tends to depress the American wage standard and to create slums, unemployment and crime" (p. 32).

M. Grant, *The Passing of the Great Race* (New York, 1916), *The Alien in Our Midst* (New York, 1930), and *The Conquest of the Continent* (New York, 1933). E. A. Ross, "Racial Consequences of Immigration," *Century Magazine*, 1914, 619. L. Stoddard, "The Mediterranean South," *Saturday Evening Post,* May 10, 1924, pp. 8, 198, and 206. In this article, Stoddard reaches the hasty conclusions that in all Italian movements from the Middle Ages on, the startling difference between North and South represents one of the most strikingly negative elements of Italy's socioeconomic structure: "The two halves of Italy are inhabited by very different breeds of men. The Northern half contains the best of the old Mediterranean stock, plus a strong Alpine element and a considerable leavening of Nordic blood. The Southern half is peopled by a racially impoverished Mediterranean stock, long since drained of its best strains and in places mongrelized by inferior Levantine elements."

5. A *New York Times* editorial of May 24, 1921, stated that the new immigration policy was "an expression which is intelligently and clearly conceived and is held by a large majority of the American people and of their representatives in Congress." *New York Times*, May 24, 1921, 14:4. See Archivio Centrale dello Stato, Rome, Presidenza del Consiglio dei Ministri, Gabinetto, 1921, fasc. 3/11 n. 385 and 3/16 n. 365. The Archivio Centrale dello Stato will be hereafter cited as A.C.S.

6. State architect, L. F. Pitcher, who went to Italy to inspect quarantine stations at embarkation ports, paid tribute to preventive measures taken by Italian Health Officials in Naples and Genoa. *New York Times*, May 20, 1921, 18.
7. A.C.S., Doc. cit. (see note 5).
8. H. C. Lodge, "A Million Immigrants a Year: Efforts to Restrict Undesirable Immigration," *Century Magazine*, 1904, 466–67; F. P. Sargent, "The Need of a Closer Inspection and a Greater Restriction of Immigrants," *Century Magazine*, 1904, 471–73; H. C. Lodge, "Lynch Law and Unrestricted Immigration," *North American Review*, May 1891, 602–12. "Should Immigration Be Further Restricted?" Symposium, Boston, Feb. 1896, *Donahoe's Magazine*, Feb. 1896, 125–33; W. D. Foulke, "A Word on Italian Immigration," *Outlook*, Feb. 20, 1904, 460–61; G. C. Speranza, "Solving the Immigration Problem," *Outlook*, April 16, 1904, 930–31. L. Villari, "L'Emigrazione italiana negli Stati Uniti d'America," *La Nuova Antologia*, Vol. 143, Sept. 1909, 294–311; "L'emigrazione Italiana vista dagli stranieri," *La Nuova Antologia*, Vol. 257, Feb. 16, 1928, 475–84. "L'opinione pubblica americana e i nostri emigrati," *La Nuova Antologia*, Vol. 148, Aug. 1, 1910, 497–517; P. H. Douglas, "Is the New Immigration More Unskilled Than the Old?" American Statistical Association, n. 125, March, 1919, 393–405; W. J. Lauck, "The New Immigration," *Review of Reviews*, Vol. 62, July–Dec., 1920, 618–24; L. Block, "Occupations of Immigrants Before and After Coming to the United States," *American Statistical Association*, Vol. 17, 1920–21, 750–64; J. J. Davis, "How the Immigration Laws Are Now Working," *Review of Reviews*, Vol. 65, Jan.–June, 1922, 509–11; J. M. Gillman, "Statistics and the Immigration Problem," *American Journal of Sociology*, Vol. 30, July 1924–May 1925, 29–48; E. Weare, "Our Immigration Problems," *America*, April 21, 1923, 7–9; April 28, 31–32; May 5, 55–56; A. M. Rose, "A Research Note on the Influence of Immigration on the Birth Rate," *American Journal of Sociology*, Vol. 47, 1941–42, 614–21; P. J. Campisi, "Ethnic Family Patterns: The Italian Family in the United States," *American Journal of Sociology*, Vol. 53, 1947–48, 443–49. C. E. Silberman, *Crisis in Black and White* (New York, 1964), 25. *Catholic World*, Vol. 116, Jan., 1923, 548, reported several anti-Catholic organizations forming with the purpose of further limiting immigration. These organizations maintained that, on the whole, immigration to the United States favored Catholics, and for them this was a sufficient reason to limit it.
9. *New York Times*, May 13, 1921, 4:6.

214   FASCIST AND ANTI-FASCIST PROPAGANDA IN AMERICA

10. Those who returned to Italy after emigrating to the United States in the first two decades of 1900 took home an estimated average of 1,000 to 5,000 lire per person. In comparison, those returning to Italy from European countries carried a mere 300 to 500 lire per capita. The comparison illustrates the important economic and financial contributions funding Italy from overseas. Vincenzo Tangorra, Finance Minister under Mussolini, offered the following assessment of Italy's financial situation from 1918 to 1922: in 1918, 7 billion; in 1920, 27 billion; and in 1921, 15 billion. During this period, the government faced severe unemployment in the "Terre Redente." See A.C.S. *Presidenza Consiglio dei Ministri, 1920–21, Gabinetto*, Fascicoli, 7/1, n. 94, 1921 and 7/1, n. 290, 1921.

11. The memorandum is in A.C.S., Rome, *Pres. Con. Min, 1921, Gabinetto*, fast. 13/4 n. 687. The General Commissariat for Emigration was instituted by law in 1901, by Visconti Venosta, who was at that time Minister of Foreign Affairs. Royal decree came first on Nov. 13, 1913, n. 2205, and was converted into law on April 17, 1925, n. 473, in which the powers and functions of the General Commissariat for Emigration were clearly defined. It is worth mentioning Article 81 "In those States where Italian migration is directed, will be instituted, in accord with other governments, offices of protection, information and possible employment. See V. De Martino, *Leggi di Uso Comune* (Rome, 1958), Vol. III, 2677–2692.

For more on price indexes see the interesting essay by A. Tenderini, *Analisi sui Prezzi in Italia dal 1901 al 1932* (Padova, 1936) and G. A. Tesoro, "The Bankruptcy of Fascist Economy through the Eyes of Italian Economists," *Rivista Internazionale di Scienze Economiche e Commerciali*, XIII, Aug. 1966, n. 8, 714–41.

12. A.C.S., Doc. cit. (see note 10).

13. A.C.S., Doc. cit. (see note 10).

14. A.C.S., Dispatches of May 21 and 26, 1921. The dispatches bore Giolitti's and Berio's signatures.

15. *Il Giornale d'Italia*, September 26, 1922, 1. Argentina Altobelli, a reformist socialist, and Benito Mussolini, a revolutionary socialist, were two influential members of the Socialist Party. Both took part in the agrarian class conflicts of 1910 in Romagna. In 1922, Altobelli wrote a profile of Mussolini's personality in her article "Fascista Proletario." She described Mussolini as ambitious, impetuous, revolutionary, and a supporter of violence. See Michelangelo Ingrassia, "Argentina Altobelli, Politica e Sindacato dal Risorgimento al Fascismo," *Rassegna Storica del Risorgimento*, Anno XCIV, Fascicolo II, Aprile-Giugno 2007, 244–275.

16. *Il Giornale d'Italia*, September 27, 1922, 6. On Fascist burning and destruction of cooperatives and Popular and Socialist associations, see *Fascismo, A Socialist Inquiry into Fascist Operations in Italy* (Milan, 1963).
17. Paratore issued a report on March 1, 1922, on Italy's economic condition. Associazione Bancaria Italiana followed with another report on August 2, 1922. A.C.S., Presidenza Consiglio dei Ministri, Gabinetto, 1922, Fasc. 1/3–4, n. 578 and 185/5, n. 1362.
18. A.C.S. *Presidenza Consiglio, Gabinetto*, Fasc. 2/29 n. 2474, 1922.
19. Ibid.
20. Ibid.
21. See note 15.
22. L. Salvatorelli, *Nazionalfascismo* (Turin, 1923), 16–20. For the programmatic fluctuations of Fascism, see M. Vinciguerra, *Il Fascismo visto da un solitario* (Turin, 1923), 19, 27, and 28.
23. G. DeMaria, "L'Origine e la Genesi dei Movimenti Fascista e Nazista nelle Intuizioni di un Economista del Tempo," *Rivista Internazionale di Scienze Economiche e Commerciali*, XIII, n. 8, Aug. 1966, 709–13.
24. F. S. Nitti, *Bolscevismo, Fascismo e Democrazia* (New York, 1927), 46–47; and *The Decadence of Europe* (New York, 1923).
25. G. A. Chiurco, *Storia della Rivoluzione Fascista*, 1919. (Florence, 1929), Vol. 3, 468–70.
26. F. Turati and A. Kuliscioff, *Carteggio*, Vol. 5 (*Dopoguerra e Fascismo*, 1919–22), (Turin, 1953), 576 and 582.
27. A. Tasca, *The Rise of Italian Fascism* (New York, 1966), 89.
28. G. Salvemini, "The Problem of Italian Over-population," *Contemporary Review,* Vol. CXXXIV, 1928, 708–15; and *Mussolini Diplomatico* (Bari, 1952), 157–74.
29. Highlights from these magazines appear in a set entitled "La cultura italiana del '900 attraverso le riviste,'" (Turin, 1960–1963). The following volumes are now available: Vol. I, *Leonardo, Hermes, e Il Regno,* introductory note by D. Frigessi; Vol. III, *LaVoce,* introductory note by A. Romano'; Vol. IV, *Lacerba e La Voce Politica,* introductory note by G. Scalia; Vol. V, *L'Unita' e La Voce politica,* introductory note by F. Golzio and A. Guerra; and Vol. VI, *L'Ordine Nuovo,* introductory note by P. Spriano. On the crisis of postunification Italy, see analysis by R. DeMattei, *Dal Trasformismo al Socialismo* (Florence, 1940), especially Chapter I and Appendixes I and II: "Cultura e letteratura anti-democratiche dopo l'unificazione."

A vast literature exists on the position held by the Socialist and Catholic parties during the downfall of Liberalism. Nevertheless, the majority of historians see Socialist-Catholic collaboration as the only

valid alternative to Fascism. The two parties, although divided by heterogeneous ideologies, had a common denominator in that they referred
to popular masses as their main political stream. On the advent of Fascism as consequence of a "crise de paresse," especially on the part of
the Socialist Party, see R. Mondolfo, *Il Fascismo ed i Partiti Politici*
(Bologna, 1922), I–XXV.

30. E. R. Tannenbaum, "The Goals of Italian Fascism," *American Historical
Review*, Vol. LXXI, n. 4 (April 1969), 1183–1204. On the lost generation complex, it seems that Tannenbaum's analysis of early Fascism
reflects that of Anna Kuliscioff of almost fifty years ago. See note 26.

31. C. Giglio, *Mercantilismo* (Padua, 1940), 119–22: F. Carli, *Le Basi
Storiche e Dottrinali della Economia Corporativa* (Padua, 1938).

32. On the matter of Fascist dissent (*dissidentismo fascista*), see A.C.S,
Ministero dell'Interno. Direzione generale di P.S. Div. aff. gen. e ris.,
1924, busta 86. Especially the enclosed buste: Pavia (C. Forni's dissent),
Naples (A. Padovani's dissent), Rome (Gino Calza-Bini's dissent,
and the committee led by Luigi Reni and Fossi Camillo), Perugia
(A. Misuri's dissent) and his program Per la Riconstruzione Nazionale
(Rome, 1923). Moreover, for a national outlook on Fascist dissent, see
the well-documented letter sent by the Prefect of Naples D'Adamo on
March 9, 1924, (*Ministero dell'Interno, Direzione Generale di P.S. Div.
Affari gen. e ris.*). The letter addresses "Gruppi ed associazioni effimere
in margine e contro il partito fascista."

33. *Il Cannocchiale*, nn. 1–3, 1966, 85–113. The proceedings of the
symposium held on the occasion of the publication of Aquarone's book
L'Organizzazione dello Stato Totalitario (Turin, 1965). Participants
R. Romeo, F. Gaeta, P. Ungari, R. DeFelice, C. Paone, A. Aquarone,
and A. Riosa seem to agree that Fascism never carried on a revolution. Rather, Fascism established in Italy a police state ruled by self-
appointed leader Mussolini. F. Chabod, *L'Italia contemporanea,
1918–1948* (Turin, 1961), 63.

34. B. Mussolini, *Discorsi Politici* (Milan, 1928), Vol. 1, 154.

35. Ibid., 318.

36. *Congressional Record, Proceedings and Debates of the First Session of
the 68th Congress*, Vol. LXV, Part 6, 5855–57.

37. Telegram Gab. S. 1011–188 from Washington, July 3, 1924, 19:40 p.m.
in *I Documenti Diplomatici Italiani, Settima Seria, 1922–25*, (Rome,
1959), Vol. 3, 207–8.

38. B. Mussolini, *Discorsi Politici, 1924* (Milan, 1924), Vol. III, 584f.
According to Damiani, the advent of Mussolini in Italy must be
interpreted within the context of a double crisis, crisis of the democratic

institutions and the parallel crisis of the economic system (p. 7). As far as the Quota Acts of 1921 and 1924, Damiani concludes: "The Johnson Act signified the end of the Italian mass emigration and the beginning of a new Italian strategy based on three objectives: (1) Diligent use of natural resources; (2) Opening of Italian emigration to new countries and (3) Colonization of new territories through protected emigration (Emigrazione Tutelata)" in Claudia Damiani, *Mussolini e Gli Stati Uniti 1922–1935*, Casa Editrice Cappelli, Bologna 1980, p. 7 and Chapter III, pp. 31–71.

In examining my essay on the Quota Act, published in *Gli Italiani negli Stati Uniti* (Firenze, 1970), Gian Giacomo Migone writes that "the international context was such to produce a crisis of the liberal system and favor the advent of Fascism in Italy" in *Gli Stati Uniti e il Fascismo, Alle Origini Dell'Egemonia Americana in Italia*, Editore Feltrinelli, Milano, 1980, pp. 47–48.

On the issue of economic conditions and unemployment in Italy up to 1930, see Gaetano Salvemini, *Under the Axe of Fascism*, Howard Fertig, New York, 1969 pp. 220–73.

A. James Gregor, *Italian Fascism and Developmental Dictatorship*, Princeton University Press, 1979, Chapter V: Alfredo Rocco, Nationalism and the Economic Policy of Fascism; Fascist Economic Policy from 1922 until the Great Depression and Fascist Economic Policy after the Great Depression, pp. 133–71.

On the Quota Act and the Fascist Emigration see Monte S. Finkelstein. "The Johnson Act, Mussolini and Fascist Emigration Policy: 1921–1930," *Journal Of American Ethnic History*, n.1, August 1988, pp. 38–55.

39. C. A. Tesoro, op. cit., 730–32; E. Di Nolfo, *Mussolini e la Politica Estera Italiana, 1919–1933* (Padua, 1960), 139–206: G. Salvemini, *Mussolini Diplomatico*, see note 28.

CHAPTER 2

1. *La Stampa Unita*, April 27, 1923, 6. On the role of the Italians in America, see De Ritis, "Gl'Italiani in America," *La Stampa*, September 26, 1924. The article was translated into English and appeared in *Living Age*, November 22, 1924, 423–26. On the issue of Italian national identity and consciousness among Italian-Americans, Gaetano Salvemini wrote that "national consciousness awoke in them when they came in touch (which often meant to blows) with groups of different national origins in America. Italy became in their mind a land of whose past glories they felt proud." See Gaetano Salvemini, *Italian Fascist Activities in*

the United States, edited with introduction by Philip V. Cannistraro, Center for Migration History, New York, 1977, p. 4.

Also, John Patrick Diggins writes: "Psychologically the Italian immigrant was conditioned to respond positively to Fascism even before Mussolini's regime dazzled his mind. Doubtless, Fascist propaganda provided the fertilizer, but American society had planted the seed...Despite protests on the part of educated Italians, the ugly, stereotyped impressions persisted since they were deeply ingrained in the anxious minds of rural, native, Protestant Americans who felt threatened by the inundation of an alien canaille." See J. P. Diggins, *Mussolini and Fascism, The View From America,* Princeton University Press, 1972, pp. 79–81.

2. *New York Times*, January 14, 1923, 2:2.
3. *New York Times*, January 24, 1923, 3:6.
4. *New York Times*, March 21, 1923, 20:1.
5. *New York Times*, March 21, 1923, 20:2.
6. *New York Times*, March 21, 1923, 20:2.
7. Mario Missiroli, *What Italy Owes to Mussolini* (Rome, 1937), 194.
8. Benito Mussolini, *Opera Omnia*. Edited by Eduardo and Duilio Susmel (32 Vols., Florence, 1951–61), XIX, 406, hereafter cited as OO.
9. *Il Gran Consiglio del Fascismo nei Primi Cinque Anni dell'Era Fascista,* (Rome-Milan, 1927), 11–14. OO., XIX, 141. For goals of Fascism in foreign countries, see Appendix I. See, also, Salvemini's *Italian Fascist Activities in the United States,* containing the dispositions issued by Mussolini on January 28, 1928, for all Fascists living abroad, pp. 57–58. According to Cannistraro (note 1), "The regulations for the fasci abroad cited by Salvemini conform in their essential points to the statement issued by the Fascist Grand Council in Rome on July 28, 1923."
10. Caetani to Mussolini, *Estratto di Rapporto della Regia Ambasciata Italiana in Washington,* January 18, 1923, n. 396/74, *Italian Foreign Minister Documents.* T.586, roll 429, nn. 014592–93. United States National Archives and Record Services, Washington, D.C., hereafter cited as I.F.M.D.
11. Telegram Caetani to Mussolini, January 28, 1923, n. 58. I.F.M.D. nn. 014646–47. The issue was presented again to Mussolini in a telegram sent on March 20, 1923. I.F.M.D. n. 014630.

CHAPTER 3

1. Memorandum from Caetani to Mussolini, March 22, 1923, n. 1253/230 I.F.M.D. nn. 014606–12; telegram on the same day, n. 1416 I.F.M.D. nn. 014631–32.

2. *New York Call*, Editorials of March 29, 1920 ("The Invisible Empire of Albany"); March 30, 1920 ("Hist: the Revolution of 1922"); March 31, 1920 ("The Report of the Notorious Seven"); April 22, 1920 ("Anti-Socialist Bills Pass"); April 23, 1920 ("Cultivating the Red Terror"); and May 24, 1920 ("Fusion to Beat the Socialists"). Marcus Duffield, "Mussolini's American Empire," *Harper's Magazine*, November 1929, Vol. 159, 661–72. *Congressional Record, Proceedings and Debates*, Vol. LXXI, Part 5, 4921.

3. See note 1. In *Blackshirts in Little Italy, Italian Americans and Fascism, 1921–1929*, (Bordighera Press, Purdue University, 1999), Cannistraro writes that Agostino De Biasi, Umberto Menicucci, and G. Passamonti were the three individuals who signed the telegram sent to Mussolini on March 2, 1921, before the March on Rome. Cannistraro states that De Biasi should be considered the pioneer and the founder, or one of the founders, of Fascism in New York and that "Mussolini's reaction to the Fasci in the United States indicates that it was the American experience that shaped his general policy toward the Fasci abroad." Cannistraro concludes that "The De Biasi story is a revealing perspective from which to examine the general history of Italian American Fascism." pp. 8–23 and passim.

4. *New York Times*, March 26, 1923, 3:2.

5. *New York Times*, March 30, 1923, 14:3.

6. *New York Herald*, March 20, 1923, 1 and 6.

7. August R. Odgen, *The Dies Committee: A Study of the Special House Committee for the Investigation of Un-American Activities, 1938–1944* (Washington, 1945). J. M. Dies, *The Trojan Horse in America* (New York, 1940). See particularly Chapter XXVII, "Mussolini's Trojan Horse in America," 332–46.

8. Alan Cassels, "Fascism for Export: Italy and the United States in the Twenties," *American Historical Review*, LXIX, April 1964, 708–10, and *Mussolini's Early Diplomacy* (New Jersey, 1970), 194–98.

9. *Papers Related to the Foreign Relations of the United States, 1928*, Vol. 3 (Washington, 1943), 112.

10. "Italy's Black-Shirt Government," *Literary Digest*, November 11, 1922, 20.

11. Benito Mussolini, "Primo dell'Anno, Prima Divagazione," *Il Popolo d'Italia*, January 1, 1920.

12. Benito Mussolini, "Il Nostro Mito," *Il Popolo d'Italia*, July 5, 1922.

13. Enrico Corradini, "Nostri Maestri," and "Per Coloro che non Credono," *Il Popolo d'Italia*, May 17, 1923, and February 12, 1924; and, "Italian Imperialist Doctrine," *Living Age*, March 1924, 403–5. Later, Perfetti Francesco analyzed the myth of Italian Imperialism with reference to the doctrine of Italian Nationalism in "Il Mito Imperialista e il Nazionalismo

Italiano," *Storia e Politica* (January–March 1971) 98–111. The author compares Theodore Roosevelt's doctrine of economic expansion to that of Italian Nationalism.

14. Ibid.

15. Telegram, Caetani to Mussolini, March 24, 1923, n. 1462 I.F.M.D. n. 014628.

16. Ward J. Price, *I Know These Dictators* (New York, 1938), 190.

17. Telegram, Caetani to Mussolini, April 14, 1923, n. 1605/298 I.F.M.D. n. 014620.

18. Caetani to Mussolini, *Memorandum*, April 6, 1923, n. 1454/275 I.F.M.D. nn. 014616–18.

19. Mussolini to Caetani, April 12, 1923, n. 3584, I.F.M.D. n. 014623.

20. Child to State, *Confidential Report*, Rome, May 15, 1923, Archives of the Department of State, Washington, D.C., Decimal File 811.00F/1. The Archives of the State Department will be hereafter cited as U.S.D.S. The document is reported in Appendix II.

21. Fletcher to State, *Confidential Dispatch*, Rome, May 9, 1924, U.S.D.S., Decimal File 811.00F/12. See Appendix I.

22. 00, Vol. XIX, 289.

23. Mussolini to Vittorio Emanuele III, Rome, June 29, 1923, *I Documenti Diplomatici Italiani, Settima Serie: 1922–35,* Vol. 2, 68–69. For diplomatic developments of the King's visit to the United States, see Alexander De Conde, *Half-Bitter, Half-Sweet: An Excursion in Italian-American History* (New York, 1971), 186–87.

24. 00., Vol. XX, 157.

25. 00., Vol. XX, 188.

26. Mussolini to Caetani, Rome, February 3, 1924, *I Documenti Diplomatici Italiani,* Settima Serie: 1922–35, Vol. 2, 428. "As Italy Sees the Shattered Entente," *Literary Digest,* February 10, 1923, 23.

27. 00., Vol. XX, 181.

28. Alexander De Conde, (*Half-Bitter*), 182.

29. *Times*, March 3, 1923, 9.

30. The article published in the newspaper *Impero* was reprinted in *La Stampa Unita,* April 27, 1923, 6.

31. H. H. Maxwell Macartney and Paul Cremona, *Italy's Foreign and Colonial Policy, 1914–1937* (New York, 1938); Muriel I. Currey, *Italian Foreign Policy, 1918–1912* (London, 1932); and Luigi Villari, *Italian Foreign Policy Under Mussolini* (New York, 1956). On Italian-American relations from 1922 to 1940, see two Ph.D. dissertations: Belleri Claudia, *Le Relazioni fra l'Italia e Stati Uniti dal 1922 al*

1933 and Di Felice Anna, *Rapporti Italo-Statunitensi nella questione adriatica secondo i documenti diplomatici italiani.* Both works, supervised by the late Professor Mario Toscano, were presented to the Facoltá di Scienze Politiche at the University of Rome, Italy.

CHAPTER 4

1. *I Documenti Diplomatici Italiani, Settima Serie, 1922–1935*, vol. 3, 160.
2. *I Documenti Diplomatici Italiani, Settima Serie, 1922–1935*, vol. 3, 163.
3. *I Documenti Diplomatici Italiani, Settima Serie, 1922–1935*, vol. 3, 182.
4. *New York Times*, June 27, 1924, 21:7.
5. *Saturday Evening Post*, June 26, pp. 1, 2, 156, and 158; July 12, pp. 5, 55, 56, 57, and 58: July 26, pp. 23, 87, 88 and 90, 1924.
6. *Documenti Diplomatici Italiani, Settima Serie, 1922–1935*, vol. 3, 201.
7. *New York Times*, June 29, 1924, 4:6, and June 26, 1924, 22:2.
8. *Outlook*, July 2, 1924, 340–41 and 348–51.
9. *Outlook*, August 6, 1924, 538–39.
10. *Literary Digest*, July 5, 1924, 18.
11. *Current History Magazine*, August, 1924, 858–59.
12. *Nation*, July 30, 1924, 114–15.
13. *Current History Magazine*, September, 1924, 1029–31.
14. *Literary Digest,* August 9, 1924, 16–17, and September 13, 1924, 21.
15. *Il Martello*, December 5, 1925, 1. Gaetano Salvemini made a significant contribution to the condemnation of Fascism and Mussolini's responsibility for the brutal assassination of Giacomo Matteotti. See Chapter V, "The Matteotti Murder" and Appendix: *The Finzi Memorandum in the Fascist Dictatorship in Italy,* Holt, Rinehart and Winston, (1927) reprinted by Howard Fertig (1967) pp. 231–319. *Luigi Sturzo, Italy and Fascism,* translated by Barbara Barclay Carter, Farber and Gwyer, New York, 1926, reprinted by Howard Fertig, New York, 1967, Chapter VII, "The Murder of Matteotti," pp. 177–86. J. P. Diggins writes that the murder of Giacomo Matteotti "caused an emotional earthquake throughout the little Italys in the United States." Op. cit, p. 121.
16. *Il Lavoratore*, July 1, 1924.
17. *Il Popolo*, May 9, 1925, 3.
18. *Unione Figli D'Italia*, August 24, 1925.
19. *Il Corriere del Popolo*, July 24, 1925.
20. Ministero dell'Interno, Dir. Gen., P.S. Div., AA.GG. e Riser., 1924, Cartella 86, Cat. F.4. *Stampe Sovversive Provenienti dall'Estero.*

21. Giacomo Di Tella to Mussolini, *A Letter From Pueblo, Colorado*, June 10, 1923. I.F.M.D. n. 3262, 014661–64. Vanni Buscemi Montana, *Amarostico, Testimonianze Euro-Americane*, Prefazione di Aldo Garosci, Bastogi Editore, Livorno, 1975. In his memoirs, Montana reports on the role, the activities and the leaders of the anti-fascist organizations of the United States. Also, Montana recalls the visit of Giuseppe Emanuele Modigliani and his wife Vera to the United States from France for the celebration of the 15th anniversary of the foundation of the Local 89 of the International Ladies' Garment Workers Union (p. 156).

According to Garosci, Montana's memoirs contain significant, direct and personal recollections of facts and events along with some important unpublished documents.

22. *New York Times*, June 30, 1924, 14:7.

23. *New York Times*, July 4, 1924, 6:7.

24. *Il Lavoratore* covered the anti-Fascist meetings and demonstrations extensively. See: July 1924, issues: 1, 17, 19, 23, 24, 25, 28.

25. *New York Times*, July 27, 1924, 31:4.

26. *New York Times*, November 21, 1924, 21:4.

27. *New York Times*, January 12, 1925, 15:2.

28. For the mentioned articles, see *Il Progresso Italo-Americano*, December 28 and 30, 1923; July 5, 6, 13, 16, 18, and August 5, 10, 1924.

29. *La Stampa Unita*, May 15, 1925, 1.

30. *Il Lavoratore*, October 25, 1924, 2.

31. *New York Times*, October 1, 1925, 2. The following authors have covered in a comprehensive and detailed analysis Mussolini's foreign policy in the 1920s and 1930s: Gaetano Salvemini, *Mussolini Diplomatico*, Laterza, Bari, 1952, pp. 14, 43, 58, 147–56 (Chapter X, Il viaggio verso l'avvenire) and 157–74; (Chapter XII, Espandersi o esplodere) and p. 538. Ennio Di Nolfo, *Mussolini e la Politica Estera Italiana* (1919–1933) Cedam, Padova, 1960, Chapter 4 ("Politica dell'Espansione, dal Mediterraneo alla penisola balcanica") pp. 139–206.

Claudia Damiani, *Mussolini e Gli Stati Uniti, 1922–1935,* Cappelli Editore, Bologna, 1980, Chapter IV ("La Corsa ai Petroli Albanesi"), pp. 74–95. Gian Giacomo Micone, *Gli Stati Uniti e Il Fascismo, alle Origini dell'Egemonia Americana in Italia*, Feltrinelli Editore, Milano, 1980, pp. 81–216.

32. *New York Times*, October 30, 1925, 20:5.

33. *New York Times,* November 8, 1925, 14:5.

CHAPTER 5

1. Memorandum for the Secretary of State, December 27, 1929. U.S.D.S., 811.00F/89; *New York Times,* October 30, 1925, 20:5.

2. *La Stampa Unita,* March 25 and April 6, 1923. The quotation appeared in the April 6 issue.
3. *Il Corriere di Syracuse,* February 6, 1923.
4. Ibid., November 17, 1922.
5. Ibid., December 8, 1922.
6. Ibid., January 5, 1923.
7. Ibid., January 28, 1923.
8. Ibid., February 24, 1924.
9. Giuseppe Sposato, *Fiamme* (Syracuse, 1935), pp. 34 and 45. The poems printed in Appendix III have been translated by the author.
10. Ministero degli Affari Esteri, Gabinetto del Ministro, *Memorandum from the Italian Embassy to Mussolini,* July 28, 1923, I.F.M.D., nn. 014665–71.
11. On the activities of Luigi Borgo, see memos sent to Dino Grandi, through the Italian Consul in Philadelphia, August and September 1925, I.F.M.D., 014733–34.
12. See note 10.
13. Caetani to Mussolini, memorandum, March 27, 1924, U.S.D.A., nn. 014720–27. Frank S. Brunelli's explanatory letter in Italian was attached to the memorandum, which contained a copy of the *Certificate of Incorporation.* The Certificate of Incorporation appears in Appendix IV. For information on Paterson as a center of radicalism, see "L'assassinio di Umberto I e gli Anarchici di Paterson," by L. V. Ferraris, *Rassegna Storica del Risorgimento,* Anno LV, January–March, 1968, 47–64.
14. See note 10.
15. Ibid.
16. Memorandum from the Italian Embassy to Mussolini, probably composed in early 1925. I.F.M.D., nn. 014728–33.
17. See note 10.
18. Ibid.
19. Ibid.
20. Ibid.
21. Ibid.
22. Ibid.
23. Ibid.
24. P.N.F., *Il Gran Consiglio Nei Primi Cinque Anni Dell' Era Fascista* (Rome, 1927), 76–77.
25. *New York Times,* May 31, and June 2, 1927.
26. Memorandum from De Martino to Benito Mussolini, October 1, 1926, I.F.M.D., 014844–48: Agostino De Biasi to Mussolini, July 26, 1926, and nn. 014850–51.
27. Caetani to Mussolini, October 13, 1923, I.F.M.D., nn. 014676–95.
28. Consul Ferrante to De Martino, I.F.M.D., March 17, 1926, nn. 014739–763.

29. Caetani to Mussolini, January 13, 1923, I.F.M.D., nn. 014598–604.
30. See note 1.

CHAPTER 6

1. "Our Black Shirts and the Reds," *Literary Digest,* April 7, 1923, 16–18.
2. Telegram, Caetani to Mussolini, February 2, 1923, n. 717, I.F.M.D., n. 014644. On the Caetani-Bastianini conflict and the role played by De Biasi considered "destroyer of ambassadors" see Cannistraro's *Blackshirts in Little Italy, Italian Americans and Fascism, 1921–1929*, pp. 32–71.
3. Telegram, Caetani to Mussolini, February 6, 1923, n. 141, I.F.M.D., n. 014629.
4. Telegram, Caetani to Mussolini, February 18, 1923, n. 716, I.F.M.D., n. 014643.
5. Mussolini to Caetani, February 24,. 1923, n. 582, I.F.M.D., n. 014642.
6. See the above-mentioned telegrams of February 2, 6, and 18, 1923. See also the decoded telegrams from Washington, n. 1067, March 1, 1923, and n. 1069, March 3, 1923, I.F.M.D., nn. 014636–37.
7. Barone Russo to Bastianini, Ministero Affari Esteri, n. 547/15, February 25, 1923, and n. 736/22, March 7, 1923, I.F.M.D., nn. 014641 and 014634–35.
8. Bastianini to Russo, February 27, 1923, n. 1179–74, I.F.M.D., n. 014640.
9. Mussolini to Ambasciata Italiana in Washington, March 3, 1923, n. 700, I.F.M.D., n. 014639.
10. Caetani to Mussolini, Fasci Negli Stati Uniti, November 26, 1923, n. 4069/769, I.F.M.D., nn. 014696–014700.
11. Ibid.
12. *New York Times*, January 21, 1923, 16:4.
13. Ibid.
14. *New York Times,* June 22, 1924, VIII, 12:8.
15. "Italy's Economic Reconstruction," and "Caetani Explains Italy's Recovery," *New York Times,* March 20, 1924, 18:4 and 19:4.
16. Memorandum to Mussolini from New York (unsigned), April 3, 1923, I.F.M.D., n. 014651.
17. Memorandum to Mussolini from New York (unsigned), April 6, 1923, I.F.M.D., n. 014652–53.
18. Molossi to Mussolini, memorandum, New York, June 6, 1923, n. 3011, nn. 014655–014660.

19. Caetani to Bastianini, telegram, Washington, September 29, 1923, n. 3874/654, I.F.M.D., nn. 014672–014675.
20. Ibid.
21. Telegram, Mussolini to Pugliese, September 29, 1923, I.F.M.D., n. 014675.
22. Caetani to Mussolini, memorandum, February 29, 1924, n. 991/67, I.F.M.D., nn. 014826–014830.
23. Letter from Bastianini to Mussolini, March 24, 1924, n. 1179/74, nn. 014713–014719.
24. *Il Lavoratore*, July 25, 1924, p. 1.

CHAPTER 7

1. Ministero Affari Esteri, Gabinetto del Ministro, doc. 3416, July 29, 1923, I.F.M.D., nn. 014665–71.
2. *New York Herald*, March 22, 1923, 4.
3. *New York Herald*, March 23, 1923, 3.
4. *New York Herald*, March 31, 1923, 9.
5. *New York Herald*, March 22, 1923, 4.
6. "Senator Cotillo Is a Duce," editorial by C. G. Lanni, *La Stampa Unita*, April 20, 1923, 1.
7. *New York Times*, January 21, 1923, 16:4.
8. *Literary Digest*, April 7, 1923, 16–18.
9. "Fascists in the United States," *Nation*, April 25, 1923, 502–3.
10. *New York Times*, February 17, 1925, 312.
11. "Does Mussolini Rule U.S.,?" *New Leader*, February 2, 1924.
12. "Carlo Tresca Enters Jail; Declared Fascist Victim," "The Tresca Case," and "Carlo Tresca Home From Jail," *New Leader*, January 6, February 21, and May 16, 1925.
13. *New York Times*, February 18, 1925, 2:7.
14. Girolamo Valenti, "A Bit of Fascism in America," *New Leader*, July 11, 1925.
15. "Our Fascist Bullies," *New Leader*, July 12, 1925.
16. "America. Where Mussolini Rules," *New Leader*, August 22, 1925.
17. "Does Mussolini Rule Here?" (Editorial), *New Leader*, August 27, 1925.
18. "Berger Hits At Fascism," *New Leader,* January 30, 1926.
19. The Declaration was signed by the following political and union leaders: Carlo Tresca, Pietro Allegra, Alberto Guabello, Alberto Pullini, Gerolamo Valenti, Gioacchino Artoni, Eduardo Molisan, J. La Rosa, Natale Cuneo, J. S. Cavallo, G. Cannata, Luigi Quintiliano, Francesca

Coco, Enea Sormenti, Giuseppe Artieri, Francesca Canvellieri, Arturo Giovannitti, Luigi Antonini, Giuseppe Genovese, Brutus Pertiboni, Leonardo Frisina. "Thousands in America Renounce Mussolini's Italy: Brigand of Predappio We Toss It at Your Feet," *New Leader*, March 27, 1926.

20. "Usurers Love Fascism," *New Leader*, January 30, 1926.
21. "St. Benito and St. Nick," *New Leader*, March 28, 1926.
22. "The Why Of Fascism," (Editorial), *New Leader*, May 22, 1926.
23. "Mussolini," *New Leader*, July 31, 1926.
24. Adam Coaldigger, "The Why Of Fascism," *New Leader*, May 27, 1926.
25. Attilio Tamaro, Venti Anni di Storia, 1922–1943 (Rome, 1953), Vol. 2, 97–98.
26. "Il Manifesto degli Intellettuali Antifascisti," in Paolo Alatri, *L'Antifascismo Italiano* (Rome, 1961), 407–12.
27. "The Manifesto of the North American Anti-Fascist Alliance," *Il Nuovo Mondo* of New York, August 26, 1926, p. 3., Rome, Archivio Centrale dello Stato, Ministero dell'Interno, Dir. Gen., P S., AA.GG. and Riser, 1924, Cartella 85–86 Cat. F.4, "Stampe Sovversive Provenienti dall'Estero." Translated by the author. A preliminary version of the Manifesto appeared in *Labor History*, Vol. 13, No. 3, Summer 1972, 418–26. Reprinted by permission, *Labor History*.
28. "Anti-Fascist Split," *New Leader*, July 31, 1926.
29. "Anti-Mussolini Group Forming," and "New Anti-Fascist Alliance Bars Communists," *New Leader*, August 7 and 14, 1926.
30. "Anti-Fascist Group Formed," *New Leader*, September 4, 1926.
31. "Italian Socialists Here Explain Organization Of New Anti-Fascists," *New Leader*, September 4, 1926.

CHAPTER 8

1. "Memoranda sent by two Italian-American doctors from New York and Chicago to Mussolini," May 1924, I.F.M.D., nn. 014736–38. In August 1923, the Anti-Fascist Workers Alliance of North America (*Alleanza Operaia del Nord America*) changed its name to the Anti-Fascist Alliance of North America (*L'Alleanza Antifascista del Nord America*), AFANA. Moreover, the Fascist Central Committee (*Consiglio Centrale Fascista*) became the Fascist League of North America, FLNA. See J. P. Diggins, op. cit., 37–47 and 59–62. Also see Appendix II in this book.
2. *New York Call*, June 30, 1922.
3. *Il Lavoratore*, November 12, 1924.

4. Ibid., November 20, 1924.

5. Ibid., July 17, 1924, p. 3. The Manifesto is signed by Enea Sormenti.

6. Ibid., July 17, 1924, p. 3. The document is signed by the Committee for the Diffusion of *Il Lavoratore*.

7. Ibid., October 11, 1924. However, protests continued through 1930.

8. Ibid., July 29, 1924. The appeal is signed by the Workers of the Communist Party of America.

9. Ibid., October 9 and 10, 1924. Serrati's articles "Toward the End of Fascism," appeared as an editorial.

10. Ibid., November 12, 1924, p. 3.

11. Ibid., July 19, 1924.

12. Ibid., July 24, 1924.

13. Ibid., July 20, 1924.

14. Ibid., July 24, 1924.

15. Ibid., July 25, 1924.

16. *Il Lavoratore* and *Daily Worker*, October 25, 1924.

17. "Camorra Consolare Fascista," and "Al Console Rappresentante di Mussolini," *Il Lavoratore*, July 19 and 24, 1924.

18. Ibid., July 18 and 21, 1924.

19. Ibid., October 9, 1924.

20. Ibid., October 9, 1924.

21. Ibid., November 20 and 22, 1924, Editorials: "Dedicato al Console Italiano di Chicago, Comm. Zunini," and "Al Console Italiano L. Zunini."

22. *San Francisco Chronicle*, November 4, 1922.

23. "American Friends of Italian Liberties," Letter of protest, May 3, 1929, U.S.D.S., 811.00F/57, file no. 702.6511/697.

24. *Christian Science Monitor,* June 4, 1929. For the governmental investigation, see U.S.D.S., 811.00F/62 and 811.00F/64.

25. *New York Herald Tribune*, November 19, 1929.

26. Confidential Conversation with the Italian Ambassador, November 19, 1929, U.S.D.S., 811.00F/84.

27. Confidential dispatch from Rome to the Secretary of State, December 7, 1929, U.S.D.S., 811.00F/103, and Memorandum for the Secretary, from Mr. Cotton, December 27, 1929, U.S.D.S., 811.00F/89.

28. Dispatch #875: Carosso, Severino et al. U.S.D.S., 811.00F/18.

29. *New York Times,* May 31, 1927, 1:7.

30. Castle's Memorandum to De Martino, June 17, 1929, U.S.D.S., 811.00F/281/8. The document appears in full in Appendix VI.

31. *New York Herald Tribune,* May 17, 1929. "City Trust Crash Linked to Drug Case Blackmail," by M.Jay Racusin.

32. Ibid., May 18, 1929, "Court Holds Two for Contempt in City Trust Crash," by M.J. Racusin, p. 2.
33. Italia, *Bulletin Bimensuel d'Information*, Edite par la Concentration Antifasciste Italianne, Paris, June 30, 1929.

CHAPTER 9

1. "Modigliani, Italian Socialist Hero, Arrives Here Tuesday," *New Leader*, November 24, 1934.
2. Vera Modigliani, *Esilio* (Milan, 1946), 245.
3. Modigliani contributed 13 articles to the *New Leader* from June 1927 to October 1938. They all dealt with Fascism and Mussolini's methods in Italy. "Fascist Charter Adds Industrial Slavery to its Political Tyranny," June 14, 1927; "Dictator Mussolini Consolidates Power at Home by Decrees Aimed at Professional Classes," March 17, 1928; "A Would-Be Assassin," November 27, 1929; "Italian Socialist Unity," August 23, 1930; "The Blackshirts Tribunal," September 27, 1930; "The Fascist Trade Unionism," October 4, 1930; "While the Planes Soar, Italy Falls," February 28, 1931; "The Vatican and Fascism," June 27, 1931; "A Great Financial Operation," November 28, 1931; "Filippo Turati-Herald of New Italy," April 23, 1932; "And Meanwhile the Horrors of Italian Fascism Go on," December 29, 1934; "Fascist Italy on the Brink of Complete Economic Ruin," April 17, 1936; "Duce Launches Jew-Baiting Drive to Cover Wide Internal Fascist Chaos," October 15, 1938. The 13 articles on Modigliani's visit to the United States can be read in their entirety in P. Nazzaro, "Modigliani's Visit to the United States and the Origins of the American Labor Party," *Rivista di Studi Politici Internazionali*, Anno LII (1985), n. 206, 241–78.
4. "Modigliani Urges Labor Party," *New Leader*, December 8, 1934.
5. Ibid.
6. "Modigliani Hailed By Local 89," *New Leader*, December 8, 1934.
7. Ibid.
8. A. N. Kruger, "Mussolini's Intrigues In America," and "Mussolini's Long Arm Reaches Into Every Italian Home in the United States," *New Leader*, November 22 and December 1, 1934. Larry S. Davidow, "Mussolini's Long Arm Reaches Detroit," *New Leader*, September 15, 1934.
9. Ibid.
10. "Fascist Squads Fight For Exploiters," *New Leader*, August 11, 1934; "Socialists Face Fascist Bands In Oregon," *New Leader*, August 11, 1934; Phil Hitts, "American Fascism Bares Its Teeth," *New Leader*, August 25, 1934.

11. "Khaki Shirts Of America," *New Leader*, June 3, 1933.
12. On the Terzani case, see *New Leader,* August 5, September 16, 23, December 2, 16, 1933. For Norman Thomas' comments on the case, see *New Leader*, April 7, 1934. On the Terzani case see J.P. Diggins, *Mussolini and Fascism*, Op. cit., pp. 131–133 and Vanni B. Montana, *Amarostico,* "La battaglia di Astoria," pp. 124–27.
13. "Khaki Shirts Now A Joke But Are Getting Ugly," *New Leader*, June 23, 1933. A protest was sent to Governor Gifford Pinchot, of Pennsylvania, and to the Department of Justice at Washington by Earl White, Secretary of the United Workers' Federation of Pennsylvania. The protest read as follows: "The Khaki Shirts headed by Art J. Smith, a purely Fascist organization with headquarters in Philadelphia, threatens civil insurrection and security of peace by armed forces and munitions all over the State of Pennsylvania. Progressive political bodies and labor unions, particularly those engaged in cleaning up sweatshop evils, are threatened with extermination as Communist. Futile tyranny and persecution of innocent citizens will inevitably result unless officials charged with enforcement of law guaranteeing citizens civil rights and liberties, disarm and squelch the present threatening menace. We demand an immediate investigation of individuals in command, the outfit itself and the boasted store of munitions and that the facts unearthed be made known to the public."
14. Ibid.
15. "A. F. of L. Fights Fascism," *New Leader*, October 13, 1934; Samuel H. Friedman, "New York Organized Labor Cheers Citrine's Plea for Fight on Fascism," *New Leader*, October 27, 1934.
16. Ibid.
17. "Wall Street Plots Fascist Coup," *New Leader*, November 24, 1934.
18. *New Leader*, December 8, 15, 22, and 29, 1934 and January 8 and 15, 1935.
19. S. Romualdi, "Modigliani's Tour Stirs Masses of Italian Workers," *New Leader*, March 23 and 30, 1935.
20. Ibid.
21. *New York Times*, November 28, 1935.
22. *New York Times*, July 23, 1936; Hugh A. Bone, "Political Parties in New York City," *American Political Science Review*, April, 1947, 277; Louis Waldman, *Labor Lawyer* (New York, 1944), 284–99: James Oneal, *The American Labor Party, An Interpretation* (New York, 1947).
23. *New Leader*, August 8, 1936.
24. Ibid.
25. The Manifesto was signed by Luigi Antonini, Chairman of the ALP, and by Rose Schneiderman, Alex Rose, Andrew R. Armstrong, Jacob

S. Potofsky, Elinore M. Herrick, D. Bellanca, Norbert Berger, J. B. Brennan, Joseph Breslau, Joseph Catalanotti, W. L. Darrington, Brasilio Desti, George Disney, David Dubinsky, Morris C. Feinstone, Jack Fitzerald, J. F. Gilliam, Max Goldman, Louis Hendin, Sidney Hillman, Julius Hochman, Louis Hollander, Arthur Huggins, A. J. Kennedy, Algernoon Lee, Pietro Lucchi, George Meany, Isidore Nagler, Joseph P. Ryan, J. J. Scully, Louis Waldman, H. J. Wilson, and W. S. Wilson.
26. Louis Waldman, "Roosevelt—Candidate Of Organized Labor," *New Leader*, August 29, 1936.

CHAPTER 10

1. G. Salvemini, *Italian Fascist Activities in the United States* (American Public Affairs, Washington, D.C., 1940), 6. On the Ethiopian War, G. Salvemini, *Mussolini Diplomatico,* Chapter XVIII, "Etiopia," pp. 244–50. Alexander DeConde, *Half Bitter, Half Sweet,* Chapter 11, "The Depression and Ethiopia," pp. 206–24. J. P. Diggins, *Mussolini and Fascism,* Chapter 12, "The Ethiopian War," pp. 287–312. G. G. Migone, *Gli Stati Uniti e Il Fascismo, Gli italo-americani e la Guerra d'Etiopia*, pp. 350–57.
2. *La Stampa Unita*, July 18, 1935.
3. W. Dubois, "Inter-racial Implications of the Ethiopian Crisis: A Negro View," *Foreign Affairs*, XIV, October, 1935, 82–92. See also, Robert G. Weisbord, "Black America and the Italian Ethiopian Crisis: An Episode in Pan-Negroism," *Historian*, February, 1972, Vol. XXXIV, n. 2.
4. C. Lanni, "Proper Propaganda," *La Stampa Unita*, July 25, 1935.
5. *Il Progresso Italo-Americano*, July 7, 1935.
6. *La Stella di Pittsburg*, August 23 and September 6, 1935.
7. *Italian Echo,* Providence, September 27, 1935.
8. *Il Popolo Italiano,* Philadelphia, October 9, 1935.
9. *La Libera Parola,* Philadelphia, October 19, 1935 and *Il Progresso Italo-Americano*, October 20, 1935.
10. *La Stampa Unita*, November 5, 7, and 14, 1935.
11. See John Norman, *Italo-American Opinion in the Ethiopian Crisis. A study of Fascist Propaganda.* (Ph.D. dissertation, Clark University, 1942), 188–89.
12. *Il Progresso Italo-Americano*, December 30, 1935, and January 18 and 28, 1936.
13. "Neutrality," J. P. Higgins, *La Stampa Unita*, February 20, 1936.

14. For detailed information on the Hearing, see John Norman, (*Italo-American Opinion, Op. cit.*), 193–205.
15. "L'Opera Svolta dalla Unione Italiana d'America," *La Stampa Unita*, April 2, 1936.
16. "What Will Mussolini Do?" C. Lanni, *La Stampa Unita*, May 15, 1936.
17. *New Leader*, May 18, 1935.
18. *New Leader*, July 13, 1935.
19. G. Valenti, "The Civilization Mussolini Would Impose On Ethiopia," *New Leader*, July 14, 1935.
20. A. Giovannitti, "Who Is This Man to Bring Light to the Abyssinians?" *New Leader*, July 27, 1935.
21. "Labor International Denounces Italian War," *New Leader*, August 10, 1935.
22. W. E. Ewer, "Roman Empire Is the Dream of Mussolini," and "The Abyss of Abyssinia," *New Leader*, August 24 and 31, 1935.
23. "Socialist and Trade Union Leaders Meet In Geneva To Map Action Against Fascist Italy's Conspiracy," *New Leader*, September 7, 1935.
24. "Soviet Russia Helps Mussolini's War Plan." *New Leader*, September 14, 1935.
25. *New Leader*, September 28, October 3 and 12, 1935.
26. *New Leader*, October 12, 1935.
27. "La Divisione Italiana dello State Republican Committee," *La Stampa Unita*, September 10, 1936.

CHAPTER 11

1. Memo from the Consulate General of Italy in New York, December 13, 1938; Giordano's personal letter to the Italian Ministry of Popular Culture on December 16, 1938, I.F.M.D. nn. 015190 and 015193. On Vincent Giordano see G. Salvemini, *Italian Fascist Activities in the United States*, p. 111.
2. Generoso Pope to the Ministry of the Popular Culture, March 7, 1939, and Giordano's letter to Guido Rocco, General Director of Foreign Press, March 3, 1939, I.F.M.D. nn. 015195 and 015198.
3. Memorandum to Ministry Italian African Colonies, Rome, January 24, 1939, I.F.M.D. n. 015192.
4. Ministry of Popular Culture, May 21, 25, and June 2, 1939, I.F.M.D. nn. 015204, 015205, 015213. For Pope's letter to Dino Alfieri on July 5, 1939, I.F.M.D. n. 015222.

5. Ministry of Popular Culture, General Director Foreign Press, November 21, 1939, I.F.M.D. n. 015226.
6. Ministry of Popular Culture, November 23, 1939, I.F.M.D. n. 015227.
7. Memorandum to Mussolini through the Ministry of Popular Culture, June 6, 1939, I.F.M.D. nn. 015217-015220. For the entire document see Appendix VII.
8. Letter to Mussolini, June 9, 1939, I.F.M.D. nn. 015210–12.
9. Memo to Il Duce, Rome, June 19, 1939, I.F.M.D. n.015216.
10. *New Leader*, April 22, 1939, p. 4.
11. *Giustizia e Libertà*, Paris, February 24, 1939.
12. *New Leader*, April 22, 1939, p. 4.

CHAPTER 12

1. *Dizionario Enciclopedico Moderno,* Citta' di Fondi, Edizioni Labor, Settima Edizione, Citta' di Fondi, Vol. 2, pp. 702–3, on the attempted abduction of Giulia Gonzaga.
2. Marzieh Gail, *The Three Popes,* New York, 1969, p. 33.
3. Joseph McSorley, *An Outline History of the Church from St. Peter to Pius XII,* Saint Louis, 1945, pp. 339–40, for Popes Gelasius II and Boniface VIII. Gelasio Caetani, the 162nd successor of St. Peter, born in Gaeta, whose pontificate ran from March 10, 1118, to January 28, 1119, died at Cluny in France. *Dizionario Enciclopedico Moderno*, Edizioni Labor, Settima Edizione, Vol. 1, Milan, 1956, pp. 600–601 for Boniface VIII.

    McGraw-Hill, *New Catholic Encyclopedia,* Vol. 2., New York 1967, pp. 671–73 for Boniface VIII. Thomson, *Encyclopedia of Religion,* Sec. Ed., Vol. 2, 2005, pp. 1018–19 for Boniface VIII. Sidney Z. Heller and John B. Moral, *Chiesa e Stato Attraverse i Secoli,* Milan 1954, pp. 122–25.

    F. C. Copleston, *Medieval Philosophy,* Harper Torchbooks, New York, 1961, p.173. "The temporal sword should not be wielded by the Church, it is wielded by temporal monarchs only in subordination to the Church."

4. *Dizionario Enciclopedico Moderno* (cit.). See p. 691 for an extensive account of the Caetani family. The *Dizionario Biografico degli Italiani* offers extensive coverage of the Caetanis in Vol. 16, 1973, pp. 111–230. *Istituto della Enciclopedia Italiana,* Roma, 1973.

    Robert Peele, "Gelasio Caetani, An appreciation," *Columbia University Quarterly,* December 1935, Vol. XXVII, N.4, pp. 430–35, *Miscellania Carte G. Caetani,* Colt G. I, 5.

Necrologie, Gelasio Caetani by P. Fedele pp. 221–25. *Fondazione Camillo Caetani,* Archivio Palazzo Caetani, Roma.

Gelasio Caetani, *Caietanorum Genealogia, Indice Genealogico e Cenni Biografici della Famiglia Caetani dalle Origini all'Anno MDC-CCLXXXII,* Perugia, 1920, pp. 94–96, Documenti Dell'Archivio Caetani, Roma.

I would like to express my sincerest thanks to Luigi and Caterina Fiorani, archivists of the *Fondazione Camillo Caetani,* Palazzo Caetani, Roma, for their assistance.

5. Pellegrino Nazzaro, "The Dissidentismo Fascista and the failures of Mussolini's Fascism: 1922–1926," paper delivered at the conference sponsored by the History Department of Bloomsburg State College, Bloomsburg, Pennsylvania, April 22–24, 1971.

6. Giuseppe Bastianini, *Rivoluzione,* Roma, 1923. *Dizionario Biografico degli Italiani,* Vol. 7, Istituto della Enciclopedia Italiana, Roma, 1965, pp. 170–75. Paolo Monelli, *La Tua Patria,* Segreteria Generale dei Fasci all'Estero, Roma, 1929.

7. Alfredo Rocco, *Scritti e discorsi politici,* with a preface by Benito Mussolini, 3 Vols. Milano, 1938. Vol. 1, *La lotta Nazionale della vigilia e durante la Guerra, 1913–1918.* Vol. 2, *La lotta contro la reazione antinazionale, 1919–1924.* Vol. 3, *La formazione dello stato fascista, 1925–1934.* Alfredo Rocco, "Politica e diritto nelle vecchie e nelle nuove concezioni dello Stato," *Nuova Antologia,* December 1, 1931, pp. 356–70.

Francesco Olgiati, *Il Concetto di Giuridicita'nella Scienza Moderna del Diritto,* Societa' Editrice "Vita e Pensiero," Milano, 1943.

Paolo Ungari, *Alfredo Rocco e l'Ideologia Giuridica del Fascismo,* Morcelliana, Brescia, 1963.

Alberto Aquarone, *L'Organizzazione dello Stato Totalitario,* Giulio Einaudi Editore, Torino, 1965.

8. Dino Grandi, *Tradizione e Rivoluzione nei codici mussoliniani,* Roma, 1940. *Dizionario Biografico degli Italiani,* Vol. 58, Roma, 2002, pp. 470–77.

9. Renzo De Felice, *Breve Storia del Fascismo,* A. Mondadori, Milano, 2000, Il problema dell'identita' nazionale, pp. 125–35.

10. Giovanni Gentile, *Che Cosa e' il Fascismo, Discorsi e Polemiche,* Firenze, 1928, p. 28.

11. Ibid., p. 36.

WORKS CITED

SELECT ITALIAN BIBLIOGRAPHY

On Mussolini

Chiurco, Giorgio Alberto. *Storia della Rivoluzione Fascista*, 5 vols. Vallecchi Editore, Firenze, 1929.

D'Aroma, Nino. *Il Popolo nel Fascismo*. Casa Editrice Pinciana, Roma, nd.

Davanzati, Forges Roberto. *Cronache del Regime*, 3 vols. Arnaldo Mondadori, Milano, 1936–37.

De Felice, Renzo. *Mussolini il Rivoluzionario 1883–1920*. Giulio Einaudi Editore, Torino, 1965.

———. *Mussolini il Fascista: la Conquista del Potere, 1921–1925*. Giulio Einaudi Editore, Torino, 1966.

———. *Mussolini il Fascista: l'Organizzazione dello Stato Fascista, 1925–1929*. Giulio Einaudi Editore, Torino, 1968.

———. *Mussolini Il Duce: Gli Anni del Consenso, 1929–1936*. Giulio Einaudi Editore, Torino, 1974.

———. *Mussolini Il Duce: lo Stato Totalitario, 1936–1940*. Giulio Einaudi Editore, Torino, 1981.

Mussolini, Benito. *Sette Anni di Regime Fascista*. Libreria del Littorio, Roma, 1929.

———. *La Nuova Politica dell'Italia, Discorsi e Dichiarazioni.* A cura di Amedeo Giannini, 3 vols. Casa Editrice Alpes, Milano, 1938.

———. *La Dottrina del Fascismo*, con una storia del movimento fascista di Gioacchino Volpe. Istituto Della Enciclopedia Italiana, Roma, 1941.

———. *Opera Omnia,* edited by E. and B. Susmel, 44 vols. Firenze, 1951–1962.

On Fascism

Gentile, Giovanni. *Che Cosa e' il Fascismo?* Vallecchi Editore, Firenze, 1925.

———. *Fascismo e Cultura*. Fratelli Treves Editori, Milano, 1928.

Gobetti, Piero. *Dal Bolscevismo al Fascismo*, note di cultura politica. Piero Gobetti Editore, Torino, 1923.

Labriola, Arturo. *Le Due Politiche, Fascismo e Riformismo*. Alberto Morano Editore, Napoli, 1928.

Mandel, Roberto. *Il Duce*. Casa Editrice Sanzogno, Milano, 1929.

Nitti, Francesco Saverio. *Bolscevismo, Fascismo e Democrazia*. Edizioni del Sole, New York, 1927.

Orfei, Ernesto. *La Monarchia Fascista*. Marviana, Roma, 1944.

Rocca, Massimo. *Idee sul Fascismo*. Editrice La Voce, Firenze, 1924.

Salvatorelli, Luigi, e Mira Giovanni. *Storia d'Italia nel Periodo Fascista*. Giulio Einaudi Editore. Torino, 1964.

Solmi, Arrigo, e Vergilio Feroci. *Cultura Fascista*. Arnoldo Mondadori, Milano, 1938.

Spampanato, Bruno. *Democrazia Fascista*. Edizioni di Politica Nuova, Roma, 1933.

Susmel, Edoardo. *Mussolini e il Suo Tempo*. Garzanti, 1950.

Turati, Augusto. *Una Rivoluzione e un Capo*. Prefazione di Benito Mussolini. Libreria del Littorio, Roma-Milano, 1927.

Valeri, Nino. *La Lotta Politica in Italia dall'Unità al 1925*. Felice Le Monnier, Firenze, 1946.

————. *Da Giolitti a Mussolini*. Casa Editrice il Saggiatore, Milano, 1967.

Vinciguerra, Mario. *Il Fascismo Visto da un Solitario*. Piero Gobetti Editore, Torino, 1923.

Zerboglio, Adolfo e Dino Grandi. *Fascismo*. Editore Licinio Cappelli, Bologna, 1922.

On Nationalism

Corradini, Enrico. *Il Nazionalismo Italiano*. Fratelli Treves, Milano, 1914.

De Begnac, Ivon. *L'Arcangelo Sindacalista, Filippo Corridoni*. Arnaldo Mondadori, Verona, 1943.

Ercole, Francesco. *Dal Nazionalismo al Fascismo*. De Alberti Editore, Roma, 1928.

Gentile, Giovanni. *I profeti del Risorgimento Italiano*. Vallecchi Editore, Firenze, 1923.

Giovannetti, Eugenio. *Il Tramonto del Liberalismo*. Laterza, Bari, 1917.

Oriani, Alfredo. *La Rivolta Ideale*. Prefazione di Benito Mussolini. Casa Editrice Cappelli, Bologna, 1926.

Papini, Giovanni, e Giuseppe Prezzolini. *Vecchio e Nuovo Nazionalismo.* Milano, 1914.

Piccoli, Valentino. *Oriani.* Edizione Augustea, Roma-Milano,1929.

Salvatorelli, Luigi. *Nazionalfascismo*. Piero Gobetti Editore, Torino, 1923.

Sighele, Scipio. *Pagine Nazionaliste.* Fratelli Treves, Milano, 1910.

On Fascism and Anti-Fascism

Alatri, Paolo. *L'Antifascismo Italiano,* 2 vols. Editori Riuniti, Roma, 1961.

Associazione Volontari di Guerra. *Il Decennale, X Anniversario della Vittoria,* Raffaele, Firenze, 1929.

Balbo, Italo. *Stormi d'Italia sul Mondo.* Arnaldo Mondadori, Verona, 1934.

Bastianini, Giuseppe. *Rivoluzione.* Roma, 1923.

Bonavita, Franco. *Primavera Fascista, dall'Avvento Fascista all'Impero Africano.* Milano, 1937.

Brighenti, Angelo. *Uomini ed Episodi del Tempo di Mussolini.* Società Editrice Internazionale, Milano, 1939.

Capasso, Carlo. *Italia e Oriente.* La Nuova Italia, Firenze, 1932.

Casucci, Costanzo. *Il Fascismo.* Il Mulino, Bologna, 1966.

Curcio, Carlo. *L'Esperienza Liberale del Fascismo.* Alberto Morano Editore, Napoli, 1924.

Damiani, Claudia. *Mussolini e Gli Stati Uniti 1922–1935.* Cappelli Editore, Bologna, 1980.

Della Somaglia, Lena Trivulzio. *Vomere e Spada.* Pensieri e Massime di Benito Mussolini. Editore Ulricho Hoepli, Milano, 1936.

Di Nolfo, Ennio. *Mussolini e la Politica Estera Italiana 1919–1933.* Cedam, Padova, 1960.

Dorso, Guido. *Dittatura, Classe Politica e Classe Dirigente.* Giulio Einaudi Editore, Torino, 1949.

————. *Mussolini alla Conquista del Potere.* Giulio Einaudi Editore, Torino, 1949.

Ferri, Enrico. *Il Fascismo in Italia e l'Opera di Benito Mussolini.* Edizioni Paladino, Mantova, 1928.

Forti, Raul, e Giuseppe Ghedini. *L'Avvento del Fascismo.* Cronache Ferraresi, Editrice Taddei, Ferrara, 1923.

Gobetti, Piero. *La Rivoluzione Liberale.* Giulio Einaudi Editore, Torino, 1966.

Gustarelli, Andrea. *L'Impero Italiano Fascista.* Vallardi Editore, Milano, 1938.

Lojacono, Luigi. *Il Fascismo nel Mondo.* Roma, 1933.

Monelli, Paolo. *La Tua Patria.* Segreteria dei Fasci all'Estero, Roma, 1929.

Mussolini, Arnaldo. *Polemiche e Programmi* (Anno 1926). A cura di Valentino Piccoli. Milano, 1928.

The Opera Nazionale Balilla. (In English) Palazzo Viminale, Roma, 1927.

Partito Nazionale Fascista. *Le Origini ello Sviluppo del Fascismo dall'Intervento alla Marcia su Roma.* Libreria Del Littorio, Roma, 1928.

Riccardi, Raffaele. *Pagine Squadriste.* Unione Editoriale d'Italia, Roma, 1940.

Salvemini, Gaetano. *Mussolini Diplomatico.* Laterza, Bari, 1952.

Sestan, Ernesto, Rosario Villari, Armando Saitta, Eugenio Garin, e Enzo Tagliacozzo. *Gaetano Salvemini.* Editori Laterza, Bari, 1959.

Segreteria Generale dei Fasci all'Estero. *Inni e Canzoni della Patria e del Fascismo.* Roma, 1928.

Sinibaldo, Nino. *Il Trentennio Fascista.* Casa Editrice il Saggiatore, Milano, 1965.

Tamaro, Attilio. *Venti Anni di Storia, 1922–1943*, 3 vols. Editrice Tiber, Roma, 1953–54.

Treves, Paolo. *Quello che ci ha fatto Mussolini.* Giulio Einaudi Editore, Roma, 1945.

Volpe, Gioacchino. *L'Italia in Cammino, l'Ultimo Cinquantennio.* Fratelli Treves Editori, Milano, 1937.

On Alfredo Rocco

Aquarone, Alberto. *L'Organizzazione dello Stato Totalitario.* Giulio Einaudi Editore, Milano, 1965.

Forresu, Ciro. *Il Fondamento Filosofico del Rapporto tra Diritto e Stato.* Cedam, Padova, 1940.

Franchi, Luigi, e Vincenzo Feroci. *Codice Penale e Codice di Procedura Penale.* Editore Ulrico Hoepli, Milano, 1953.

Istituto di Studi Legislativi, Studi di Diritto Penale Comparato. *Il Progetto Rocco nel Pensiero Giuridico Contemporaneo.* Saggi Critici, Casa Editrice Cedam, 1930.

Liuni, Francesco. *La Concezione Italiana dello Stato.* Vecchi & C. Editori, Trani, 1934.

Olgiati, Francesco. *Il Concetto di Giuridicita'nella Scienza Moderna del Diritto.* Vita e Pensiero, Milano, 1943.

Pannese, Gerardo. *L'Etica nel Fascismo e la Filosofia del Diritto e della Storia.* Edizioni La Voce della Stampa, Roma, 1942.

Panunzio, Sergio. *Il Sentimento dello Stato.* Libreria del Littorio, Roma, 1929.

Rocco, Alfredo. "Politica e diritto nelle vecchie e nelle nuove concezioni dello stato," *Nuova Antologia,* December 1, 1931, 356–70.

———. *Scritti e Discorsi Politici,* 3 vols. Prefazione di Benito Mussolini. Vol. 1, *La lotta nazionale della vigilia e durante la Guerra, 1913–1918.* Vol. 2, *La lotta contro la reazione antinazionale, 1919–1924.* Vol. 3, *La formazione dello stato fascista, 1925–1934.* Milano, 1938.

Ungari, Paolo. *Alfredo Rocco e l'Ideologia Giuridica del Fascismo.* Morcelliana, Brescia, 1963.

Vanzetti, Adriano. "Alfredo Rocco e l'Ideologia Giuridica del Fascismo," *Rivista di Diritto Pubblico,* Anno XI, n. 2, 1965, 119–29.

On Fascism and Corporativism

Assante, Augusto. *Dal Sindacato alla Corporazione.* Alberto Morano Editore, Napoli, 1934.

Bellomo, Probo Bini. *Dallo Stato Liberale alla Politica Corporativa.* Cedam, Padova, 1936.

Bottai, Giuseppe. *L'Economia Fascista.* Roma, 1930.

———. *Le Corporazioni.* Mondadori, Milano, 1933. (This work contains a lengthy bibliography on the subject).

———. *L'Ordinamento Corporativo.* Mondadori, Milano, 1938.

Cerrito, Corrado. *Aspetti Etici del Corporativismo Fascista.* Edizioni Politica Nuova, Roma, 1937.

Paoloni, Francesco. *Sistema Rappresentativo del Fascismo.* Editrice Rispoli, Napoli, 1937.

Viglietti, Vitale. *Corporativismo e Cristianesimo.* Edizioni lo Stato Corporativo, Napoli, 1934.

On Southern Italy (Il Mezzogiorno)

Centro Studi Emigrazione. *La Societa' Italiana di Fronte alle Prime Migrazioni di Massa.* Morcelliana, Brescia, 1968.

Dore, Grazia. *La Democrazia Italiana e l'Emigrazione in America.* Morcelliana, Brescia, 1964.

Dorso, Guido. *La Rivoluzione Meridionale, Il Mezzogiorno d'Italia da Cavour a Mussolini.* Alberto Mondadori Editore, Milano, 1969.

Gramsci, Antonio. *La Questione Meridionale.* Editori Riuniti, Roma, 1966.

Rizzo, Franco. *Luigi Sturzo e la Questione Meridionale.* Editoriale di Cultura e Documentazione, Roma, 1957.

———. *F.S. Nitti e il Problema del Mezzogiorno.* Universale Studium, Roma, 1960.

Rodanò, Carlo. *Mezzogiorno e Sviluppo Economico.* Giuseppe Laterza, Bari, 1954.

Sturzo, Luigi. *I Discorsi Politici.* Istituto Luigi Sturzo, Roma, 1951.

Trimarchi, Giovanna. *La Formazione del Pensiero Meridionalista di Luigi Sturzo.* Morcelliana, Brescia, 1965.

Villari, Rosario *Il Sud nella Storia d'Italia, Antologia della Questione Meridionale.* Editori Laterza, Bari, 1961.

SPECIALIZED BIBLIOGRAPHY ON FASCISM AND ANTI-FASCISM IN AMERICA

Albrecht-Carrié, René. *Italy From Napoleon to Mussolini*. New York and London: Columbia University Press, 1968.

Bayor, Ronald H. *Neighbors in Conflict: The Irish, Germans, Jews and Italians of New York City, 1929–1941*. Baltimore and London: The Johns Hopkins University Press, 1978.

Bosworth, Richard J. B. *Mussolini*. New York: Oxford University Press, 2002.

———. *Mussolini's Italy, Life Under His Dictatorship, 1915–1945*. New York: Penguin Press, 2006.

Cannistraro, Philip V. *Blackshirts in Little Italy: Italian Americans and Fascism, 1921–1929*. West Lafayette, IN: Bordighera Press, 1999.

Chabod, Federico. *A History of Italian Fascism*. Murial Grindrod & Howard Fertig, (trans.). New York: H. Fertig, 1975.

Damiani, Claudia. *Mussolini e gli Stati Uniti*. Bologna: Cappelli Editore, 1980.

De Conde, Alexander. *Half Bitter, Half Sweet: An Excursion into Italian-American History*. New York: Charles Scribner's Sons, 1971.

Diggins, John P. *Mussolini and Fascism: The View from America*. Princeton, NJ: Princeton University Press, 1972.

———. *The Rise and Fall of the American Left*. New York, London: W. W. Norton, 1992.

Fascismo. *Inchiesta Socialista Sulle Gesta Dei Fascisti in Italia*. Milano: Edizione Avanti, 1963.

Federal Writers' Project, New York City. *The Italians of New York*, a survey prepared by the workers of the Works Progress Administration in the City of New York. New York: Random House, 1938. Reprinted 1969, Arno Press, New York, and the *New York Times*.

Finkelstein, Monte S. "The Johnson Act, Mussolini and Fascist Emigration Policy: 1921–1930," *Journal of American Ethnic History*, n. 1, August 1988, pp. 38–55.

Iorizzo, J. Luciano, and Salvatore Mondello. *The Italian-Americans,* Third Edition. Youngstown, NY: Cambria Press, 2006.

Kessner, Thomas. *The Golden Door, Italian and Jewish Immigrant Mobility in New York City, 1880–1915*. New York: Oxford University Press, 1977.

Kirkpatrick, Ivone. *Mussolini, A Study in Power*. New York: Avon Books, 1964.

Lagumina, Salvatore J. *Vito Marcantonio, The People's Politician*, Dubuque, IA: Kendall/Hunt, 1969.

————. *WOP: A Documentary History of Anti-Italian Discrimination in the United States*. San Francisco: Straight Arrow Books, 1973; distributed by Quick Fox, New York.

————. *The Immigrants Speak: The Italians Tell Their Story*. New York: Center for Migration Studies, 1978.

Luconi, Stefano. "The Italian Language Press, Italian American Voters and Political Intermediation in Pennsylvania in the Interwar Years," *International Migration Review*, Vol. 33, N. 4 (Winter 1999), pp. 1031–61.

————. *The Italian-American Vote in Providence Rhode Island*, 1916–1948. Cranbury: Fairleigh Dickinson University Press, 2004.

Mack Smith, Denis. *Mussolini: A Biography*. Vintage Books Edition. New York: Random House, 1983.

————. *Mussolini's Roman Empire*. London: Longmans, 1976.

Mangano, Antonio. *Italian Colonies of New York City*. Masters thesis, Columbia University, New York, 1903.

Migone, Gian Giacomo. *Gli Stati Uniti e il Fascismo, Alle Origini dell'Egemonia Americana in Italia*, Milano: Feltrinelli Editore, 1980.

Montana, Vanni Buscemi. *Amarostico, Testimonianze Euro-Americane*. Prefazione di Aldo Garosci. Livorno: Bastogi Editore, 1975.

Nazzaro, Pellegrino. "L'atteggiamento della stampa cattolico-moderata Americana verso il Fascismo prima e dopo la Conciliazione," *Storia Contemporanea*, Anno II, N. 4 (Dicembre 1971), pp. 717–37.

———. "L'Immigration Quota Act del 1921, la crisi del sistema liberale e l'avvento del Fascismo in Italia," Gli Italiani Negli Stati Uniti, Atti del III Symposium di Studi Americani, Firenze, 27–29 Maggio 1969, Istituto di Studi Americani, Universita' Degli Studi di Firenze, 1972, pp. 323–64.

———. "L'Atteggiamento della stampa cattolico-moderata Americana verso il Fascismo prima e dopo la Conciliazione," *Modernismo, Fascismo, Comunismo,* Aspetti e figure della cultura e della politica dei cattolici nel '900, a cura di Giuseppe Rossini. Bologna: Societa' Editrice il Mulino, 1972, pp. 47–67.

———. "The Manifesto of the North American Anti-Fascist Alliance, New York, August 26, 1926," *Labor History.* Vol. 13, N. 3 (Summer 1972), pp. 418–26.

———. "Italy from the American Immigration Quota Act of 1921 to Mussolini's Policy of Grossraum: 1921–24." *Journal of European Economic History,* Vol. 3, N. 3 (Winter 1974), pp. 705–23.

———. "Il manifesto dell'Alleanza Antifascista del Nord America," *Affari Sociali Internazionali,* Franco Angeli Editore, Anno II, n. 1–2 (Giugno, 1974), pp. 171–85.

———. "Fascist and Anti-Fascist Reaction in the United States to the Matteotti Murder," in Studies in *Italian American Social History, Essays in Honor of Leonardo Covello* (pp. 50–65). Edited by Francesco Cordasco. Totowa, NJ: Rowman and Littlefield, 1975.

———. "Modigliani's Visit to the United States and the Origins of the American Labor Party (13 Articles for the *New Leader,* June 18, 1927–October 15, 1938)," *Rivista di Studi Politici Internazionali,* Anno LII, n. 206, 1985, pp. 241–78.

Parenti, Michael John. *Ethnic and Political Attitudes: A Depth Study of Italian Americans.* New York: Arno Press, 1975.

Rogers, Griffin. *Fascism* (Oxford Readers). New York: Oxford University Press, 1995.

Salvemini, Gaetano. *Italian Fascist Activities in the United States.* Edited and with an introduction by Philip V. Cannistraro. New York: Center For Migration Studies, 1977.

INDEX

ABOUT THE AUTHOR

Dr. Pellegrino Nazzaro is professor of European History in the College of Liberal Arts at the Rochester Institute of Technology (RIT). For several years Dr. Nazzaro taught Crime and Violence and Comparative Criminal Law in the School of Criminal Justice.

Dr. Nazzaro holds a B.A. in Humanities from the Liceo Classico Pietro Giannone of Benevento, Italy (1951), and a Ph.D. in Jurisprudence (Law and History) from the University Federico II of Naples (1956). In the biennium 1956–1958, he registered at the University's Facolta' di Lettere e Filosofia for postdoctoral research in History and Philosophy.

Dr. Nazzaro has been a member of the Ordine Avvocati e Procuratori of Naples, the Centro di Studi Sturziani of Naples, a member of the Christian Democratic Party (DC), and president of Catholic Action of Montesarchio (Benevento). Dr. Nazzaro also received appointment as vice-correspondent for the newspaper *Il Quotidiano* and collaborator for *La Vita del Mezzogiorno*. He was nominated by the Provveditorato agli Studi di Benevento to teach at the Istituto Magistrale Statale Benedetto Croce within the Italian state school system.

Appointed a member of Milan's COI (Centro Orientamenti Immigrati), Dr. Nazzaro is a *socio vitalizio* (lifetime member) of the *Istituto per la Storia del Risorgimento Italiano* of Rome, Italy.

Dr. Nazzaro arrived in the United States and began teaching in 1962. In 1974, he received RIT's Eisenhart Outstanding Teacher of the Year Award; an award as Outstanding Educator of America in 1975; and inclusion in *Marquis Who's Who in the East* and the *International Who's Who in Education* in 1981 and 1982. During 1975–1977, Dr. Nazzaro was nominated chair of the Distinguished Faculty Award Program of the Commonwealth of Pennsylvania at the Edinboro State College.

From 1974 to 1980 he chaired the History Department at RIT. In 1976, Dr. Nazzaro organized and directed the International Symposium on Costantino Brumidi for the Bicentennial Celebration of the United States of America, and in 1977 he chaired a section of the international conference, "Italian Immigrant Women in North America" in Toronto, Canada.

Dr. Nazzaro has served on the Executive Council of the American–Italian Historical Association and as a member of the European Community Studies Association (ECSA) and the American Historical Association.

Dr. Nazzaro has done extensive scholarly research in national and international archives, including: the *Archivio Centrale dello Stato*, Rome; the *Archivio della Sapienza*, Rome; the Secret Archives of the Vatican; the Library of the Vatican; the Office of the Extraordinary Affairs of the State of the Vatican; and the John F. Kennedy Library, in Boston, among others.

Dr. Nazzaro has published over 40 scholarly essays in national and international journals, including *Storia Contemporanea* and *Affari Sociali Internazionali*, directed by the late Renzo De Felice, internationally acclaimed authority on Fascism. Also, Dr. Nazzaro has published in *The Journal of European Economic History*; the *Rivista di Studi Politici Internazionali; Labor History*; *Encyclopedia International Grolier*; *Dictionary of American Immigration History*; *Great Lives From History*, Twentieth Century Series; *Research Guide to American Historical Biography*; *Research Guide to European Historical Biography*; and *The United States in the First World War: An Encyclopedia*. Dr. Nazzaro contributed to the book *Modernismo, Fascismo, Comunismo, Aspetti e Figure della Cultura e della Politica dei Cattolici nel '900;* and to *Studies in Italian American Social History* and *Gli Italiani negli Stati Uniti.*

From 1970 to 1980, Dr. Nazzaro published scholarly essays in *Current History* with international scholars Arthur P. Whitaker, Gerald Braunthal, Norman A. Graebner, Pierre Henry Laurent, Michael E. Bradley, Guy De Carmoy, Richard H. Laech, Walter

H. M. Frohlich, and Edward Whiting Fox, among others. In 1998, Dr. Nazzaro contributed to the book *Constantino Brumidi, Artist of the Capitol* (U.S. Government Printing Office, Washington, 1998). Finally, Dr. Nazzaro is the author of the textbook *The European Union*, which is in its 8th Edition (Thomson, Ohio).

Printed in the United States
201655BV00002B/1-63/P